CHURCHES
AND PEOPLE IN
AUSTRALIA
AND NEW ZEALAND
1860–1930

CHURCHES AND PEOPLE IN AUSTRALIA AND NEW ZEALAND

1860–1930

H.R. JACKSON

Allen & Unwin/
Port Nicholson Press

First published in 1987 by
Allen & Unwin New Zealand Limited
in association with the Port Nicholson Press,
60 Cambridge Terrace,
Wellington, New Zealand

Allen & Unwin Australia Pty Ltd,
NCR House, 8 Napier Street,
North Sydney, NSW 2060, Australia

Unwin Hyman (Publishers),
40 Museum Street, London
WC1, England

George Allen & Unwin Inc.,
8 Winchester Place, Winchester,
Mass. 01890, USA

© H.R. Jackson 1987

National Library of Australia Cataloguing-in-Publication Entry
Jackson, H. R. (Hugh R.).
Churches and people in Australia and New Zealand
1860–1930.

Bibliography.
Includes index.
ISBN 0 86861 698 2 (pbk.).

1. Christian sects – Australia – History. 2. Christian
sects – New Zealand – History. 3. Protestants –
Australia -- History. 4. Protestants – New Zealand –
History. 5. Catholics – Australia – History. 6.
Catholics – New Zealand – History. I. Title.

280'.0994

Designed by Missen and Geard
Typeset by Graphicraft Limited, Hong Kong
Printed in Hong Kong

CONTENTS

List of Illustrations　vi
List of Tables　vii
List of Graphs　vii
Acknowledgements　viii

Introduction　1
1. Religion and the Immigrants　5
2. In a New World　23
3. Revivalism　48
4. Separation and Identity　77
5. Sunday　104
6. Doctrine　125
7. The Family　142
Conclusion　167

References　174
Bibliography　199
Index　206

LIST OF ILLUSTRATIONS

1. From the mining districts   9
    Punch, or the London Charivari, vol. 28, 1855, p. 8

2. Irish emigrants leaving home   14
    National Library of Australia, from *Illustrated London News*, 1851

3. Opitonui coffee-palace   27
    William Morley, *The History of Methodism in New Zealand*,
    Wellington, 1900

4. A bark-sheet church   29
    Photograph by William Boag, John Oxley Library

5. A view of Tambaroora, New South Wales   31
    Holtermann Collection, Mitchell Library

6. Bishop Marsden visits Gulgong   32
    Holtermann Collection, Mitchell Library

7. The First Church of Otago, Dunedin   46
    National Museum of New Zealand

8. California Taylor   52
    Morley, *The History of Methodism in New Zealand*

9. The Helping Hand Mission Hall, Balmain, Sydney   59
    James Colwell, *The Illustrated History of Methodism in Australia* . . .
    Sydney, 1904

10. Patrick Hennebery   67
    Author's possession

11. An early colonial Wesleyan class ticket   79
    Colwell, *The Illustrated History of Methodism in Australia*

12. The climax of the Eucharistic Congress in Melbourne,
    1934   95
    Souvenir of the National Eucharistic Congress . . ., Melbourne, 1934

13. How the Loyalist League of Victoria saw Archbishop
    Mannix, *c.* 1919   96
    Anon., *The Menace of Mannix and Co.*, n.p., n.d.

14. Children of Mary   99
    Auckland Catholic Diocesan Archives

15. Sunday school children, Reefton, New Zealand   106
    Morley, *The History of Methodism in New Zealand*

16. Sunday afternoon in the Botanical Gardens   107
    Sydney Punch, 20 Oct. 1866

17. Premier Murray proposes to put the fire out   111
    The Bulletin, 13 Oct. 1910

18. Consolation   118
    The Bulletin, 29 Sept. 1910
19. A Catholic rural congregation with their bishop   123
    Adelaide Catholic Archdiocesan Archives
20. Richard Davies Hanson   130
    Lithograph by S. T. Gill, *c.* 1856, National Library of Australia
21. The paterfamilias leads his family at prayer   149
    Cutting from Rev. J. Saunders's Letter-book 1834–56, Mitchell
    Library
22. A Protestant family, *c.* 1921   152
    From a family album in possession of Mr H. G. C. Merritt, Auckland
23. For Catholic homes   156
    Anon., *The Good, the Unctious, or 'Jelly Fish' and the Bad Catholics*,
    Sydney, n.d., Mitchell Library

LIST OF TABLES

1. Percentages of the overseas-born of the colonists in
   1891 born in England and Wales, Scotland and
   Ireland by colony.   6
2. Percentages of population in each colony adhering to
   the principal denominations in 1860–61.   20
3. In-marriage patterns by denomination, New South
   Wales, 1891.   83
4. In-marriage patterns by denomination, New South
   Wales, 1891 and 1921.   85
5. Social class and church attendance, Melbourne,
   1887.   105
6. Protestant churchgoing in New Zealand,
   1891–1926.   117
7. Average issue of native-born wives of all
   denominations and Irish-born wives of all
   denominations in New South Wales in 1901.   145

LIST OF GRAPHS

1. Wesleyan and united Methodist annual growth rates,
   South Australia, 1856–1930 (per cent).   50
2. Trends in church attendance in selected New
   Zealand counties, 1891–1926.   116

ACKNOWLEDGEMENTS

Professor K. S. Inglis by occasional remarks in articles set me wondering about the possibilities of a systematic historical comparison of the Catholic and Protestant experience in Australia. Living in New Zealand made it seem a natural progression to widen the historical stage. The result is this book. In the process I have drawn heavily on the work of fellow historians and on none more so than that of Professor Patrick O'Farrell.

Dr F. B. Smith, who supervised my PhD thesis, provided expert criticism. My wife, Sandra, commented on my drafts from the earliest stage. Dr David Hilliard rendered assistance at many points. For help in various ways I also thank Selwyn Dawson, Jim Docherty, Marie Therese Foale, Clyde Griffen, Pat Grimshaw, David and Lyn Hall, Ken Inglis, Sybil Jack, Doreen Jackson, Jan Kociumbas, Hugh Laracy, Warren Limbrick, Peter Lineham, Ken Lockridge, Behan McCullagh, Hugh McLeod, Elsie Muhlhan, Barry Reay, Deryck and Paddy Schreuder, George Seber, Chris and Joy Selby-Smith, Ernest Simmons, Niven and Val Sowerby, John Stagg, Andrew and Carolyn Thornley.

This book would not have been possible without a PhD scholarship which I held at the Australian National University. I am grateful to the Australian taxpayer for the opportunities that scholarship afforded. The research entailed much travelling. I was assisted here by grants awarded by the Auckland University Research Committee. My wife and children bore with my absences and accepted the other sacrifices I asked them to make. I am deeply grateful.

A large part of Chapter 6 has appeared previously in the *Journal of Religious History*.

H. R. *Jackson*
University of Auckland, 1986

Illustrations The following institutions and individuals gave permission to reproduce illustrations in their possession: Mitchell Library, National Library of Australia, John Oxley Library, *The Bulletin*, *Punch*, Adelaide Catholic Archdiocesan Archives and Father G. Carmody, Auckland Catholic Diocesan Archives, the Merritt family (Auckland), Society of the Precious Blood (Carthegena, Ohio), St John's College (Auckland), National Museum of New Zealand.

To My Mother and Father

INTRODUCTION

In two hundred years of European presence in Australia and New Zealand two religious traditions have counted most: the British Protestant and the Irish Catholic. So different in ethos, they both reached Australasia from the British Isles and both had to struggle to establish themselves in a new environment. This book is an attempt to follow Protestants and Catholics from the old world to the new and to investigate the extent to which the children and grandchildren of the immigrants assimilated their respective religious heritages. It is a study of two kinds of religion.

It is also a study of old-world influences in the new. For England, Scotland and Ireland were not left behind when people left for Australasia; they carried home with them in their hearts and minds. Furthermore cultural dependence was by no means confined to the immigrant generation or, indeed, to their children. Ideas and attitudes in the new world continued to be modified by innovations transmitted from the old. Nor were the British Isles the only source of change. For Protestants the United States was another, though less important. Catholicism in Australasia, as elsewhere, looked to Rome.

There is no attempt here to write a comprehensive history of Protestantism and Catholicism in Australia and New Zealand. Rather there is a sharp focus on the relationship between people and churches. The word church may stand for a building, a denomination or even the Christian faith itself. But so far as historians are concerned, churches are primarily people, meaning individuals in their corporate religious life, whether that life be strong or weak, extensive or exiguous, almost wholly devotional or with pronounced social and recreational elements. So I have looked at churchgoers both individually and jointly, and the centre of interest has been whether the ties between individual and group slackened or tightened and whether a different movement can be traced for Protestants and Catholics. In the first two chapters I discuss the religion of the immigrants and the distinctive nature of their new environment. I consider changes over time in the next five, taking up different aspects of the relationship between individuals and churches: revivals, the drawing of boundaries between insiders and outsiders, Sunday observance, doctrine, and religion in the family. In the final chapter I look back to see whether any general patterns can be defined and what their significance might be.

In Australasia Protestants and Catholics shared a culture which from the beginning was notably this-worldly and which became more so. By early this century religious observance was ceasing to be a cachet of social respectability. Already many Protestants had begun that wholesale disengagement from church life which has been taken so much further in our own day. I began by wanting to show that in the secular colonial environment Irish Catholicism triumphed where British Protestantism failed. The truth turned out to be not so simple.

I have tried to drive Protestant and Catholic in tandem throughout (Catholic will mostly follow behind Protestant!). Too often religious historians of Australia and New Zealand have studied either one or the other. The notable exceptions tend to be those who write about sectarianism, and this in its own way can leave the impression that Catholics and Protestants lived behind their different fences and only came out to fight. Folklore often appears to support this. Many a Catholic family has a story about the rotten Masons, many a Protestant about the grandparent who would slight a Catholic by walking on the opposite side of the street. No doubt these stories point to some past realities but they do not ring true to the complexities of human behaviour as most of us experience it. The truth about Protestant–Catholic relations in Australia and New Zealand has been more subtle than we have often been led to believe.

In describing Protestant developments I have rarely gone beyond the Church of England, Presbyterians, Methodists and Congregationalists. The first three constituted between them around nine out of every ten Protestants in Australasia. In 1901 Congregationalists accounted for but 3.7 per cent of the population of South Australia, the Australasian colony in which they were proportionately strongest. They get here more attention than their numbers would seem to require because this book grew out of a PhD thesis on Australian Congregationalism. The thesis was conceived of and executed as a case study of Protestantism in the late nineteenth and early twentieth centuries. The aim was to illuminate what happened to the relationship between Protestants and their churches through a detailed examination of one denomination, an examination which could not be so easily carried off with a much larger religious group. It is reasonable to regard evidence pertaining to Congregationalists as normally providing a good guide to what was happening within Presbyterianism and Methodism. From early this century the three denominations were engaged in discussions about church unity.

Two kinds of religion? Were there not three: Catholic on the one hand, Protestant on the other, and the Church of England

2

somewhere in between? Certainly the Church of England in Australia and New Zealand retained 'Catholic' elements, especially in its liturgy. But again and again, so far as the relationship between people and churches is concerned, churchgoing Anglicans approximated to a general Protestant pattern. Developments were not always so marked but they were usually present: there was an Anglican difference of degree but not of kind.

I have not hesitated to draw on material pertaining to any part of Australia when it has suited my purpose, but this has rarely meant going beyond New South Wales, Victoria and South Australia. I have treated these three as forming with New Zealand one natural unit. Large-scale free settlement began in all four at about the same time. They were also geographically contiguous, since the Tasman Sea was a highway, not a barrier. The immigration programmes of the Australian and New Zealand governments after World War II were different and did introduce a degree of cultural divergence, but right through to the 1940s social and cultural homogeneity in the European populations was undisturbed.

There were some religious differences. In proportion to population as well as in absolute numbers the Catholic body was much smaller in South Australia and New Zealand than in New South Wales and Victoria. This made for a more accommodating public stance by the South Australian and New Zealand bishops. The Protestant Bible Class movement early this century was more successful in New Zealand than in Australia. But there do not seem to have been any significant variations in the ways in which Protestants or Catholics related to their local churches. The essential religious homogeneity of Protestantism and Catholicism in Australia and New Zealand was displayed in some close organizational links. It was not until 1899 that the Catholic bishops of New Zealand held their first provincial council as a hierarchy fully independent of Australia. It was not until 1913 that Wesleyan Methodism in Australia and New Zealand ceased to be under the authority of a single Australasian General Conference.

I would like to have said more about class and religion. I have certainly had vague notions at the back of my mind – for instance that Protestant churchgoers in Australia and New Zealand have been predominantly 'middle class' and that Catholic attenders have tended to be located a little lower down the social scale – but I have tried to keep these assumptions under control and not to pretend to know where really I am ignorant. The class analysis of religion in Australia and New Zealand is in its infancy.

I would also have liked to have dealt with the religious orders.

Presumably the religious orders attracted and still attract many of the most religiously committed Catholics; my exclusive concentration on ordinary parish life may therefore give a misleadingly bad impression of the spiritual health of the Catholic body in its fullness. It would also have been interesting to compare the fortunes of the corporate lives of the religious orders with the very different corporate lives of ordinary Catholic parishes.

Australia and New Zealand lack the social diversity of much larger societies. Yet smallness of scale can have advantages too. Within the compass of a single book it is possible to make a quite detailed Australasian survey covering many decades. With both Catholics and Protestants I have followed developments to about 1930. For at least three decades after the onset of the Great Depression Catholicism in Australasia seemed to flourish. The travails of the Protestant churches continued, with some alleviation during the period of the Cold War. So 1930 does not provide a natural cut-off point. The following study, however, is offered in the belief that the period covered does yield significant results in terms of trends and patterns. The breakdown of corporate religious control over the individual has been carried further in our own day, but to fully understand what is happening we need to go back. This is equally true of the two kinds of religion.

Chapter One

RELIGION AND THE IMMIGRANTS

In the nineteenth century European churches in Australia and New Zealand were churches of immigrants. As late as 1891 a majority of adult colonists had been born overseas.[1] Thirty years earlier the predominance of immigrants over native-born was overwhelming. It could not have been otherwise, since large-scale free settlements had not begun until after 1830. The total European population of all the colonies of Australasia was a mere 73 000 in 1830; by 1860 it was well over one million.[2]

Our knowledge of the immigrants in any aspect of their lives in their homelands is at present primitive. By and large before their arrival in Australasia they constitute what one historian of migration to North America has called a 'blur'.[3] Nevertheless it is possible to make some worthwhile generalizations about religion and the immigrants once we take into account the nature of the societies from which they were drawn and the social groups to which they belonged.

England was the country of origin of about half of all the people who settled in the nineteenth century in New South Wales, Victoria, South Australia and New Zealand. In the four colonies in 1891 the highest proportion of English-born amongst all those born overseas was to be found in South Australia. New Zealand was the only one of the four in 1891 to have more people born in Scotland than in Ireland. In each case the number who came from Wales was negligible.

Between about 1790 and 1840 the Protestant churches in England experienced extraordinary growth and vitality. As always within evangelical Protestantism, revitalization was marked by renewed concentration on the conversion experience. The way to religious authenticity became once again the passage from conviction of sin to personal knowledge of forgiveness. For many this was an emotional affair. The theology was simple and powerful, straight out of the central Protestant tradition. Man had sinned so greatly against the holy God that left to himself there could be no salvation, only eternal punishment; God in his unfathomable mercy had offered as expiation the sacrifice of his Son; in conversion man appropriated the merits of Christ. The Pauline emphasis was pervasive. Yet the theologically homogeneous world of English evangelical Protestantism was socially divided. There were in fact

5

Table 1: Percentages of the overseas-born of the colonists in 1891 born in England and Wales, Scotland and Ireland by colony

	England & Wales	*Scotland*	*Ireland*	*Total British Isles*	*Other Overseas-born*	*Total*
New South Wales	47.9	11.4	23.3	82.6	17.4	100.0
Victoria	46.9	14.6	24.6	86.1	13.9	100.0
South Australia	53.3	9.7	15.7	78.7	21.4	100.1
New Zealand	48.9	21.3	19.5	89.7	10.3	100.0

Note: Those born outside the respective colonies but born within Australasia are not included in the table. 'Other Overseas-born' includes all born overseas except where the birthplace was specified to be within the British Isles.

Source: Colonial censuses

two revivals. One occurred within the Church of England, the other outside it; one involved the governing classes, the other, groups who were governed.

The revival in the established church can be traced to a handful of conversions in the late 1780s. The French Revolution furthered the movement by frightening the English upper classes and leading them to equate political radicalism with irreligion. The Evangelicals, as the upper class converts came to be called, campaigned for the abolition of slavery but they eschewed radicalism at home. Mrs Trimmer recommended her Sunday schools to upper class patrons because they taught docility to the lower orders. 'If you are civil you will behave with respect to ladies and gentlemen', children were told in her model Sunday school. 'You will say, Sir, or Madam, when you speak to them; you will rise from your seat when they come into a room where you are sitting; you will make a curtsey to them when you meet them.'[4] It is difficult to tell how long it took for Evangelical recruits to affect the tone of the English ruling class. The *Annual Register* of 1798 carried a report that the carriages of the fashionable were being seen outside London churches in unprecedented numbers.[5] On the other hand William Romaine was reputedly the only Evangelical preacher in London until the end of the century.[6] Probably at its zenith around 1815, by the late 1830s the conservative evangelical revival was over. One sign of this was the success of the Catholic-leaning Oxford Movement, which began in 1833. Bright young men from Evangelical families provided some of the leading figures of the Oxford Movement.

Religious dissent had long been in England a means of expressing deviance from the values of those who ruled. It was so again in the early nineteenth century when there were many who were aggrieved with their lot or who sensed the possibility of improvement. The utility of religion as a means of social protest and advancement was not the sole or main cause of the revival among the dissenters but it did much to boost it.[7] Between 1790 and 1840 total membership of Congregational, Baptist and Methodist bodies increased from about 100 000 to around 650 000, a rate of growth twice as great as that of the total population.[8] The very existence of the Church of England as the established church of the land seemed to be in peril as it became less and less plausible to dismiss dissent as the choice of a tiny minority. At the 1851 census of public worship, the first and only such official census conducted in England, the number of chapelgoers about equalled those who attended the services of the Church of England.[9] Fortunately for the established church the period of rapid expansion for the dissenters ended in the late 1830s. Zeal in religious practice, so highly valued in the various dissenting traditions, persisted much longer. Two religious censuses were held in Liverpool in 1881, one of religious affiliation and the other of separate acts of attendance at public worship. In 1881 total Church of England attendances in the Liverpool area were around 55 000, constituting about eighteen acts of attendance for every 100 persons who professed to belong to the established church. Total attendances for all other groups, excluding the Roman Catholics, were 68 000. This was about 65 acts of attendance for every 100 persons who were professèd nonconformists, as the dissenters had come to be called.[10]

Many rural folk were among the Anglicans seldom to be found at public worship. In the heavily rural district of South Lindsey in Lincolnshire perhaps less than one third of the total population worshipped in a parish church on census Sunday in 1851.[11] Holy Communion services were especially badly attended. In 1800 some Evangelical clergymen published a report on a survey they had made of 79 parishes in the diocese of Lincoln. Fewer than one in six of persons over fourteen years of age in these parishes received Holy Communion.[12] In the South Lindsey district, statistics for 1873 suggest that about eight out of every ten adults abstained from receiving Holy Communion.[13] Nor did attending the parish church guarantee even a modicum of religious knowledge or commitment. A communicant taking the chalice in Dorset in the early nineteenth century wished the vicar a Happy New Year. At another village church when a newly arrived vicar administered communion one man touched his forelock and said 'Here's your good health, sir'.[14]

Uncompromised by the Church of England's intimate association with the governing classes, dissenting preachers appealed powerfully for a time to craftsmen, farmers and miners. They did not reach rural labourers on any significant scale. The Primitive Methodists were not really an exception here. The Primitives attracted a disproportionately large number of labourers to membership of their churches – disproportionate that is to the Wesleyans, Congregationalists and Baptists – but they were too small a body to make a substantial impact; the total Primitive Methodist membership in England in 1840 was but 74 000.[15]

The only form of religion genuinely popular amongst English rural labourers in the early nineteenth century seems to have been a loose collection of immemorial folk practices. These have often been dismissed as superstition and not religion at all, yet they presupposed a lively belief in a supernatural order. The best study is that of James Obelkevich, who has documented for Lincolnshire spells for curing ailments and winning sweethearts, horseshoes for keeping away Old Nick, telling the bees when their master had died, consulting 'wise men' about lost or stolen property and so on. Obelkevich has concluded that these practices were on the wane in Lincolnshire by the middle of the nineteenth century.[16]

Labourers and their families probably constituted the bulk of emigrants from the countryside to the rapidly growing towns; therefore the tenuous hold of the Church of England and nonconformist bodies upon rural labourers was fraught with significance for the future. Nearly two out of every three residents of English towns in 1851 had been born in the country.[17]

In the large towns labourers were poor church attenders compared with the middle and upper classes. At the religious census of 1851 attendances were lowest where there were the largest concentrations of labourers – London and the manufacturing towns.[18] The religious census of London conducted by the *Daily News* in 1902 and 1903 is especially revealing. Taking London as a whole there was a close correlation between the affluence of areas and the rate of religious practice of residents: the higher the proportion of households with servants, the more people went to church or chapel. In poor areas of London hardly more than one adult in ten was attending public worship at the time of the *Daily News* census.[19]

Urban labourers on the whole were not atheists or anti-clerical. They normally sent their children to Sunday school and many would themselves occasionally be in church for weddings, funerals and special festivals. But regular attendance at public worship was not a strand of the working class cultural pattern. The cultural gap between church and chapel life on the one hand and the unskilled

FROM THE MINING DISTRICTS

AN ATTEMPT AT CONVERTING THE NATIVES

Assiduous young curate. '*Well then, I do hope I shall have the pleasure of seeing you both next Sunday!*'

Miner. '*Oi! Thee may'st coam if 'e wull. We foight on the Croft, and old Joe Tanner brings th' beer.*'

on the other was sometimes extraordinarily wide. Henry Mayhew met a London costermonger who told him 'religion was a regular puzzle' to his folk.

> They see people come out of church and chapel, and as they're mostly well dressed, and there's very few of their own sort among the church-goers, the costers somehow mix up being religious with being respectable, and so they have a queer sort of feeling about it. It's a mystery to them.[20]

9

From the late 1790s there began in Scotland a revival of evangelical religion that roughly corresponded to the revival in England. Initially there was the same upsurge of itinerating evangelism.[21] There was also the same shift of opinion amongst the upper classes encouraged by developments in revolutionary France. Gustave d'Eichthal who visited Britain in 1828 commented on the increase of religious practice in Scotland as well as England.[22] About this time Lord Cockburn observed that religion had become 'certainly more the fashion' in Scotland.[23] Yet through to the 1830s the dynamism and disruption of revival English-style was missing. Though John Wesley had made 22 trips to Scotland between 1751 and 1790 Methodism never caught on there. The Baptists and Congregationalists in Scotland did not enjoy the prodigious growth of their English co-religionists.

There was no hope of thorough-going revival within the Church of Scotland so long as the Moderates were in control. Men of the Enlightenment, theirs was a cool reasonable religion. Opposed to them were the Evangelicals – the Scottish counterpart of the English party with the same name. The centre of the power struggle between the two was patronage. The Moderates firmly supported, the Evangelicals wished to curtail the right of lay patrons to appoint to congregations the minister of their choice. In 1833 Thomas Chalmers moved in the General Assembly of the Church of Scotland that congregations be able to veto ministers presented to them by lay patrons. Chalmers had been a Moderate clergyman until a conversion experience in 1811, whereupon he quickly became a leader of the Evangelicals. Chalmers's motion was defeated, but in the next year the Moderates were toppled. The Evangelical party passed a veto act which aimed to severely limit though not to abolish lay patronage. This same 1834 Assembly appointed Chalmers convener of the committee on church extension, formed in 1828. Previously this committee had achieved little by seeking government aid. Chalmers appealed to private generosity. In the seven years when he was convener the committee raised £306 000 and built or began building 222 churches. In the late 1830s there was also a new enthusiasm for foreign missions.

The civil courts declared the 1834 veto act beyond the power of the Church Assembly. What happened then best demonstrates the power of the evangelical energies now unleashed within the Church of Scotland. Chalmers and his followers abandoned hope of reform through parliament in the short term; they were in a hurry and they believed that the choice was whether or not to capitulate to an Erastian establishment. The price of not capitulating was to make the immense sacrifice of forgoing all state money. This is what one third of the ministers and one third of the congregations chose to do in 1843. At the Disruption the ministers who went out had no manses, no stipends, and there were but 50 churches they could call their own. Within a year 470 new churches had been completed. By 1847 there were over 700 Free Church congregations worshipping in churches of their own. Within 25 years the Free Church raised not less than £600 000 for education and had nearly 600 schools.[24]

Alongside the Church of Scotland, and the Free Church after the Disruption, there were other smaller Presbyterian bodies corresponding to the dissenters in England. Speaking generally, evangelical religion had the stronger hold in Scotland. The Sabbath rest was more rigorously observed and churchgoing higher. There was also a stronger tradition of bible reading and prayers within the family circle. Piety within the Church of Scotland was not intense, especially after the Disruption had taken away the warmest souls. Yet the Church of Scotland was more evangelical than the official church in England. The Church of England was an attempt at a *via media* between Rome and Geneva; the Church of Scotland was definitely Genevan.

In Scotland, as in England, religion went hand in hand with social respectability and labourers appear to have been largely estranged from the churches. Amongst many rural labourers a folk religion only tinged with Christianity persisted into the nineteenth century.[25] There were the same problems as in England with the rapidly expanding working class districts of the large towns. At work in one of these areas in Edinburgh in the late 1830s, the Reverend Thomas Guthrie observed he might as well have gone to be a missionary among the Hindus on the banks of the Ganges.[26]

Class differences within the churchgoing population in Scotland have been but slightly examined by scholars compared with those in England. Nevertheless there is little doubt that there were broad social differences between the main religious bodies. The eighteenth-century seceders and their ministers were of humbler origin than those who led the Church of Scotland. A. A. McLaren has studied the social composition of the supporters of the Free Church in Aberdeen, where in 1843 all fifteen ministers left the establishment. McLaren concluded that middle class entrepreneurs were especially attracted to the Free Church. These were new men who were challenging the established well-to-do families linked to the gentry. The social comment of Free Church spokesmen was attuned to the urban middle classes.[27] The Free Church became strong also in the highlands.

In the early nineteenth century about 80 per cent of the population of Ireland were Catholic. The Protestants were heavily concentrated in Ulster where they were about half the population. As in England and Scotland, the Protestant churches in Ireland experienced a revival in the early nineteenth century. But there was an Irish variation: evangelicalism confronted by a Catholic majority of four to one took on a harsher, more combative edge. By the 1830s there were calls within the established Anglican Church of Ireland for a drive to convert 'Popish idolaters'. In the late 1840s a determined Protestant crusade was launched from England and for a few years it looked as though proselytism might succeed on a large scale. By the 1860s the intense mutual suspicion between Protestant and Catholic in Ireland had superseded the relative tolerance of the first quarter of the century.[28] Both England and Scotland had their indigenous Catholic traditions but by the middle of the nineteenth century these were struggling for survival in the face of heavy migration across the Irish Sea. In four Lancashire towns that have been studied by John Bossy, as early as 1834 the Catholic congregations were 62 per cent Irish.[29]

The Catholic church in Ireland in the early nineteenth century faced an enormous pastoral problem with the landless or virtually landless poor who constituted at least two thirds of rural families. Priests ministering to these people had to compete with folk beliefs and practices. Labourers working cultivated fields often left standing certain kinds of bush believed to be favoured by the fairies. Hundreds at a time gathered at wells and other sacred places for activities that were more pagan than Catholic. The Irish wake of the countryside had little to do with affirming a Christian understanding of death, for it seems to have been widely believed that the spirit of the dead person presided over the gathering and was honoured by the festivities. These wakes sometimes included games celebrating sexual vitality.[30]

Population increase compounded the task of making Catholicism a living faith to the rural poor. In 1772, when it had already been growing for a generation, the population of Ireland was about 3.6 million; in 1841 it was 8.2 million. In 1731 there were 1587 Catholics in Ireland for every parish priest or curate; by 1840 there were 2996 for every parish priest or curate.[31] In a poor country it was impossible to build enough places of worship for such an expanding population. As an expedient, priests said masses in private houses, but this inhibited priestly independence and kept local gatherings small. Attendance at mass in the mid-1830s was lowest in proportion to population in the north-west, west and south-west, where priests and chapels were least well provided.[32]

There were other problems. The Catholic church in Ireland had its share of the abuses and inefficiencies that seem to have characterized churches in many parts of Western Europe in the eighteenth century. Parish priests were unaccustomed to vigorous episcopal oversight: in theory, at least, between 1698 and 1782 a Catholic bishop discovered in Ireland was liable to arrest and deportation. By the 1830s and 1840s some bishops were tightening discipline but others were senile, incompetent or uninterested. A national synod held in 1850 was unable to resolve bitter, public and long-held episcopal differences of opinion over education.[33]

Members of the dissenting Protestant churches were strongly associated with the cause of Irish nationalism through to the late 1790s. Actual insurrection against the British Crown, culminating in the battle at Vinegar Hill in 1798, brought a realignment of Protestant sympathies. From this time Catholicism became progressively and peculiarly identified with nationalist aspirations and thereby enhanced its influence upon Irish society. The parliamentary act of Catholic emancipation in 1829 was won in part through work in the constituencies by Daniel O'Connell's Catholic Association. The clergy of the Association, one historian has written, 'acted as local and constituency organizers, passed down directives, and above all gathered, led and steadied the voters on the day of polling'.[34] This identification of the church with the cause of the people was strengthened in the campaign against the tithe which even half-starved labourers on potato patches were compelled to pay to the Church of Ireland. The Catholic bishops were not as unqualified in their support of the campaign for the repeal of the Act of Union of 1800, but the Repeal movement was widely seen as an anti-Protestant cause and priests were prominent in it.

Following a partial failure of the potato crop in 1845 there was a complete failure in 1846. By 1851 perhaps one million people had died, thousands from starvation but most of fever they were too weak to resist. Another million had become emigrants. There were further lesser famines and further emigration. At any time between 1850 and 1900 more than two million Irish-born were living overseas. Economically as well as demographically there was extraordinarily rapid change. A subsistence economy had predominated in many rural parts before the Famine and had

Irish emigrants leaving home, with the priest's blessing.

existed in others almost side by side with a commercial sector. The proportion of holdings between one and five acres is a rough guide to the shrinking and virtual disappearance of this large subsistence sector: at the 1841 census 45 per cent of all holdings larger than one acre were between one and five acres; at the 1851 census the proportion was 16 per cent and still falling.[35]

The tragedy of the Great Famine had far-reaching religious implications. Many of those who survived and remained in Ireland were psychologically prepared for a message of salvation by observation of the starving and the dead, by personal suffering and by dislocation of life either experienced or feared. The constituency of the Catholic church was drastically altered, providing more malleable material for the clergy. Before the Famine labourers had probably always been under-represented, large farmers heavily over-represented, amongst those who attended mass, provided their sons for the priesthood and donated money for church purposes. Yet the emigrants were recruited predominantly, though by no means exclusively, from the rural poor. Farmers in 1845 had been outnumbered more than two to one by poorer sections of the rural population; by 1881 the two broad groups were roughly equal.[36] An absolute decline in the Catholic population – 6.5 million in 1840, 4.1 million in 1871 – naturally meant that a higher proportion could be accommodated in churches, a proportion that was further enlarged by the building of many new churches. Furthermore, although the total population decreased, the number of priests increased, so that by 1870 the Catholics of Ireland were nearly twice as well off for priests as they had been 30 years before.[37] These priests were overseen by a reformed and reforming episcopacy. The national synod of Thurles in 1850 began a series of administrative reforms which tightened the bishops' supervision of their dioceses. In the parishes devotions that were new to most Irish Catholics became popular in the decade or so after the Famine, including the rosary, the forty-hours adoration, blessed altars, benediction and vespers, and devotion to the sacred heart.[38]

To judge from some defective government statistics, in 1837 perhaps two in every three adults who were within easy reach of a Catholic church went to Sunday mass.[39] According to one early nineteenth-century observer Irish peasants so strictly observed public worship that 'the man must be very far gone in crime who disregards it'.[40] So there was a strong base for further effort. Even so the religious progress made in the aftermath of the Famine was phenomenal. By the 1890s probably 90 per cent of the Catholic population was regularly at mass.[41] The British Protestant churches at the height of their revivals earlier in the century never matched this drawing power.

Founded in 1788, the colony of New South Wales for the first 40 years of its existence was primarily a receptacle for convicts. At the census of 1828 two in every three persons were either convict or ex-convict. Transportation to New South Wales did not cease until 1840. All told about 80 000 men, women and children arrived in New South Wales following sentences of transportation by British courts.[42]

Large-scale free settlement of Australasia did not begin until the second third of the nineteenth century. In 1831, when the British government decided to assist free migration to New South Wales, the population of the colony was only 51 000. It was not until 1834 that the occupation of Victoria by pastoralists began. The pioneers of settlement in South Australia did not begin to arrive until 1836. When Britain annexed New Zealand in 1840 the total European population was probably not more than about 2000.[43] Victoria, South Australia and New Zealand were either totally or almost totally given over to free migration.

In the British Isles convicts were notorious for their irreligion. Sydney Smith, for example, claimed that the gaols of England, and especially those of London, were filled with those who 'have never entered a church, who have never heard a pastor, who have never heard God's law mentioned but when it was broken, nor

God's name invoked but when it was blasphemed.'[44] Many of those transported to New South Wales were drawn from a floating population which moved within and in and out of London. According to Henry Mayhew, who knew them well, there were many distinct types of these nomads, from the half-thief, half-beggar to those with skills; yet they were all 'more or less distinguished . . . for their use of a slang language – for their lax ideas of property – for their general improvidence – their repugnance to continuous labour – for their disregard of female honour – their love of cruelty – their pugnacity – and their utter want of religion.'[45] Clergymen working as chaplains on the transports to Australia sometimes made energetic attempts to reform their charges. They made little progress. The male convicts were known to use Bibles and prayer books to make cards, the women to turn tracts into hair curlers.[46] If convicts on transports displayed piety, they were usually shamming to get favoured treatment. Not all the Irish Catholic convicts were hardened against religion, though this was probably the rule. Peter Cunningham, a surgeon superintendent on five transports in the 1820s and a man not easily fooled, once saw a group of Catholic convicts at their prayers and thought them genuine.[47] When the first Catholic bishop of Sydney, John Bede Polding, began to minister to Irish Catholic convicts newly arrived in Sydney, officials were impressed by the moral improvement which occurred.[48]

The radical Protestant revival of the early nineteenth century encountered in Britain tenacious social and religious privilege. In 1828 the Test and Corporation Acts were repealed and in the next three or four years it seemed to some that all religious inequalities would be swept away along with rotten boroughs and aristocratic sinecures. But in the late 1830s, when the tide of radical reform was receding, the dissenters were still, by force of law and custom, second-class citizens. In England they faced restrictions at the ancient universities; if they wished to bury their dead in an Anglican churchyard – and often no other burial ground was available – the service had to be conducted by an Anglican clergyman; chapel records of baptism, marriage and death were not admitted as evidence in courts of law; they had to pay rates for the support of the established church.[49]

One possibility for frustrated radicals was to begin settlements overseas in which their civil and religious aspirations could have free play. Some saw South Australia this way, and one in particular, George Fife Angas, was well placed to influence events. Angas was a member of the Colonization Commission charged by the British government with overseeing the establishment of the colony; he was active too in the South Australian Company, which had interests in whaling, agriculture and livestock. Though keen to make money out of South Australia, Angas was sincere when he declared his main purpose to be 'to provide a place of refuge for pious Dissenters of Great Britain, who could in their new home discharge their consciences before God in civil and religious duties without any disabilities.' Of the 12 204 persons who got free passages during the first five years of settlement in South Australia, Angas and the men whom he got appointed emigration agents were responsible for sending out one third. Angas represented only one kind of influence upon early South Australia. Hindmarsh, the first governor, and Fisher, the resident commissioner, were both staunch Church and Crown men. Most of the men of capital who arrived in the early years were less attracted by religion than by the consideration that land-buyers got free passages for their labourers.[50]

The Otago settlement in New Zealand was begun in 1848. Initially Otago was controlled by a Lay Association, which was in theory an arm of the Free Church of Scotland. The two principal leaders in the early years were the Reverend Thomas Burns and Captain William Cargill, both of whom were fervent Free Churchmen and both of whom saw themselves as making a godly experiment after the model of the Pilgrim Fathers two centuries earlier. But Burns and Cargill and others in the Lay Association got only token support from the Assembly of the Free Church of Scotland. Furthermore, the Association was disbanded in 1853 when the population of Otago was only a few thousand.[51] Perhaps most who sailed for Otago, even in the first few years, came for wholly secular reasons.

In its original conception the Canterbury settlement was to be a new-world exemplar of an Anglican state. J. R. Godley who led the infant settlement had come under the influence of the Oxford Movement and his dream of Canterbury as a Church of England colony was the antithesis of Angas's of South Australia as a haven for dissenters. Even more than in the cases of South Australia and Otago secular influences mastered the original vision. Within five years of Canterbury's founding in 1850, church and state had been separated there.[52]

Albertland, north of Auckland on the Kaipara harbour, was another failure as a religious settlement. Conceived of as a 'nonconformist' colony, the first three ships carrying the pioneers arrived in late 1862 in time to mark the bicentenary of the ejection from the Church of England of nonconforming ministers. Other ships followed but the scheme never recovered from early bungling. Albertland was never an exclusively nonconformist settlement.[53]

The religious element was strongest amongst a few small groups of immigrants. In 1839, 537 persons arrived in South Australia after running foul of the state in Prussia because of their religious views. These pietists had originally intended to go to America, but were diverted when their leader made contact with George Fife Angas.[54] A similar group was a community of Scots that settled in New Zealand between 1854 and 1860. They were Calvinists of a stricter kind than the Otago people and belonged to a group that had broken with the Church of Scotland long before 1843. Their leader was Norman McLeod, an intelligent and autocratic Presbyterian minister. They were in search of a land where they could fish, work timber, farm, and freely practise their faith. These Scots had migrated initially to Nova Scotia and had been settled at St Annes, Cape Breton Island, since 1820. In 1848 Norman McLeod's son, Donald, wrote from South Australia recommending that the community remove there. Crops. had failed and American competition was threatening the fishing, so at the age of 71 McLeod made a second migration. Over 850 in all, the people came in six ships, some of which they had built themselves. The *Margaret*, on which McLeod sailed, led the way in 1851. After an attempt to acquire land on the coast of South Australia was unsuccessful, the *Margaret* went on to Melbourne. McLeod and some of his band remained in Victoria for a year and a half, again seeking suitable land. After a second group of the Nova Scotians had negotiated with Sir George Grey in New Zealand, a permanent settlement was made at Waipu, north of Auckland.[55]

But for two factors it is highly likely that many more British Protestant radicals would have found their way to the antipodes. The first is that since North America was so much closer to home there had to be a special reason for preferring the long and costly voyage south. Secondly, free migration occurred almost entirely after 1830 and to a very large extent after 1850. This is important because those Protestants intent on religious settlements overseas left the British Isles predominantly in the *early* nineteenth century. By the late 1830s English dissent had lost much of its earlier dynamism. Thus *free* settlement in Australasia only began in time for the colonial churches to receive the backwash of the English dissenting revival. New South Wales, founded in 1788, was in a position, chronologically speaking, to receive the maximum impact of evangelical energies. Yet, as a convict colony, revival, naturally, passed it by. Botany Bay might have been a second

Massachusetts Bay; it is a great irony of Australian history that, instead, it became a byword for depravity and irreligion. In Queensland in the early 1860s Bishop James Quinn and Father Patrick Dunne established an immigration society which catered largely for Irish Catholics. But no Catholic entrepreneur, Irish or otherwise, succeeded in launching a settlement that was physically apart and exclusively Catholic. Any attempt to do so would have been unlikely to secure approval from the Colonial Office and from Protestant dominated colonial governments. Even Quinn's scheme had to be wound up after a few years in the face of Protestant objections. The bishop's boast about turning Queensland into Quinnsland did not help.[56]

Ireland was the chief source of Catholics by a long way. Defining Europe to include the British Isles, Ireland was the place of birth of 72 in every 100 Catholics who had migrated from Europe and were living in Australia in 1911. Catholics seem to have accounted for around one in twenty of English immigrants. Other sources of Catholic immigrants during the nineteenth century included Scotland, France, Germany and Italy.[57]

Irish emigration statistics kept by the British government provide a good guide to the flow of Irish Catholics to the colonies. In 1841–50 there were 23 000 departures from Ireland for Australia and New Zealand. Roughly half of all departures for Australia and New Zealand during the nineteenth century were in the next two decades: 1851–60 102 000, 1861–70 83 000. Declining during the 1870s and 1880s, by the early 1890s the flow had been reduced to a trickle.[58] This variation was much the same as that in the flow of Protestant migration to the antipodes from all over the British Isles. But the Catholic Church in Australasia stood to benefit much more from the largely late nineteenth-century nature of the immigration. After about 1860 it would have been hard for any Catholic in Ireland to have remained uninfluenced by the heightening of piety that followed the Famine. Sixty-three in every 100 Irish departing for Australia and New Zealand between 1841 and 1900 came *after* 1860.[59]

Colonial censuses regularly included a question about religious affiliation. Though there was some transfer of denominational allegiance within the colonies, the censuses of 1860–61 may be taken as a rough guide to religious professions upon arrival of the immigrants of the preceding 30 years.

New South Wales and Victoria were the most Catholic of the colonies, which is not surprising since they were also the most Irish. At least a quarter of the immigrants to New South Wales before 1860 had been Catholic. This was a substantially larger

Table 2: Percentages of population in each colony adhering to the principal denominations in 1860–61

	Church of England	Presbyterian	Methodist	Roman Catholic	All Others	Total
New South Wales	45.6	9.9	6.7	28.3	9.5	100.0
Victoria	38.1	16.1	8.6	20.3	16.9	100.0
South Australia	36.9	8.9	18.8	13.2	22.2	100.0
New Zealand	44.9	21.4	8.5	11.0	14.2	100.0

Source: Colonial censuses

proportion than Catholics formed of the total population of the British Isles.[60] New Zealand was the most Presbyterian colony. South Australia stood out for its large number of English dissenters, especially Methodists. The Cornish who came to mine silver, lead and copper had done much to boost the Methodist presence in South Australia.[61] They were also likely to be found anywhere in Australia that mining skills were in demand. When a visiting British Wesleyan Methodist leader addressed a large gathering of Wesleyans at Ballarat in the early 1860s he judged that two thirds of those present were from Cornwall.[62]

Not all the immigrants from the British Isles professed some form of Christian belief. Alexander Harris, who was later to write *Settlers and Convicts*, had become an atheist before sailing for New South Wales in 1825.[63] Thomas Arnold was brother of that great Victorian doubter Matthew Arnold, and friend of A. H. Clough, another poet who experienced religious unsettlement. Thomas Arnold himself had already abandoned religious orthodoxy when he left on the *John Wickliffe* for New Zealand in 1847.[64] Charles Southwell, who emigrated to Victoria in 1855, was one of the most notorious British freethinkers of his day. In 1841, following the fourth number of his journal *The Oracle of Reason*, he had been sentenced to gaol for a year for blasphemy.[65] But professed unbelievers were a minute element amongst those who emigrated before 1860. In Victoria, for example, at the census of 1861 the enumerators discovered only 441 persons who declared themselves to have no religion. This was in a population of half a million.

Because social position conditioned religious attitudes so heavily in the nineteenth century (as indeed it does now) occupational statistics regarding the immigrants deserve a rapid review. For New South Wales and Victoria before 1850 the most detailed information we have is for 1838–41. During these years the occupations were recorded of 14 308 adult male immigrants, comprising both assisted and unassisted. Six out of every ten were recorded as being agricultural labourers.[66] In the first two decades of settlement in South Australia three out of every four arrivals were assisted and almost certainly a majority of the assisted males were labourers.[67] British officials kept records of the occupations of *all* adult males departing from the United Kingdom between 1854 and 1876 for Australia and New Zealand. Upwards of six in every ten of the adult male immigrants during these years were classified as agricultural or other labourers.[68] All these statistics should be regarded as approximate but unquestionably the unskilled and semi-skilled predominated. Furthermore it seems certain that most of the immigrant families had recent experience of the countryside, even if they did not come directly from it. In other words most immigrants were from precisely those social groups – the rural and urban labourers – which the Protestant churches had found hardest to reach at home. Victoria is something of a special case. To an extraordinary extent its nineteenth-century immigrants arrived during the gold rushes of the 1850s. About half of Victoria's migrants during the 1850s were skilled tradesmen, professionals or those with commercial or financial backgrounds.[69]

Dissent tended to go with skills. Victoria in the 1850s took both an unusually large share of skilled immigrants and an unusually large share of dissenters. In Victoria between the censuses of 1851 and 1861 the combined numbers of English and Scottish dissenters increased almost three times as fast as those who adhered to the established churches of England and Scotland. The same phenomenon can be observed in South Australia. In that colony the unassisted constituted 17 per cent of the arrivals between 1836 and 1846. Between 1846 and 1855, when the share of the unassisted increased to 27 per cent, the number of English and Scottish dissenters in South Australia increased twice as fast as did adherents of the established churches.[70]

In New Zealand it was Scottish not English dissent that was especially well represented amongst the immigrants. At the New Zealand census of 1858 there were almost twice as many Presbyterian dissenters as adherents of the 'auld kirk' amongst those who specified to which Presbyterian body they belonged.[71]

For two years we have detailed information on the occupations of all Irish arrivals in Australia and New Zealand. In 1857 eight out of every ten of the males whose occupations were specified were labourers, in 1867 slightly under three out of every four. In both years the women with occupations specified were almost universally domestic servants.[72] Other evidence is provided by a random sample made by N. Coughlan of 3200 migrants entered on shipping lists of vessels arriving in Victoria between 1853 and 1870. Eighty-nine per cent of the Irishmen in this sample were unskilled and the bulk of these were described as 'labourer'. (Coughlan found that 50 per cent of his English and Scottish immigrants were unskilled.)[73]

Summing up the religion of the immigrants is not easy. On the one hand, New South Wales and Victoria received large numbers of Irish Catholics; on the other, South Australia and New Zealand received relatively few. On the one hand, convicts provided New South Wales with the worst possible religious foundations; on the other, there were attempts at religious settlements. On the one hand, at least half of the immigrants were from labouring families and therefore likely to be slow in responding to the churches in the colonies; on the other, there was a substantial minority of dissenters, a people renowned for their church involvement.

Professor Patrick O'Farrell has written that very few who were really religious came to Australia.[74] Undoubtedly true, and undoubtedly equally true of New Zealand. But in any country how large is the proportion of those who are 'really religious'? Churchmen were to lament the convict origins of Australia. With more force they might have said if only free Protestant settlers had arrived in large numbers during the revivals of the early nineteenth century; if only all the Catholics had been imbued with the heightened piety characteristic of the church in post-Famine Ireland; if only more of both Catholics and Protestants had been well-to-do. Yet these comments would have been one-sided: though pilgrim mothers and fathers were few, most of the immigrants had backgrounds that predisposed them towards some degree of continuing contact with the churches. The England, Scotland and Ireland, from which the immigrants were drawn, were during the nineteenth century amongst the most religious societies in the history of European civilization. Presbyterianism in New Zealand was in a position to benefit from the Free Church revival. South Australia has been aptly called a 'paradise of dissent'. The Catholic arrivals were nearly all Irish and therefore habituated to linking their faith with their Irishness. Unless the physical and social environment of the new world turned out to be extraordinarily tough the churches seemed assured of a future.

Chapter Two

IN A NEW WORLD

A Wesleyan wrote from Adelaide in 1848, 'We are receiving many emigrants, who left England as professors of religion, but comparatively few unite themselves to us or other of Christ's Churches.'[1] Reporting on the state of Presbyterian religion in Otago in 1890, the Reverend Dr Michael Watt commented on the 'multitudes who had been brought up in Christian homes, who had been members of the Church in the Old Country' yet whose only connection with church life in the colony was through their children's attendance at Sabbath school.[2] Similar complaints were made time and again within the colonial Protestant churches.[3] Though there were fewer comments in the Catholic press, Catholic bishops and priests also worried about 'leakage'.[4] The problem was recognized too by some of the Catholic laity. A writer for the Irish Catholic *Freeman's Journal* published in Sydney did not bother to elaborate on how Catholic immigrants fell away from the practice of their religion; many of his readers, he observed, were well aware of what happened.[5] In all these laments there was a solid basis of truth but also probably an element of exaggeration: many immigrants did not so much abandon the churches as sit more loosely to them.

The religious unsettlement of colonial life was anticipated on the voyage out: the immigrant's vessel was a little colony in itself. People from different backgrounds were thrown together, the pious along with the indifferent. Routines broke down in enforced idleness; frequently there was slackness of tone and a relaxation of moral conventions. Religious services lacked the solemnity provided by a building set aside for public worship; sometimes there would be no regular services.[6]

For those immigrants who had a churchgoing background landfall was a testing time. Some immigrants carried letters of introduction to ministers, but who was to see that a single unaccompanied young man or woman was going to use them?[7] Some immigrants took months after arrival to settle down – some never did – and in the meantime it was easy to get out of the habit of churchgoing. A new arrival was also exposed to new ways of behaving and seeing the world, since in the colonies people from all over the British Isles and with different local traditions were brought into contact. Going along with a new circle of friends often induced departure from family religious traditions.

23

John McGlashan, on the eve of Otago's founding, urged that it should be an exclusively Free Church colony; in this way, he believed, its settlers could counteract or avoid 'the evils which have arisen in other colonies from the heterogeneous mixture of all creeds and persuasions, and the spiritual destitution which in consequence has so much characterised them.'[8] But Otago itself proved to be no exception to the rule of heterogeneity. Free Church adherents constituted no more than half of the settlers to 1860.[9] Then came the gold rushes. At the census of 1891 Presbyterians were a minority in Otago and in not one county or borough of the province did they constitute two thirds of the population.

A South Australian Protestant colonist complained in 1859 that fellow-believers had allowed their children to mix too freely with the children of the ungodly and even encouraged them to do so. 'In the recreations of our religious families there is too often an utter want of society congenial to pious associations and moral restraints. The rule seems to be to choose the most mixed and promiscuous society as the most desirable for innocent and profitable enjoyment.'[10] Many evangelical Christians undoubtedly did acquire a taste for social intercourse with the unconverted. Still, this criticism was not completely fair; in the colonies 'bad' company was not easily avoided.

After extensive experience in the Australian colonies in the 1830s James Backhouse wrote that people who had never been plunged into an entirely new environment were little aware how much of what they counted their own good character they owed 'to the oversight of those by whom they are continually surrounded.'[11] In the middle and upper middle classes oversight at home was especially strict about how Sunday was observed. Alexander Harris, who travelled about New South Wales during the late 1820s and 1830s, heard many people say 'There is no Sunday in the bush.'[12] A minister in New South Wales in 1848 reported the saying 'No Sunday beyond the mountains.' It was used, he claimed, on a particular pass, by men as they descended westwards onto the plains.[13] In the early years of settlement people were similarly careless about Sunday in the New Zealand backblocks and the squatting districts of Victoria. Even Scots succumbed on the frontier, without other Sabbatarians about them to keep them up to the mark. Sometimes these Presbyterians ignored the Sabbath altogether; sometimes they made it what one of their New Zealand ministers called 'a handy day' for doing miscellaneous tasks of a smaller kind.[14]

The pious who moved into sparsely settled and remote districts could find their faith frighteningly insecure. William Hamilton, a Presbyterian minister, reported in the late 1830s that the 'ungodly conversation' in the Goulburn district 'chills my piety and tends to degrade my discourse'. In 1837 a Wesleyan was warned by his friends against settling his family in Maitland because of what it might do to their faith. Backhouse found that religious conviction waned on the frontier as people stopped saying their prayers.[15] Time and again outback ministers were engulfed by a spiritual indifference that was omnipresent. It was partly in self-defence that some enterprising Church of England ministers began brotherhoods through which outback parsons might give one another support. Urging a brotherhood for New Zealand, the Reverend W. Bullock in 1923 wrote that to send a young man into the backblocks unaccompanied by a wife or a fellow minister was 'a form of not very refined cruelty'.[16]

A primary cause of frontier irreligiosity was a shortage of women. They were missed as people who were churchgoers. They were missed, too, as moderating and softening influences on male behaviour. Where women were few, drinking, gambling and swearing were likely to abound and readiness for religion to be slight.

The clergy too were in short supply in frontier districts. People absorbed in pioneering were often unable or unwilling to support a regular ministry, and city congregations were uninterested or miserly about funding the work. It was also an inherently difficult task ministering to a thinly spread population and nowhere was this more so than on the great inland plains of eastern Australia. To give just one illustration, the Reverend E. Synge made a tour of inspection of the south-western part of New South Wales for his bishop in the late 1850s. This was then one corner of the Church of England diocese of Sydney. Synge took ten months to do the trip by horse and had to travel 4700 miles.[17] It is hardly surprising that some colonists in the 1850s had not seen a minister for ten or fifteen years; some of their children never.

Some did not miss a parson. In 1859 at Okains Bay on New Zealand's Banks Peninsula saw-millers organized dog fights to try to put an end to the first church services there.[18] C. H. S. Matthews, who served as a parson in the New South Wales outback, had a story told him by a clerical friend, which, whether true or not, is similarly revealing. A bushman had been brought into hospital from a township 400 miles away. The clergyman asked the man whether there had been a religious service in his town. The man replied that on one occasion the boys had heard a religious bloke was on his way. They got worried, held a meeting and decided that, since they had done without religion for so long, they could do without now. So they took up a collection which came to ten quid and then one of the boys went to meet the religious bloke and told him that he could take his money and clear or they would keep their money and they'd clear. The clergyman is supposed to have taken the money.[19]

But this is not the whole picture. We need to be wary of ministers who talked only of frontier irreligion. The standards of these ministers were high and they often wanted to shock city people into providing them with financial support for bush work. There were parsons whose ministry was welcomed. The Abercrombie district in New South Wales had been without a minister until the Reverend Richard Leigh arrived in the late 1850s. On learning that the dead had been buried up till then without religious rites Leigh let it be known that he was willing to make good the lack. Soon afterwards, a young man turned up on his doorstep about seven o'clock on a Sunday morning to ask him to bury a woman who had died in childbirth. The man had ridden all night upwards of 40 miles. When Leigh went on the Monday as arranged he found at the place fifty or sixty horses scattered over the hillside. Their owners walked down to greet him. It was cold and raining heavily as it had been all day. Leigh conducted the service over a shallow grave, an old man insisting on holding over him his cabbage tree hat. The service over, he was shown the baby. Would he baptize it? The baptism was conducted by the grave, the riding skirt of one of the women present stretched over Leigh and the baby.[20]

During a journey of 1874 the Reverend F. B. Boyce arrived at Wilcannia after sunset on a Saturday evening. He left 48 hours later. In the meantime he held a Sunday morning service, a children's service, an evening service so crowded that some could not get in, christened children, married two couples and held a public meeting at which those present agreed to pay for a clergyman to come every quarter from Bourke, to support a resident minister when one could be sent, and subscribed at the same meeting £385 for a church. Before Boyce left Wilcannia he and a committee had selected the site.[21]

In all the colonies where the land was suitable for farming, by the end of the nineteenth century the sheep runs were being broken up. In these districts a religious evolution occurred. The infrequent service in a homestead, woolshed, or cottage was followed by regular services in a school or some other public building. These were taken by any minister who happened to be available. As a general rule churches were erected by congrega-

Opitonui coffee-palace. Colonial Methodists used a variety of buildings as preaching stations. This temperance refreshment house was in the Coromandel circuit, New Zealand.

tions formed along denominational lines as soon as the population became sufficiently large to allow such specialization. One Anglican clergyman who knew the Canterbury plains charmingly named the different stages in the religious evolution of that district after the vegetation which characterized each: first the eucalypt for the gum trees about the lonely sheep station, at which an infrequent service might be held; then the pine for the plantations around the farms, whose folk might have regular worship but in some temporary accommodation; finally the macrocarpa for the hedges which divided the sections in the village, where there stood a proper church with its cross and other sacred emblems.[22]

Conditions for worship during the transition could be primitive. We have a description of a Wesleyan service held near today's Canberra on a Sunday afternoon in January 1878. About 25 people were gathered in the disused outhouse of a farm. The walls were roughly split slabs through which lines of sunlight showed; the roof was stringy bark; the floor was earth. The seats were slabs of split timber with pegs driven in at either end to make legs and put in at an angle to ensure stability. To preach, the minister stood behind a hardwood table. For hymns one person gave out the note and the congregation sang unaccompanied.[23] How much did makeshift reduce the attractiveness of public worship? Probably Catholics and Anglicans felt the more cheated because they, more than adherents of the other denominations, had been brought up to draw sustenance from ceremony. A Catholic mass in a schoolroom might have to make do with the teacher's table as an altar, no flowers or ornaments, candles stuck by their own grease on the lids of tobacco tins; the congregation would have to pull themselves awkwardly out of children's desks to kneel on the floor.[24]

When a church building did go up its first setting was sometimes a clearing, the earth still raw about the base and stumps of trees round about. Or the church might be in a paddock, just back from a dusty road, stock kept away by straggling fences. Or, if it was in the main street of an infant settlement, ugly shop fronts were often circumjacent. The church itself was sometimes just a small timber box, designed to house the Sunday school at a later stage. If the building had an iron roof it was intolerably hot in an Australian summer.

The principle of having an established church was quickly overthrown in the colonies. As early as the 1830s Wesleyans, Catholics and Presbyterians in New South Wales were in receipt of public monies for ministers' stipends and churchbuilding. The accession of Queen Victoria to the throne was officially announced in

A Presbyterian congregation stands outside their bark–sheet church at Stanthorpe, Queensland, in 1872. Though the building materials are primitive, the dress of most of the congregation is formal.

Hobart from the steps of 'Westella', a mansion that overlooked the harbour and belonged to a wealthy Congregational merchant, Henry Hopkins.[25] In Victoria, South Australia and New Zealand there never was a time when the Church of England was plainly the official church. When the second son of Queen Victoria visited the colonies in the late 1860s the Wesleyans of Adelaide solicited the governor of South Australia to request the prince to lay the foundation stone of their new college. The governor did so and the prince agreed.[26]

Old-world habits amongst some of the Church of England clergy died hard. One likened the gap between the Church and Nonconformity to the social distance between a cultured graduate and a converted prize fighter who dropped his H's and picked his teeth with a fork at the dinner table.[27] 'My Lord' was still heard when bishops were addressed in speech or letter.[28] Rural deans continued to wear gaiters.[29] To non-Anglicans, in the free air of the colonies such behaviour was ludicrous. In South Australia especially there were struggles to ensure that at official gatherings the bishop of the Church of England should not be given precedence over other denominational leaders.[30] Another field of combat was nomenclature. In the 1850s the Wesleyans, the Baptists and the Congregationalists began to call their places of worship churches not chapels, and even to denounce the word 'chapel'.[31] A South Australian colonist in 1858 declared 'dissenter' to savour of 'antiquity, bigotry and absurdity'.[32] Non-Anglicans sometimes denied the validity of the term 'Church of England', substituting 'Episcopal Church' or 'Episcopal sect' to avoid suggesting that Anglicanism was in any way a national church in the colonies.

Another galling adjustment for many Church of England clergymen (and those of the Church of Scotland) was that their social status was reduced vis-à-vis their own people. An Englishwoman who was visiting Australia once tried to give her brother's parishioners some old clothes and kitchen left-overs just as she would have done at home. She was sharply rebuffed. The clergyman's wife, commenting on this episode, observed that 'what they loved was to bring *us* little presents of new-laid eggs or poultry or what not, and to charge us less than they charged the laity for what they did for us in the way of business.' She was bitter about 'that tinge of contempt and patronage' that went with these favours.[33] Also, in a church which was disestablished, the financial pressure which the laity could bring to bear on their minister was immense. When the Reverend Vicesimus Lush of Thames in New Zealand had tea at the Goodalls in 1871 Mrs Goodall told him that they would only give £1 to the new church;

Tambaroora, New South Wales. An example of how raw and ugly the setting of colonial churches could be. The marks of goldmining are everywhere. Tambaroora / Hill End was a gold field that boomed in 1871–72.

Bishop Marsden visits Gulgong. Samuel Edward Marsden was Anglican Bishop of Bathurst, New South Wales, 1869–85. A Cambridge graduate, he came into a pioneering settlement as an agent of refinement and respectability as well as religion.

if the site had been where Mr Goodall had wished, she said, they would have given £50. Lush noted in his journal that the Goodalls were being like Reid the draper, who had gone off to the Wesleyan chapel and had boasted that he would have given £20 to the new Church of England church if it had been erected nearer his house. One observer of the church in New Zealand reported that there were 'a few in most congregations' who were inclined to treat their pastor 'not only as a hireling, but as *their hireling*; and by continual threats, either open or implied, of withdrawing their support, they try to make him feel his dependent position.'[34]

A further twist of the knife was that adherents of the Church of England were not accustomed at home to supporting the ministry by direct personal giving. In consequence the Wesleyan minister in a colonial town might occupy a larger house and have a better turnout of horses. As one historian has remarked, it was a topsy-turvy world.[35] In Christchurch in 1864, while the Church of England was floundering, the Methodists opened a stone church that was of cathedral proportions.[36]

It was not all gain for those who had been dissenters at home. They had in part defined who they were through their struggle against the establishment principle: with religious equality a present reality in the colonies they lost a measure of their *raison d'être*. A Baptist minister told his co-religionists in 1872 that they were suffering from lack of cohesion in consequence of religious equality.[37] The Reverend Dr Bevan, when he first arrived in Australia, believed that the absence of an established church was an advantage enjoyed by colonial Congregationalism; experience caused him to change his mind.[38]

The voyage out might well have been for many Irish Catholic immigrants the first time they had ever spoken to a Protestant. In western Ireland in the 1830s perhaps fewer than five people in every 100 were Protestant.[39] Even where Protestants were more populous there was often a strong tendency for the Protestant and Catholic communities in Ireland to keep apart.[40]

Irish Catholic encountering British Protestant on an immigrant ship sometimes produced conflict. Sometimes there was good fellowship.[41] Always on a mixed ship there was a possibility that Catholic and Protestant stereotypes of one another might crumble. Father Patrick Dunne, who had been a chaplain on an immigrant ship, saw the risk from the Catholic point of view and described it luridly to Archbishop Cullen in 1859: 'Only think My Lord of pure, innocent, Irish country girls being placed in the closest contact, such as sleeping in the same berth, with English protestants of the lowest class and some of them selected from the streets of London, think of them being thus placed under the care of a protestant Doctor & Captain all perhaps combining to destroy their faith and morals.'[42]

Arrival in the new land provided no abatement of the Protestant danger. Of all the principal religious groups Irish Catholics had to make the most far-reaching adjustments. British Protestants left a land which was predominantly Protestant for colonies which were the same: most Irish Catholics left a largely or wholly Catholic environment for one in which alien influences had the upper hand.

Though in a minority the immigrant Irish might still have kept Protestants at a distance if they had made one or two regions their own and settled there exclusively. But no little Irelands got established. In the 1840s and after, the Irish gathered on the tablelands of New South Wales around Yass and Bathurst.[43] The Kilmore district in Victoria was a Catholic stronghold. In 1857 Kilmore's representative in Victoria's lower house, John O'Shanassy, became premier of the colony. On the west coast of New Zealand's South Island there was a clustering of Irish who had arrived during the gold rushes of the 1860s. But at the censuses held in all four colonies in 1871 there was but one electoral district in which Catholics accounted for even half the population. That was Kilmore in Victoria.

Seclusion from Protestants was possible on a small scale and for a short period, as is proved by Waitohi Flat, which Helen Wilson knew as a young schoolteacher in the 1880s. Apart from the teacher sent in by the Department of Education, the only regular contact that this community of agricultural labourers had with the outside world was the weekly visit by a grocer. Helen Wilson described the Flat in her novel *Moonshine*: 'a little bit of "Ould Ireland" – minus the rent collector – a stagnating, isolated, self-contained backwash, standing aside from and apart from the changing, vigorous life of young New Zealand.'[44] The more usual experience was to live in a district where fewer than one person in four was a Catholic.

The situation was the same in the cities. Take Melbourne, for example. Melbourne had around 100000 Roman Catholics at the end of the nineteenth century so an Irish Catholic sub-community was demographically possible. Yet there was in Melbourne nothing like the Irish enclaves that existed in Liverpool or New York. Irish Catholics did show a fondness for living in north and west Melbourne around the railway yards where so many of the Irish found work, but even in North Melbourne fewer than 50 in every 100 residents at the end of the century were Catholic.[45]

The explanation for the remarkable diffusion of the Irish Catholic immigrants in city and country seems to lie chiefly in the nature of the immigrants of the 1850s and 1860s. These were largely single men and women who frequently arrived under government-assisted schemes and who were not dependent upon remittances from relations already settled in the colonies. Many could not have had any members of their family already present because the pre-1850 arrivals were so few in number compared with the flood of the 1850s and 1860s. Especially was this so in Victoria. Consequently many immigrants slipped free of Irish Catholic networks upon arrival and became dispersed amongst the general population. By contrast, in the United States the more general practice was for new arrivals to be received by relatives who had sent remittances for the voyage and who helped with jobs and accommodation, both of which might be found within an Irish enclave.[46]

It was a colonial saying that a young man migrated to get a job and a young woman to get married.[47] Irish Catholic women were no exception and many were not fussed about the religion of a potential partner.[48] So the mixed society of the colonies produced many mixed marriages. Of the Irish brides who married in Victoria in 1870–72, 48 per cent took a non-Irish husband.[49] In a sample of Irish brides who married in Canterbury province between 1850 and 1879 the number marrying men born in Ireland did not much exceed those who married men born elsewhere in the British Isles.[50] This level of out-marriage is much higher than has been found for the Irish who migrated to Greenock, Scotland.[51]

Some Irish Catholic immigrants positively preferred Protestants as husbands either for themselves or their children, because Protestant men had better worldly prospects or higher social standing.[52] Irish Catholic immigrant men married non-Catholics much less frequently.[53]

Another consequence of diffusion was that time and again a Catholic ended up with a Protestant employer. Mother Mary McKillop writing to Rome in the early 1870s observed that one of the ways in which a Catholic spirit was diminished was through Catholics being afraid to lose the favour of their Protestant employers.[54] Servants in Protestant homes were especially at risk. J. F. Hogan claimed that it 'rarely' happened that an employer insisted that his Irish Catholic servant not go to mass or vespers.[55] Father Julian Tenison Woods was more worried. In 1871 he presented as 'no uncommon picture' this dialogue.

'Bridget, clear the tea things away and then come into prayers.'
'I cannot come to prayers', says Bridget firmly but respectfully. 'I am a Catholic.'
'Oh, nonsense, you must do what you are told. It is all the same, our prayers won't hurt you.'
'I will not come into your prayers', says Bridget more decidedly, with a little flush in her countenance and a trifle of fire in her eyes.
'Why, what nonsense and bigotry is this, Bridget. We all adore the same God. Tell me why you won't come in?'
'My Church tells me I must not', says Bridget, 'and I will not, and it is a shame for you ma'am to ask me to disobey my Church.'
'Oh, I thought so. It is the old story. It is because your priests tell you to do this or that, that you do it, that is how you poor Catholics are kept in your ignorance and superstition.'[56]

Reporting to Cardinal Barnabo in Rome in the early 1870s Bishop James Quinn commented that Catholic bazaars in Brisbane had had vice-regal patronage and had been heavily supported by Protestant ladies and gentlemen. During Quinn's last visitation of his diocese, Protestant gentlemen had supplied the horses he rode and provided him with accommodation, even to the extent of giving up their own residences in the more remote districts.[57] Such helpfulness on the part of Protestants was by no means

unusual. Many Protestants contributed to Catholic church building funds and sometimes attended the opening services.[58] Protestants were estimated to constitute a third of the congregation at
the consecration of St Patrick's, Ballarat.[59] During a Redemptorist
mission at Oamaru in 1884, many Protestants gave their choicest
flowers to decorate the sanctuary and altar for a solemn exposition
of the Blessed Sacrament.[60] The goodwill was mutual. Father
Geoghegan, the first Catholic priest in Melbourne, subscribed to
Protestant church building funds. So did some of the later Catholic clerical arrivals in Melbourne.[61] Father O'Reily, Wellington's
first Catholic priest, had as a close friend Thomas McKenzie, an
elder of St John's Presbyterian church. Once, when the minister
of St John's was sick, O'Reily took an unmodified Presbyterian
service with the agreement of the elders.[62]

In small bush settlements Catholic priests often took their turn
with other visiting clergy to hold services attended by all or nearly
all the worshippers of the place. If no regular services were held,
Protestants might even seek out a visiting Catholic priest. In his
history of the Catholic church in South Australia, Father Byrne
told a story of how once in the early days he got to the small
town of Streaky Bay on a Sunday afternoon. When the news of
his arrival spread he was waited upon by a deputation of Protestants. At the service he held that evening in the pub all but four or
five of the congregation were Protestants. As Byrne remembered
it, he had begun his service with the Lord's Prayer, given a
sermon on prayer and finished with the Litany of the Holy Name.
All had been pleased to be present.[63]

Such friendly feeling was but an extension of what happened
Monday to Saturday in small pioneering communities. With pur-
suits and interests in common, Protestants and Catholics tended to
think of themselves as belonging to one family. There was a
strong feeling that old-world religious divisions ought not to be
transferred to the colonies; perhaps partly in response to this
pressure many colonists seem to have kept their religion to
themselves.[64] Before the 1860s episodes of sectarian ill-feeling
were infrequent in the larger towns, and virtually unknown outside them.[65]

James Buller, a Wesleyan minister with long experience in New
Zealand, believed that many Catholics shed their prejudices regarding Protestants upon close contact with them. Roman Catholics, so far as he had known them in New Zealand, were 'liberally
minded, except the very lowest of the classes, who submit to be
priest-ridden.'[66] Buller did not specify the liberal views held by
colonial Catholics, but almost certainly he had in mind, among

other things, the belief that it did not matter to what church a person belonged so long as he or she lived a decent life. Implicit here, of course, was a denial of the teaching authority of the Catholic church and of some Catholic dogmas. To their dismay the Catholic bishops found this 'indifferentism' or 'liberal Christianity' well entrenched among their laity. The joint pastoral letter issued by the Provincial Council of bishops in 1869 called indifferentism 'the mother heresy and pestilence of the day'.[67] Archbishop Redwood in 1890 detected the presence within the church of those who wished to commend themselves to 'the more cultivated members of society': 'You hear Catholics say, if not in so many words, at least in a guarded and insinuating way, "All religions are pleasing to God; it matters little what church a man belongs to so long as he lives honestly".'[68]

Some Irish Catholic immigrants so absorbed the spirit of community that they regularly attended Protestant services. In South Australia the practice of Catholics attending Protestant worship was sufficiently extensive for Father Woods to warn Catholics against it.[69] In 1885 Bishop Luck of Auckland referred to Catholics attending Protestant services out of curiosity and using the 'excuse' that where there was no Catholic service it was better to go to a Protestant service than stay at home.[70]

Indifferentism flourished among Catholics in mixed marriages. A Catholic woman married to a Protestant was foolish to flaunt her Catholicism in the home and she might come to see much good in the religion of her husband. Children of mixed marriages often grew up only nominally Catholic.[71] But all Catholics who wished to please Protestants – whether because Protestants were employers, customers, friends, or for some other reason – faced subtle pressures to trim their distinctive religious principles. A layman from Ipswich, Queensland, commented in 1872 that those Catholics were at risk who could not have frequent recourse to the sacraments. When Protestants made jibes about Catholic doctrine these isolated Catholics kept silent 'either from social considerations, from personal regard, or other kindred motives, until at length, through a mistaken notion of liberality, opinions at variance with Catholic doctrine are not only heard and discussed with indifference but prejudices and false principles contrary to faith are imbibed.'[72]

Assimilation of non-Catholic or anti-Catholic assumptions was all the more likely to happen because of the defectiveness of the Catholicism which the immigrants brought to the new environment. This was especially true of those who had left Ireland before the Famine. Their religion could be almost ludicrous in its reliance upon outward forms. Alexander Harris recounted an incident he observed in a bush hut in up-country New South Wales one evening before 1850. In the corner of the hut a Roman Catholic began saying his prayers half aloud. The conversation in the hut went on and three times the Catholic broke in with an oath, returning immediately to his prayers. This occasioned much laughter.[73] It was treatment which might lead to the abandonment of private prayer.

Nineteenth-century Catholicism was a religion centred upon the sacraments; Catholic identity was sustained by the sacraments. Without priests there could be no sacraments. So it followed in almost syllogistic fashion that any shortage of priests undermined the laity's sense of being Catholic. In a printed appeal made in Ireland in 1859 Archdeacon McEncroe explained that one of the principal objects of his return home after 27 years was to recruit missionary priests for New South Wales: without them hundreds, if not thousands, would lapse from the faith just as they had in the United States of America.[74] In 1887 Father Hurley singled out want of access to the sacraments and inability to attend mass frequently as among the chief reasons why Catholics in New Zealand lost their faith.[75] In Victoria a lag between the arrival of Irish Catholics and an adequate provision of priests was almost inevitable given the rapidity and scale of immigration after 1850. There were about 18 000 Catholics in Victoria at the beginning of 1851 and 170 000 twenty years later.

Bishops and priests who encountered bush Catholics left for years without a regular ministry were appalled by what they observed. The spiritual destitution, they said, had to be seen to be believed. 'Religion in tears' one priest called it.[76] Often the Irish bishops and priests who made these comments were seeking to draw attention to the shortcomings of English (or, in the case of New Zealand, French) episcopal oversight.[77] But there can be no doubt that their reports were substantially accurate. Father Woods, who was experienced in country parish work in South Australia, commented that it was only when he started holding missions in the bush of New South Wales that he became aware of the full extent of the ignorance of religion amongst Catholics in the sparsely settled districts. There was, he found, an 'extraordinary neglect of parents to teach their children religion, or to bring them to the sacraments'.[78] In the New South Wales bush, where Woods worked in the 1870s, the faith of Catholic settlers was almost devoid of social or spiritual supports: not even the vestiges of a Catholic community, mixed marriages common, Catholics habituated to being without a priest, children who were without even the protective memories of Catholic Ireland.

The colonies were democracies. Under the New Zealand Constitution Act of 1852 any male over 21 could vote provided he held a very small amount of property. By 1860 adult male suffrage had been introduced in the other three colonies. There continued to be very large differences in income, in the size of houses people lived in, in their conditions of work, the quality of their education and so forth, yet colonists had a well founded conviction that things were more equal than in the old land. That Jack was as good as his master was a common saying. As for Jill she might work as a servant but, if she did, she was likely to be less deferential than her counterpart at home. The hierarchical principle of the Catholic church ran counter to this colonial democracy.

Challenges to episcopal authority occurred in the 1850s and 1860s. Archbishop Polding of Sydney saw himself as threatened by an incipient 'presbyterianism' within his own church.[79] In Victoria Bishop Goold had to fight hard against disaffected and openly critical Catholics.[80] The laity criticized Bishop Pompallier for mismanagement of the Auckland diocese and some wanted more say in the running of their denomination's schools.[81] In the late 1860s a Catholic bishop might well have been apprehensive about even more resistance to come. There had been clashes in the United States between bishops and laity who wanted to choose their own priests and had applied as a lever the legal powers of lay trustees of church property. Bishop Henry Conwell had lost his job after he had tried to do a deal with dissidents at St Mary's, Philadelphia.[82] Nothing so serious developed in the Australasian colonies. Why it did not is a puzzle. It may be related to the better disciplined Catholicism of the migrants who left Ireland after about 1860.

Reverence for the priest was second nature to many Irish Catholics who embarked for the colonies. A French writer, Alexis de Tocqueville, who visited Ireland in 1835, was struck by the reception given to a priest whom he accompanied one day in the west of Ireland. 'On seeing him the women curtseyed and crossed themselves devoutly, the men respectfully took off their hats' while the priest himself 'saluted nobody'.[83] Not everything the priest said was law in Ireland. Many a priest exhorted in vain against agrarian secret societies, or lewd games at wakes, or the Irish thirst for poteen. But the priest did have an awesome spiritual authority over those peasants who saw his ministry of the

sacraments as an incarnation of supernatural power. Some attri-
buted the power of magic to him.[84] A habit of deference to the
priest was fostered by the fact that hardly ever in a rural parish
was there to be found another Catholic of equal education or
experience of the world. An English traveller in Ireland, J. E.
Bicheno, declared in 1830 that priests acted for the people as 'their
physicians in remote districts, and the lawyers everywhere' and
that they were 'very competent advisers in matters of business'.[85]
Over 70 years later another observer wrote 'in many parts of the
country the priest is the match-maker, the arbitrator, the authority which decides whether a man shall buy or sell a farm, the price
he shall pay for it, the market at which he shall deal, the manner
in which he shall invest his savings, or in a word, the whole
business of his life.'[86] The jibe about Catholics being priest-ridden
in Ireland was not all Protestant fancy.

The priest had no more competence than the next man in
secular matters in the colonies. If he were newly arrived from
home he had less. His status in the wider colonial community was
not high; his level of education and culture might even be embar-
rassingly low compared with a Protestant professional man.
Habits of deference and submissiveness to anyone ran against the
grain of colonial life. The bulk of the population rejected the
notion of priestly authority. Lay Catholics, consciously or unconsciously, were influenced by these things.

Father Philip Ryan in 1867 told a bishop newly arrived in New
South Wales: 'They are not afraid of priests here the same as in
Ireland. You cannot persuade them to do things if they don't like
them.'[87] Father Hurley believed that New Zealand Catholics were
tempted to win favour with their Protestant friends and workmates by showing 'want of due reverence for the priestly
authority'.[88] An Irish priest who arrived in New Zealand early
this century was told by an Irish-born New Zealand layman, 'You
are not cock of the walk out here, Father.'[89] Probably the change
in attitude was most pronounced amongst the native-born children of Irish immigrants. At the First Australasian Catholic Congress in 1900 Bishop Gallagher of Goulburn, in a paper on Catholic youth, noted criticisms of Australian Catholic young men.
'Many say that you are too proud, too independent, with no sense
of reverence, and no humility.' He warned priests against holding
young men with too tight a rein.[90] Priests did adjust of course and
some commented that respect for a good priest was just as high as
at home.[91] But respect had to be earned to a much greater extent.
And the offhandedness of the colonials could be most unsettling.
A priest recalled how once he was hearing confessions in the bush.

After several penitents had come to him in the large room where
he was placed a young fellow who

> came in quite leisurely, took off his hat, gave me a familiar nod and said
> 'Good-morning.' I replied, 'Good-morning.' He said, 'Its a fine morning.' I
> agreed with him. 'Yes, 'tis a fine morning.' He then pointed over his shoulder
> and said, 'Is that your nag outside?' 'Yes, that's my nag.' 'Humph!' he said, 'fine
> stamp of a mare that!' 'Yes,' I said 'she's very good.' At this point I thought I
> would suggest if he wished to go to confession. 'Oh, yes' he said 'I suppose we
> must clean out the old pot sometimes.' After this preamble he went to
> confession right enough.[92]

'In a very brief space', lamented a colonial minister, 'the face of a
congregation becomes so entirely changed that it seems altogether
new, whereas in many of our home places of worship the child
succeeds the parent in the occupancy of the pew and the son the
father in the offices of the church and of the school.'[93] The
turnover he observed arose from the footloose character of the
colonists. The movement of the immigrants did not stop on their
arrival. As well as moving about the country districts, they and
the native-born were prone to change house within a particular
city, between city and country and often between colonies. When
the New Zealand Treasurer in 1878, John Ballance, introduced a
land tax in preference to one on income, he said it was partly
because the latter would be too difficult to collect.[94]

One Congregational minister doubted whether his denomination had an adequate conception of 'the terrible leakage to church
membership and church vitality resulting from the migratory
habits of the people'.[95] As an instance of extreme mobility we
may take Melbourne during the 1890s when thousands of people
changed house under the spur of economic depression. One in
every five persons affiliated with the Congregational churches of
Melbourne at the 1891 census had severed connection by 1901.
The Methodist, the Presbyterian and the Anglican churches of
Melbourne did not experience the same *net* loss of adherents as did
the Congregational ones. Because the Congregational churches
were relatively few and were unrepresented in many parts of the
city and suburbs they were not able to pick up movers as easily as
lose them. But the Congregational loss does suggest the extent of
transience in the local churches of the other denominations in
Melbourne in the 1890s.[96]

The consequences of physical mobility for the local church life
of all denominations were far reaching. It was difficult for ministers to plan church work when there was such a high turnover of
leaders. The financial position of a church could suddenly be
rendered precarious by departure of a single generous supporter.

Above all, personal ties between those who attended local churches were difficult to create or sustain: a sense of religious community was often non-existent.[97] There were also comments in
the religious periodicals of how moving house was sometimes the
occasion for people lapsing from church life altogether.[98]

A second enemy of the churches was mammon. At a dance in
Victoria in the 1850s a lady confided in Robert O'Hara Burke that
those in their company had come out to seek their fortunes. The
future explorer replied 'Why, my dear Mrs G——, did not you
and I come out here because we could not get so good a living at
home?'[99] Thousands of immigrants may have had only a hope
of bettering themselves. Others were obsessed. Jane Williams
observed young men on board the *Castle Forbes* in 1821 who often
occupied themselves 'talking over the readiest and shortest mode
of making their fortunes – displaying their love of country by
always taking it for granted that in a certain given number of
years they would return to spend their wealth in their native
land.'[100] Men on the make like this were perhaps unlikely to
participate in church life at all. But the same spirit affected many
who were church members. One Presbyterian clergyman believed
that if he could tell many professing Christians that multitudes
were turning to the Lord it would not give them a tithe of the
satisfaction of hearing by the next English mail that wool had
gone up twopence per pound.[101]

John Chandler was a carter who had supplied goldminers during the Victorian rushes of the 1850s and who had known Melbourne during the property boom of the 1880s. Towards the end
of his long life he reflected how often those who got rich
weakened in their faith. Referring to the members of a Baptist sect
with whom he once worshipped, he commented, 'They will not
acknowledge this, I know, but I have had experience of both
[wealth and poverty], and am sure that he lives nearest the Lord
who has to ask for his daily supply, and shines much brighter
when he is not covered with thick clay; and he has more messages
to the throne.'[102] Many Protestant clergy would have agreed but
it was difficult for them to recommend poverty to the prosperous
who paid their stipends. The president and secretary of the South
Australian Wesleyan conference gave sympathetic and tactful
counsel to laymen in 1888. They were aware of 'the necessity
for close attention to business' in a commercial depression and
aware of 'the tyrannical exactions imposed by modern commercial
modes and usages'. Yet it was their duty as pastors to remind
commercial men that there was more to life than money: 'Oh,
beware that business does not wholly swallow you up.'[103]

It was Mary McKillop's 'sad conviction that money and the comforts it brings, *even where it should not*, is one of the most formidable enemies the Catholic Faith has got in Australia.'[104] Archbishop Polding many times in his pastoral letters exhorted Catholics to beware of covetousness. It was wealthy Catholics, he believed, who stinted the church. He saw an intimate connection between money and that religious indifference which he believed was a scourge of colonial Catholicism. A Catholic who had made money could lapse in his prayers, be infrequent at mass, deaf to the needs of his brothers and sisters in Christ, give almost nothing to church funds and then when he came to confession once a year pass over all these sins. Polding's long pastoral for Lent 1861 was entirely devoted to avarice.[105] The following year, he, together with his fellow bishops, told the clergy that those who went hungry in Ireland were not so destitute as those in the colonies whom greed had taken into 'a hopeless exile' remote from those spiritual riches which were their soul's true good. 'These are our truly poor, uttering no cry, attracting no sympathy of the natural heart, because they themselves are unconscious of their misery.'[106]

Catholics were much over-represented among the unskilled of the 1860s. Catholics still had a reputation of being a largely working class people in the 1920s. And they were. But as Polding's condemnation of avarice suggests many Irish Catholics did well for themselves in the colonies. The effect of success was often to weaken the sense of solidarity with the Irish Catholic culture from which they were drawn. It is therefore significant that an increasing proportion of those of Irish Catholic stock prospered in the colonies. The 1933 Australian census is especially revealing, as Professor Oliver MacDonagh has pointed out.[107] At this census the distribution of income of male breadwinners was classified according to denomination. Twenty per cent of all Catholic male breadwinners were in either of the top two income brackets encompassing those who earned over £207 per annum. Twenty-three per cent of all Australian male breadwinners were in these two brackets. Catholics were at a relative disadvantage then in 1933, but the striking fact is how small this was.[108]

One good reason for Protestant and Catholic church leaders to condemn avarice was that money was always needed for church building, for paying ministers and for philanthropic work. Another was that young men in the grip of the money-making spirit did not find the church a promising place for a career. Throughout the nineteenth century those born in the colonies were less well represented in the ministry and priesthood than they should have been given the proportion of the native-born in the total population.[109] There were complaints that colonial parents tried to persuade their boys against becoming ministers or priests.[110]

In seeking to explain colonial absorption in money making it is worth taking account of a point that de Tocqueville made about the nature of democracy. He argued plausibly that in an aristocratic society 'desire for wealth and physical prosperity' had restricted scope: the nobility were able to take for granted their wealth and social position and the masses were so far removed from these they were not tempted. In a democracy, on the other hand, many were tempted to accumulate because nobody inherited vast estates and everybody had abundant prospects of improving themselves.[111] This new possibility of wealth was also singled out in a pastoral letter addressed to early settlers by the Presbytery of Otago. The Presbytery believed that the danger of covetousness was peculiarly strong in an 'infant colony'.

> On the one hand the enterprising settler finds himself thrown completely upon the single resource of his own personal energy – his own individual activity and toil: he sees that upon these alone depend not the comfort merely, but the very existence of himself and his rising family. Whilst on the other hand, he sees just as clearly that an ample return for his industry – a reward tempting to his cupidity, and stimulating all his powers to the very utmost – lies full in his eye, and seems but a very little way in his path before him.

The editor of the *New Zealand Presbyterian* in 1879 when publishing extracts from this early pastoral commented that the warning had lost none of its force.[112]

By the 1850s folk religion was losing hold in the British Isles, even in Ireland. The disruptions of migration and exposure to those for whom folk religion was superstition seem to have powerfully accelerated the process. Another factor working against survival was that much folk religion grew out of agricultural practices tied to the seasons, and in the colonies land use was different and the seasons back to front.

Some folk beliefs and practices managed to survive for a time in the colonies. When the grandfather of Pat Lawlor died around the turn of the nineteenth century a penny was placed over each eye and the jaw bound with a cloth after an Irish custom. Lawlor also remembered from his childhood that the Irish-born in New Zealand sometimes had wakes, during which the coffin was always left in another room, and that those present would interrupt their drinking to pay the dead person their respects.[113] This practice seems to have been a remnant of the belief, which flourished in pre-Famine Ireland, that the dead person presided over the wake.[114]

The Cornish miners of South Australia celebrated midsummer's eve with bonfires. Some of them believed that dwarfs whom they called 'knockers' lived down the mines and plied their picks and hammers in search of metal. When the Cornish heard the knocking of the knockers' hammers they believed good ore was near. One of the Cornish local preachers believed that his mother had been made bad-tempered by the Devil whom he supposed he had found in bed with her.[115] But these South Australian Cornish mining communities were exceptionally cohesive by new-world standards. If rural Irish immigrants had been situated as were many of the Cornish in South Australia – geographically remote and settled only with their own kind – who knows how many would have seen fairies? In actuality the Australasian Irish were a prosaic lot.

Church religion was found wanting in the sparsely settled and remote areas in the colonies. Yet if we consider the cities, the towns and the agricultural districts – the areas where the overwhelming bulk of the immigrants and their children lived – we are presented with a different picture. Certainly migration and settlement were religiously unsettling processes, but the far bush aside, and measured against the virtual disappearance of folk religion, institutional Christianity showed a considerable capacity to replicate itself. In virtually every settlement of any size throughout the colonies, sooner or later a building would go up devoted to the worship of the Christian God. Sunday by Sunday men, women and children attended church and gave money for the support of ministers of the Christian gospel.

The basic institutions of old-world Christianity were not merely evident in the new, the immigrants reproduced them in detail, down to the distinctive features of each denomination. A stranger landing in Auckland, Bishop Selwyn remarked in 1863, hardly twenty years after New Zealand had become a British colony,

> would see Churches and Chapels in every part of the town, and in fair proportion to the number of the inhabitants. He would see one of the principal Churches, the Church of St. Paul, in course of enlargement; and in the Parish of St. Matthew a new Church of ample dimensions, approaching to completion. On the other side of the town he would see the new Church of St. Mary, already too small for its congregation. He would find upon enquiry, that in these three Parishes daily and sunday-schools are maintained; that an income is provided for the Clergyman according to the Diocesan scale; that the Parish System is duly organized with its Churchwardens and Vestry....[116]

A Methodist minister commented about the same time that Wesleyan services in Sydney were 'so truly English, that one might have imagined they were held in the heart of Yorkshire, Lincoln-

The First Church of Otago, Dunedin. Opened in 1873, this was a Gothic church of which colonials could be proud. It was erected not by Anglican or Catholic but Free Church of Scotland settlers.

shire, or Lancashire rather than fifteen thousand miles distant from our shores.' Another minister thought it like a dream that a church building, its fittings, and the way the service in it was conducted should be 'so home-like'.[117] Under pressure of European invasion and in the face of the catastrophes of disease and the seizure of their land, the Maoris responded with many new religious forms and teachings. But no new Christian sect arose among the European settlers in New Zealand. Charles Strong in Melbourne founded the 'Australian church' but this came to be only a one-congregation denomination and was ailing within fifteen years of its formation in 1885. In his teaching Strong drew on what was standard fare in liberal circles in British and German Protestantism.[118] John Alexander Dowie was a religious man willing to experiment radically and flamboyantly but he had to go to the United States before he could gain a large following.[119] To us the general imitativeness of colonial religion may seem to express lack of originality. But originality was not the need of this generation. Reassurance was. A New Zealand colonist once observed that it was an important day for a settler when he first heard in his district a bell sounding the call to divine worship: 'it is a time that touches him very nearly, and tells him of old times, and seems to bring him a thousand miles nearer home, when the day is restored to him endeared with something of the old remembered surroundings.'[120]

Thus though the first generation of settlers sat loosely to their churches, the churches were far from abandoned. Much had changed from what had been the case in the old world and much had remained the same. What was the future going to hold? From a vantage point of around 1860 it would have been difficult to say. Church leaders, both Protestant and Catholic, might reasonably have expected to benefit as life became more settled. But there was also the possibility that the undeniably secular hue of colonial life might deepen. There was another question very much unresolved at the end of the 1850s: whatever the general social environment – whether in the future it would favour organized religion or militate against it – which kind of religion was going to do better in the colonies, Catholicism or Protestantism?

Chapter Three

REVIVALISM

'Colonial society', declared a Presbyterian clergyman in 1870, 'is composed of such heterogeneous and ephemeral elements, and is so much affected by sceptical and materialistic influences, which soon eat out the heart of its religious life, that here, if anywhere, the Churches of Christ, in order to hold their ground and make headway, need frequent times of refreshing – great waves of Religious feeling to pulsate through the community.'[1] It was natural that an evangelical Protestant should think this way in the late nineteenth century. Colonists who were nominal in their Christianity abounded. Yet within living memory the Protestant churches in England, Scotland and Ireland had experienced a series of revivals in which tens of thousands had been given a vital faith which they had previously lacked. To Protestant leaders revival readily presented itself, indeed virtually imposed itself, as the sovereign remedy to administer to colonial apathy.

Catholic leaders did not speak of the need for religious revival in the same terms as did Protestants. Revival was rather a Protestant word. But the Catholic church too had experienced periods when religious interest and religious feeling were heightened. Catholic Ireland in the late nineteenth century was experiencing a revitalization which was one of the most powerful in the entire history of the Catholic church since the days of Ignatius Loyola and Teresa of Avila. Given their knowledge of what was being done at home it was almost inevitable that the Irish Catholic bishops should promote means of energizing their many spiritually inert laity. Thus it is well worth asking of both Protestant and Catholic churches from the 1850s, first, what efforts there were to make religion come alive for the colonists, and secondly, how successful these efforts were. Perhaps the group to watch most closely of all is the labourers. The unskilled and semi-skilled constituted the bulk of the colonial workforce. These men and their families had had a tenuous relation to the churches at home, but in the colonies the churches were not so handicapped by association with social privilege or respectability. In the colonies also there were many opportunities for people to go up the social elevator and with this experience become more open to church influence. Perhaps many who had been outside the churches could in the colonies be attracted by special measures and the churches become genuinely popular institutions.

In mid-1859 news reached the colonies of religious excitement and revival among the Protestants of northern Ireland. There was news also that committed evangelicals in England and Scotland were praying that revival might spread across the Irish Sea. Almost at once a counterpart to this English and Scottish movement began in the colonies. Interdenominational prayer groups were formed in principal towns. Interest mounted in early 1860: prayer meetings were said to be thronged in Sydney; in Melbourne there was a group that met daily.[2] On 2 July 1860 the *Revival Record* was launched 'to chronicle and herald events of the most momentous character'. Published in Melbourne, it was a colonial version of the *Revival*, begun in England the previous year.[3] The *Wesleyan Chronicle*, also published in Melbourne, told its readers in March 1861, that revival had occurred in the past two or three years in Ireland, America and Sweden, and asked 'Why should not the Australasian Churches secure a Revival of religion?' To this end the writer recommended a sinking of denominational differences, an increase in personal holiness and, above all, prayer.[4]

There was no general revival. The *Revival Record* ceased publication on 15 January 1863.[5] Time and again thereafter, usually in response to reports from overseas, zealous evangelical Protestants were to pray for a general revival. It did not come.

There was never anything remotely comparable to the First and Second Great Awakenings in America which helped to shape a culture and a society. Nor, significantly, did the Primitive Methodists flourish. The Primitive Methodists had in their camp meetings a religious institution that had the potential for large popular appeal, a potential which had been realized on the American frontier. The camp meetings of the Primitives were poorly attended in the colonies and religious feelings hardly ever seem to have run high.[6]

It would not be true to say that Protestant revival failed to eventuate in the colonies, completely and always. Judged by increases in membership, quite impressive runs of local revivals sometimes occurred among the Wesleyans.[7] The adjacent graph shows the amount in proportionate terms by which Wesleyan membership increased from year to year in South Australia. The mid-1860s and the early 1880s stand out as periods of exceptional recruitment. The same is true of Wesleyanism in Victoria where the denomination's growth was even faster before about 1890. The early 1880s were also exceptional years for the Brethren in New Zealand, a significant fact, for the Brethren, like the Wesleyans, placed much emphasis on personal conversion. According

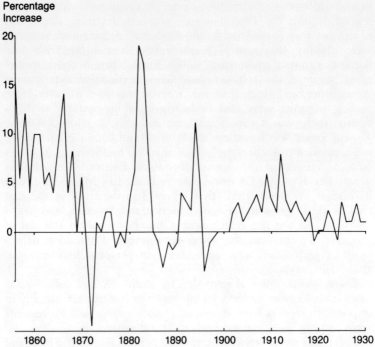

Percentage
Increase

Graph 1: Wesleyan and united Methodist annual growth rates, South Australia, 1856–1930 (per cent). (Source: Wray Vamplew *et al.*, *South Australian Historical Statistics*, History Project Incorporated, University of New South Wales)

to census statistics between 1881 and 1886 the number of Brethren in New Zealand increased from 1967 to 3179, a rate of increase which was more than three times as fast as that of the total population.[8]

The catalyst of local revival was sometimes the arrival of a gifted preacher. At Callington, in South Australia, in 1865 members of the Wesleyan church prayed for revival in the couple of weeks leading up to the anniversary services. They desired that their own children should be converted, as well as those whom they regarded as 'the unsaved people of the township'. Since the opening of the new chapel attendance at services had increased but not the number of members. The Reverend John Watsford, chairman of the Wesleyan district, arrived to take the Sunday anniversary services. Such was the impression he made that when a prayer meeting was held on 'Maze Monday' almost the whole township turned up, according to one Methodist account. In the evening it had been planned that Watsford would give a public lecture but this was changed to a sermon and prayer meeting in the chapel. At that meeting twenty persons came forward as penitents to be prayed over. Watsford stayed a further two days and after his departure revival work was continued. All told nearly a hundred conversions were claimed. Some 'found peace' in the chapel, some in their houses, some in the scrub. Many were children of church members.[9]

Watsford's services were sometimes emotional affairs. At a meeting Watsford held in the Goulburn circuit in the late 1850s a woman who had been in much distress suddenly found Christ. She stayed on her knees for a time, then sat in a chair for an hour or more, repeating again and again as the tears fell, 'Oh, I never thought it was like this. Glory be to God.'[10] On another occasion in Sydney, also in the late 1850s, Watsford held a special Monday service for those who were troubled in spirit. Some of his hearers fell to the ground, and possibly rolled about a little. So loud was the crying policemen came to see what was the matter.[11] Nonetheless most Wesleyan behaviour at colonial local revivals seems to have been less fervid than this.

The success of Watsford in gaining converts was insignificant compared with that of William Taylor in the mid-1860s.[12] An American and a full-time revivalist, 'California' Taylor arrived unannounced in Melbourne in June 1863 and sought the support of the Wesleyan leaders there. They were nervous about him but he was allowed to go ahead. After successful services in Melbourne he went on to ply his trade in Victorian country towns and in New South Wales and South Australia, making shorter visits to Queensland, Tasmania and New Zealand. He finished his tour of the colonies in February 1866.

Born in 1821, Taylor made a reputation as a revivalist in gold-rush California. With a physically powerful presence, a sonorous voice and a gift for humour, he was a man to handle crowds. And he was prepared to go virtually anywhere he thought he could draw people to hear the gospel and to buy his writings. In 1884 the General Conference of the Methodist Episcopal Church appointed him missionary bishop to Africa. Altogether he was an extraordinary man.

It was Taylor's practice in Australasia to work from the local Wesleyan church but other denominations co-operated at times. He would stay a week in a small town, a fortnight in a large one, holding services each week-evening with Friday the climax and Saturday for travelling. This series of services allowed a build-up of popular interest, which was one of the key principles of the leading American authority on revivals, Charles Grandison Fin-

California Taylor.

ney. Taylor's preaching was racy with a fund of homely illustrations. This too was after Finney's manner. So also was Taylor's
practice of separating potential converts from the rest of a congregation so that psychological pressure could be systematically
applied. At the close of a soul-winning sermon he would invite
those who desired to be reconciled to God to come forward to
kneel at the communion rail or some other convenient place.
Taylor would instruct them individually and the congregation
would pray for the penitents, as they awaited God's mercy. Soon
some of the penitents would claim experience of release and
forgiveness, and they would be examined by the superintendent
of the circuit in the vestry. If they wished to become members of
the Wesleyan church they were enrolled at once in a Wesleyan
class. If they belonged to another denomination they were advised
to see their minister immediately, or so Taylor claimed. Taylor
was keen to convert children of church members and encouraged
the colonial Wesleyans to expect these conversions. The pastoral

address of the Australasian Wesleyan conference of January 1864
noted that there had been many conversions amongst young
people in the previous year.[13]

In his autobiography Taylor claimed much of the credit for
bringing over 11 000 souls to Christ during his first Australasian
tour.[14] Taylor was an exaggerator and a self-advertiser in the
American revivalist tradition but he should not be dismissed as a
charlatan. Wesleyan Methodist membership in Victoria increased
by 2182 or 34 per cent between 1863 and 1865. Growth in the
previous three years had averaged less than 6 per cent. In New
South Wales, where Taylor also spent much time, members increased by 907 in 1864–65, a rise of 22 per cent after numbers had
been static for the three previous years.[15] But did these converts
stick? Daniel Draper, a Wesleyan leader in Victoria who had
backed Taylor initially, began to have reservations after a few
months, and in 1864 became convinced that the permanent good
Taylor effected was slight.[16] On the other hand Smith and Blamires, early historians of the Wesleyan church in Victoria, while
acknowledging that some conversions were ephemeral, were stout
defenders of the revivals of the 1860s. Their testimony is impressive because they were ministers in Victoria at the time and
because, when they came to write their history, they were able to
judge with the hindsight of twenty years. They reported an estimate that sixteen ministers working in the colonies in the late
1880s were Taylor converts.[17]

The success of Gordon Forlong was on a smaller stage than that
of California Taylor. Born into a well-connected Scottish family
in 1819, Forlong had practised as an advocate before becoming
one of Britain's leading evangelists. He arrived in New Zealand in
1876, having migrated for the sake of his health, and farmed near
Bulls in the Rangitikei district. His preaching in Bulls on a Sunday
was popular but initially that was all. After evangelistic work in
Dunedin he returned to the Rangitikei. In the meantime there had
been some conversions in the district. With Forlong preaching
again at Bulls, in 1883 about 200 persons were converted in a
couple of weeks. Many of these found their way into a Brethren
assembly of which Forlong became the pastor.[18]

However helpful a star preacher was in contributing to the
power and scope of a local revival, he was not essential. There
were local revivals in the backblocks of New Zealand's North
Island in the 1880s at which Forlong did not preach.[19] There were
local revivals in Victoria in the early 1860s which owed nothing to
California Taylor.[20] Nor was the presence of a star preacher a
sufficient condition for successful revival work: Taylor's second

tour of the colonies in 1869 and 1870 fared so badly he devoted but one sentence to it in his autobiography.[21] Plainly, the emotional and spiritual receptivity of people to the call for revival counted before all else.

But what determined this? And why was there never a major revival in the colonies? Professor Paul F. Bourke has drawn attention to the revivals in the United States in the nineteenth century and pointed out that in the United States there was no state aid to the churches. In New South Wales, under the Church Act of 1836, grants were made to the principal denominations for the building of churches and the payment of ministers. Bourke's conjecture is that taking advantage of state assistance developed in colonial denominational leaders a state of mind inimical to growth through revivalism.[22] This is plausible so long as we consider only New South Wales and Victoria, which had a similar provision. But state aid for church buildings and stipends was granted on a significant scale in South Australia only between 1847 and 1851 and in New Zealand never.[23] In any case Bourke himself is careful not to claim that without the Church Acts there would have been a religious revival. In his view the Acts were but one major inhibiting factor.

Starting with the same problem that Bourke set himself, let us see how far we can get by considering a particular local revival, and asking what forces were active to make it an exception to the general rule of colonial indifference to revival religion. As the Moonta revival of 1875 was probably the most powerful local revival ever seen in Australia and New Zealand it may provide a basis for a few conjectures.[24]

Moonta lies at the top end of South Australia's York Peninsula. In the mid-1870s about 12 000 people lived in what were really two settlements at Moonta, one in the town itself and the other at the adjacent copper mines. Nearly all were Cornish: Moonta at the time possibly constituted the largest Cornish community beyond Land's End. Since Cornwall was a Methodist stronghold it is not surprising that Moonta's religious life in the 1870s was dominated by the Wesleyans and two breakaway Methodist groups, the Primitives and the Bible Christians.

Revival amongst the Wesleyans at Moonta was precipitated by the death of a mine captain. The more powerful revival amongst the Bible Christians likewise began with a death. On Sunday 4 April 1875 a funeral sermon was preached at Moonta Mines for a young woman who had belonged to the Bible Christian Sunday school. Within a few days a crowded chapel was hearing young folk acknowledge their conversions as they held each other by the hand and sang 'Jesus, I love thee'.[25] On Sunday 11 April cries for mercy were heard from all parts of the chapel and 40 members were added to the church.[26] A rush of conversions also occurred amongst the Primitive Methodists.

On Friday 18 June revival workers and converts were ready for a show of strength in Moonta town. Around 300 persons gathered at the Bible Christian chapel in Williams Street. The Reverend Mr Casely explained that though processions with hymns were a novelty in the town they were frequent at the Mines and that Mr Stephens from the Mines would be leading the singing. The group set off down Williams Street to 'Hold the Fort', recently made famous in England during the Moody and Sankey missions. On reaching Ryan Street Mr Stephens led them in the lively 'My God, the Spring of All My Joys'. There was a circus in town that night but the procession gathered strength. Soon there were more than a thousand voices. The roll of Cornish harmony sounded over the tramp of feet, reverberated around the town and out over the wastes of the mines and the ravaged mallee scrub.[27]

By mid-July revival was over. According to one estimate 1250 people had professed conversion.[28] This figure includes those who had been converted at Wallaroo and Kadina, mining settlements close to Moonta, which had many Cornish among them. Attempts to spread revival beyond the mining communities failed.

The people of Moonta in 1875 were under stress. Accidents, sometimes fatal, were common in the copper mines. Primitive sanitation caused severe health problems including a typhoid epidemic in 1870. One piece of low lying land on the Moonta Mines was so stricken that it became known as Cemetery Flat. After a boom in copper prices in the 1860s and early 1870s there was a permanent reversal in 1874. Thereafter fear of unemployment continually haunted mining families. In 1874 there was a strike when the company reduced wages, contrary to a previous undertaking. At Moonta in 1875, we may suppose, there were many disposed to seek supernatural help and security.

It is difficult to know how much weight to give to financial stress as a cause of the Moonta revival. This is also a problem with other lesser local revivals. Real wages were falling, with agriculture being especially depressed, when California Taylor enjoyed such success in Victoria in 1863 and 1864.[29] The New Zealand economy was in depression in the early 1880s when the Brethren gained so many rural converts. The years in which Wesleyan recruiting was particularly high in New South Wales were periods of drought or bad harvest.[30] But this evidence is not much more than suggestive. We need a close examination of a number of local revivals focusing on precisely who the converts were.[31] One reason for being sceptical about any simple causal relation between economic depression and revival is that the Wesleyans and the Salvation Army did very well in Victoria during the boom in that colony in the 1880s. Another is that historians of religion in America, who have looked into the matter thoroughly, have found revivals occurring in conditions of both economic buoyancy and depression.[32]

Moonta itself ought to encourage us to look beyond a simple correlation between economic or social distress and local revival. A substantial proportion of the mining folk at Moonta had probably been involved in local revivals in the old land. In the aftermath of the French Revolution, of all English counties Cornwall had seen perhaps the most spectacular religious enthusiasm. At Redruth in 1814 two thousand persons were converted at one meeting which lasted nine days and nights. Revivals continued to occur in Cornwall into the late nineteenth century.[33] It is hardly surprising then that the Cornish at Moonta were prone to revival. Nor is it remarkable that the Cornish should have been prominent in Methodist revivals in gold-mining settlements in Victoria.[34]

What other immigrant groups came from districts in the British Isles which had recently experienced revival? There were some people from Northern Ireland in the 1860s and 1870s who may have had personal experience of the revival of 1859. There were immigrants from Wales in the early twentieth century, some of whom might have come from villages affected by the Welsh revival of 1904–05. But on the whole there were not many such immigrants relative to the total number of settlers. The bulk were English and the English by the 1840s were becoming more and more proofed against local revivals.[35] A demonstration of this came in 1859 when a determined attempt to spread the revival in Northern Ireland to England failed.[36] The number of local revivals in the colonies was therefore almost bound to be few.

But what still needs explanation is the intensity of the Moonta revival. The hazards of life there surely helped to precipitate revival in 1875. But the nature of the Moonta community was an even greater influence. The people were nearly all Cornish and, what is more, geographically isolated from people of other backgrounds. The relatively few immigrants after 1840 who came from revival-prone districts in the British Isles were as a rule exposed in the colonies to the refrigerating influence of a thoroughly heterogeneous society. Not so at Moonta.

It is interesting to compare Moonta and the Burned-Over District of up-state New York, notorious for its religious enthusiasms in the 1830s and 1840s. The Burned-Over District contained a far larger population and its revivals were more spectacular. But it was like Moonta in two respects. First, it was settled by a people who came from a revival-saturated religious culture – in the case of the District, immigrants from New England who had experienced the Second Great Awakening. Secondly, the Burned-Over District, like Moonta, had a population which was remarkably homogeneous in terms of its religious composition.[37]

Even in the mid-1860s California Taylor was not the only overseas revivalist working in the colonies.[38] From the 1870s, aided by the introduction of rapid steamships, overseas practitioners of the hot gospel became quite numerous. In the 1880s those who toured, on what had become a colonial circuit, included Mrs Hampson, George Williams, the Mountains, a husband and wife team, George Clarke, Mateer and Parker, Eli Johnson, R. T. Booth, William Noble, Matthew Burnett, Harry Grattan Guinness and Henry Varley.[39] So hot was the competition in 1886 that Mateer and Parker were forced to terminate their tour prematurely.[40] The flow was continued in the 1890s and through to the 1920s.

Taylor in the mid-1860s spent much time in small towns. Even in the cities his gatherings were normally of hundreds rather than thousands.[41] Those who came after relied more and more on the big gathering in the city. Whereas Taylor stayed for over two years, their time in the colonies was often measured in weeks. Taylor moved about the colonies in days before the railways had extended far beyond the cities; from 1883 it was possible to travel by train between Sydney and Melbourne. Taylor had been a folk evangelist; his successors of the 1880s and 1890s were of the age of mass culture.[42]

For the new age new methods. These were pioneered in Britain in 1873–75 by two Americans, Dwight L. Moody and Ira D. Sankey. Confounding the sceptics, they showed that it was possible to attract gatherings of thousands, to keep them entertained and, what is more, ensure that at each gathering there would be an impressive display of people who professed conversion. The coupling of sermon with song, of Moody with Sankey, was a key innovation during this tour. Other experiments that were to become standard were a massed choir, a solid phalanx of ministers on the platform at the front of the hall and an insistence on interdenominational support before the revivalists moved into a city.

In a remarkably short time Moody and Sankey reached the colonies in a surrogate form. Alexander Sommerville was one of the ministers who had been associated with Moody and Sankey during their Glasgow mission of 1874. By the end of 1877 Sommerville was conducting missions in the colonies which clearly showed Moody and Sankey influence: use of venues designed for mass gatherings, interdenominational support, the use of Sankey's *Sacred Songs and Solos*, and one of Sommerville's sons playing Sankey to the evangelist's Moody.[43]

Exaggerated reports of Moody and Sankey's success in Edinburgh in 1874 stimulated prayer meetings for revival in Melbourne, Sydney, Dunedin, and elsewhere. Interest in revival soon dissipated[44] but there were those who continued to hope for big things if only Moody and Sankey could themselves be persuaded to come.[45] Though the Australians and New Zealanders never got the original article, they got close. Reuben A. Torrey who toured Australasia in 1902 was a protégé of Moody and the first superintendent of the Bible Institute which Moody had established in Chicago in 1886.[46] J. Wilbur Chapman who came in 1909 and again in 1912 had been converted by Moody and had assisted him in his work.[47] Charles Alexander played Sankey to both men during these tours.

The sheer number of overseas revivalists who toured between the 1870s and World War I suggests that they were providing what large numbers of colonial Protestants wanted. The big crowds which some of them attracted confirm this. When Sommerville began his mission in Sydney in September 1877, 5000 people squeezed into the exhibition building. Mrs Hampson created a sensation in Melbourne in 1883 and in the same year hundreds of people had to be turned away from the Adelaide Town Hall on the final day of her 'Gospel Mission'. On one occasion during Chapman and Alexander's Sydney mission in 1909 a crowd of around 7000 had gathered three and a half hours before a meeting was due to begin.[48] Predictably, some denominational leaders hailed this enthusiasm as a sign that the long awaited revival was in progress. It was not. There is even doubt whether the overseas revivalists gave a fillip to churchgoing. In the New Zealand country districts where Chapman and Alexander did not go, churchgoing held up into this century; in the large centres where they did go churchgoing continued to decline.[49] It is only fair to add that there were some quite impressive, if perhaps temporary, increases in church membership associated with some of the missions. Supporters of Chapman and Alexander could plausibly claim that the duo had much to do with an 11.6 per cent increase in Methodist membership in New South Wales between 1911 and 1913 and the approximately 2000 people

The Helping Hand Mission Hall in Balmain, Sydney, grew out of a tent mission, and was opened in 1903, proof that Methodists had not wholly abandoned the attempt to reach unchurched labouring people. The front of the building also had scriptural texts along with a 13 × 9 foot picture of Peter calling on the Lord.

who became members of the Protestant churches in South Australia in 1912.[50]

Behaviour at California Taylor's gatherings in the 1860s seems to have been on the whole more restrained than during local revivals in Britain or America between about 1790 and 1840. Behaviour at the evangelistic meetings of Sommerville and Chapman and the like was more restrained still. California Taylor talked unabashedly of 'conversions'; Chapman seems to have preferred 'decisions for Christ'. Whereas Taylor preached for 'revival', Chapman conducted 'missions'.

Leaders of the Church of England were generally reserved in their attitude to Protestant revivalists. In 1923 the bishops in both Australia and New Zealand took a risk in fully supporting 'healing missions' conducted by James Moore Hickson, a layman of somewhat mysterious background. Hickson was then on a world healing tour which had begun in the USA in 1919. Thousands of sick people were brought forward to cathedral altar rails all over Australasia for the laying-on of hands. Whether there were in fact any cures was controversial but many bishops and clergy believed an immense amount of religious good had been done. In 1924 all the Australian bishops signed a pastoral letter that testified to 'the wonder of divine healing' which was in their judgement 'quite incapable of explanation on any merely physical or mental basis'.[51]

In the United States, the home of the Protestant revivalist, revivalism slumped in the 1920s. In Australia and New Zealand there was a growing feeling after World War I that the big campaign was a thing of the past. When revivalism came again in the United States in the 1950s renewed interest was shown in the antipodes and Billy Graham was invited to tour.

During the late nineteenth century there were many attempts made in Britain to turn the urban working classes into practising Christians. It was a tough nut to crack and some were convinced that it was not good enough just to provide the worker with a place of worship to attend or entertainment to draw him there: he must first be converted. Of those who sought to convert urban labourers and their families, William Booth had the largest initial success. Booth took sole control of the London-based 'Christian Mission to the Heathen of Our Own Country' in 1877. Within seven years the Salvation Army had a newspaper with sales of 350 000 a week.[52]

The first officers sent from England for what was to be Southern Command of the Salvation Army reached Adelaide in February 1881. By early 1883 the Salvation Army was recruiting in all four colonies. Advance was rapid initially. On New Year's Day 1884 about 10000 gathered at the first anniversary celebration of Victorian Salvationists in the Melbourne Exhibition Building, to enter which members of the public were expected to pay one shilling.[53] On New Year's Day 1885, about 20000 joined an Army march through the centre of Melbourne.[54] At the New Zealand census of 1886 over 5000 persons professed to belong to a movement which had been but three years in the country. In the next five years the number of New Zealand adherents almost doubled.

The religious feeling of the early Salvationists was at times intense. Ada Cross, wife of a Church of England clergyman, made a visit incognito to a service at Headquarter Barracks, Melbourne. She went with a friend out of curiosity about a new sect, ready to be disdainful of lower class religious eccentricities. The visitors were pleasantly surprised – only the excited preaching of a young woman struck a jarring note. Getting anxious because her friend's husband awaited their return, Mrs Cross leaned across to a young workingman on her left to ask the time. She never felt more ashamed. 'Wild prayers were going on, and the young man was on his knees, and his uplifted face wore a stern solemnity that showed him miles and miles above all such considerations as the time of day. At first he took no notice, as if he had not heard me; then he slowly climbed down and down from his heights and looked at me with a blank, dazed stare; and his eyes were full of tears.'[55] The early Salvationists also manifested religious enthusiasm of a more active, boisterous kind, as when they sang outside pubs, urging those within to come to the Lord, or confronted 'Skeleton Armies' who sought to mock and harass them.[56]

A year after the first corps was formed in Melbourne, Salvationists began to wait outside Pentridge Gaol to offer assistance to newly released prisoners. In the annals of the world-wide Salvation Army the forming in 1883 of this Melbourne prison house brigade is viewed as the inauguration of Army social work.[57] Creativity too marked the Army presentation of the Gospel in the early phase of the movement in the colonies. In the early 1890s a Limelight Brigade was formed around Captain Joseph Perry who had been supervisor of the prison gate home at Ballarat and who showed unusual skill with the magic lantern. The Brigade toured constantly throughout Southern Command. The work was expanded under Herbert Booth, the General's third son, and the Limelight Brigade began to produce moving pictures. By the end of 1899 short sequences of moving pictures dealing with the crucifixion were being shown in Victoria. On 13 September 1900 a Limelight Brigade production dealing with the early Christian martyrs had its première in the Melbourne Town Hall. Using slides and film, 'The Soldiers of the Cross' was one of the first efforts of its kind in the history of the cinema.[58]

Booth in England, like many a religious leader before him, had found it hard to sustain the initial enthusiasm for his movement. *War Cry* sales in England fell from 350000 per week in 1883 to fewer than 290000 in 1890.[59] Allowing for a time lag, it was the same story in the colonies. By the test of census affiliation there were fewer Salvationists in Southern Command in 1901 than in 1891. In New Zealand, where an official census was made also of church attendances, the Army's share of total attendances declined between 1891 and 1896.

To what extent did the Army attract labourers even during its brief expansionist phase in Australia and New Zealand? It is difficult to say. There were certainly some unskilled or semi-skilled workers among those who attended early meetings. An Auckland journalist described a meeting in 1883 as so mixed it was 'as if the dress-circle, stalls and pit of a theatre had been thrown together – the hoodlums in a majority'.[60] But many of the 'hoodlums' may have attended out of simple curiosity and come only once or twice: the question is what proportion of the early *recruits* were labourers, previously outside the churches. It is highly likely that many early recruits were churchgoing Methodists, keen to re-experience the experimental religion which had fallen from favour with their co-religionists as they had prospered and become socially respectable. Another type is represented by Patience Wooler, who came into the Army from the Church of England, whose services she had attended regularly. Patience was 'companion' to the wife of the Resident Magistrate in York in the early days of the Army in Western Australia. She went one evening with the family to a ball and while she was dancing saw the fallen woman of York standing outside an entrance door. Moved by the woman's plight, Patience Wooler went home to pray. Some days later she was taken to an Army meeting by a woman who did casual housework for the magistrate's wife. There she was converted. She was to tell her children how in the years immediately following her conversion she could feel the presence of God like one walking beside her, whose hand she could hold.[61]

The Keswick convention movement was another innovation in Protestant revivalism to reach Australasia from England. This was an attempt to lead practising Christians to 'a higher spiritual life' by gathering them together to hear inspiriting addresses and to pray. Personal holiness was the watchword. Mere conventional religion was to be transcended as the believer received power from on high for the daily Christian walk. Keswick was part of a wider interest in personal holiness in English Protestantism in the 1870s: in Methodism there was an attempt to recover John Wesley's doctrine of Christian perfection; the emerging Salvation Army held holiness meetings.

The Keswick movement, begun in England about the same time as the Salvation Army, belonged to a different social world.[62] Booth was after the submerged tenth forgotten by the churches; Keswick was sufficiently upper class to be acceptable to graduates of Oxford and Cambridge. Booth was too proletarian for even the Methodists; Keswick attracted many within the Church of England. Booth's army began in London; Keswick takes its name from the place in the English Lake District where the chief convention of the movement was held annually from 1875.

Robert Pearsall Smith, a glass manufacturer from Philadelphia, was a man whom organizers of the Keswick convention wanted to forget, but there is no doubt that Keswick was in part Smith's creation. He was a chief force in a series of religious conferences held elsewhere in England in 1874–75 that led up to Keswick. If he had not misconducted himself with a young lady at a conference in Brighton at the end of May 1875 he would have been the star attraction at Keswick a month later. On his 'fall', Smith was abandoned.

Pearsall Smith had sought from Christians a more committed discipleship and promised that God the Holy Spirit would himself provide the power for a truly holy life. His teaching was, from the orthodox point of view, dangerously close to antinomianism, for he claimed that fillings of the Holy Spirit could give effortless victory over all sin. As the Keswick conference got established this American emphasis on the eradication of sin was toned down.[63]

As early as 1869 a leading Baptist minister, Silas Mead, was promoting holiness teaching in Adelaide. He began to correspond with Robert Pearsall Smith and in the mid-1870s was a leader in a small holiness revival in Adelaide.[64]

In January 1875 there was a holiness rally in Melbourne, organized by Hussey Burgh Macartney, incumbent of St Mary's Church of England, Caulfield, and son of the Dean of Melbourne. One of the speakers was Dr Thomas, who had attended the convention at Oxford four months earlier.[65] Macartney became closely associated with Keswick and was one of the speakers there during a trip to England in 1878.[66]

The English interest in holiness teaching was also reflected in the colonies in Methodist conventions in the 1880s, the formation of at least one Methodist Holiness Association in the mid-1880s,[67] and the holiness meetings which the Salvation Army held from its arrival in the colonies in the early 1880s. The Salvation Army had a holiness periodical, as did the Methodists in New South Wales.[68] The periodical which Macartney began in 1873, *The Missionary at Home and Abroad*, also had a holiness orientation.

Macartney was an organizer of the Geelong 'Christian Convention' of 1891, at which the chief attraction was a man who had been commissioned in England to take the Keswick message to the colonies. He was George Carleton Grubb, an Irishman like Macartney, fervidly evangelical, an exuberant personality and a powerful speaker. Grubb made a brief visit to Australia and New Zealand in 1890, and in April 1891 was back again for over a year, conducting Keswick conventions and parish and cathedral missions.[69] From around 1889 in various centres small groups of ministers, including Anglicans, had been meeting to pray for revival, occasionally doing so throughout the night.[70] Some of these men were at Geelong in September 1891 as an economic depression deepened. They came expectant. And they became more so as Grubb took hold of those present. At last God was working among his faithful people and they were being empowered for evangelization amongst those who for so long had been heedless. Old 'Father' John Watsford described to the Geelong convention how he had seen revival come to Fiji one Saturday after the Wesleyan missionaries had known nothing but resistance from the Islanders. As the promise that water would be poured out upon dry land had been fulfilled in Fiji, so, he said, it would be in Australia. Even now he could see the floods were rising around Geelong. 'The brethren tell me that they used to pray together that the Lord would spare me to see a big revival. We have had our hands on the ropes a long while, and the bell is now going to ring. Yes, and the bells of heaven shall ring also.'[71]

The Geelong convention was quickly followed by another in Sydney at which nearly 2500 were present at one of the evening meetings in the Centenary Hall, with another thousand in overflow meetings. The Launceston convention which followed in a few days attracted about 2500 and was thought to be more successful.[72] Thereafter hopes of a national revival with holiness conventions as the chief instrument began to fade. Holiness conventions that continued to be held into this century, as at Geelong and at Ngaruawahia in New Zealand, maintained a Keswick piety in an evangelical pocket. But there was no significant outreach to the bulk of churchgoers, much less the unchurched.

Grubb and his co-workers held small prayer meetings at which they had 'glory times'. During one of these held one morning in Ballarat in 1891 with some non-Anglican ministers, the rejoicing in the Lord was so uncontained that the noise could be heard many houses away. Grubb's party also practised faith-healing and on occasions laid on hands for the imparting of the Holy Spirit.[73] Such fervid, charismatic religion was not welcome within the mainline Protestant churches. At some of the meetings of the Geelong convention of 1893 'a wave of glory seemed to roll over the audience' and there were shouts of 'Hallelujah! Glory be to God'.[74] At Belgrave outside Melbourne in 1910 there was speaking in tongues.[75] But these were exceptional episodes at Keswick-type conventions. There were Pentecostal groups in Australia before the First World War but it was not until after the Second that teaching about baptism in the Spirit was accepted into congregations within the Protestant mainstream.[76]

There was a Catholic revivalism as well as a Protestant one. Not so frequently, but often no less intensely than Protestants, Catholics were challenged with the facts of their sin, of God's judgement and of his offer of salvation. This had been so ever since the Counter Reformation. At least two religious orders, the Vincentians and the Redemptorists, had been founded with the express purpose of holding missions, which were chief instruments of Catholic revivalism.

In the middle of the nineteenth century there was an upsurge of revivalistic activity in many parts of the Catholic church.[77] In Ireland in the 1850s and 1860s parish missions conducted by religious orders were employed to spearhead a revitalization of faith.[78] Thereafter the periodic parish revival was a standard feature of Catholic religious life in Ireland.

Through to the 1870s there were not enough trained men to meet the demands in Ireland for parish missions.[79] For a time, therefore, the Irish bishops in the colonies were obliged to rely on their personal efforts or those of individual priests in reaching desultory or nominal Catholics. Archbishop Polding of Sydney was especially indefatigable in seeking out the lost, travelling vast distances to do so. In the 1870s this colonial mission work seems to have become more formalized, though the era of the professional team was still to come. In this decade there were at least two priests who gave themselves up to the work for months at a time. One was Julian Tenison Woods, who conducted bush missions up and down eastern Australia.[80] The other was Patrick Hennebery.

Invited by Bishop Redwood of Wellington, Father Hennebery arrived in New Zealand in October 1877.[81] He was 47 years old. Born in Ireland, he spent his boyhood in Wisconsin, and, after a move to Ohio, had there joined the Society of the Precious Blood. The Ohio priests of the Society were Germans who specialized in conducting missions to settlers on the American frontier, using methods developed in Europe. After much experience of this work and after helping to found a seminary in California, Hennebery tried his hand at revivalism overseas, taking in New Zealand, Australia, South Africa, England and India. One of his purposes was to raise money for his struggling seminary. He did this through sale of literature during his missions, thus resembling California Taylor before him.

Between October 1877 and May 1879 Hennebery conducted missions in virtually every New Zealand town of any size. It was one mission after another, travel over often atrocious roads, and each mission normally a week or more of three addresses a day, the first often at five or five-thirty in the morning. He did get help in hearing confessions but it was he whom the people came to see and to hear. It was his responsibility that each mission be a success.

The early and late morning addresses that Hennebery gave were usually quiet in tone and often addressed to the special needs of particular groups of Catholics: working men, mothers, unmarried girls and so forth. The evening sermon was the big one, often of an hour or more. Hennebery's subjects were the standard ones of the Catholic European and American parish missions: a sermon bringing home the reality of God and the imperative necessity that men and women should be right with God, a sermon on death and judgement, one on God's mercy, one on the sacraments as aids to a persevering faith. Hell does not seem to have been a constant preoccupation, though when he spoke about it he could draw, according to one observer, 'a fearful picture of the tortures and torments of the damned'.[82]

A reporter for Auckland's *New Zealand Herald*, who heard Hennebery preach, wrote that he told numerous anecdotes, some of which were funny or made so by the way he told them, and that his language was 'sometimes rugged'.[83] An editorial in the same paper, the day before, commented: 'There is a great deal in Father Hennebery's style and manner and language resembling that of Protestant revival preachers.'[84] Like the Protestant revival-

Patrick Hennebery.

ist Hennebery called men and women to receive new life in Christ. Like his Protestant counterpart he relied on emotional preaching to elicit decision. He used the same term 'mission' to describe his work. He too counted those who had been saved through his work. There were also differences. One was that the

Protestant revivalist often did not work closely with denominational leaders; sometimes they barely tolerated him. Hennebery conducted his missions in a diocese with the authority of the bishop behind him; sometimes a bishop participated in a mission. Another difference was in the procedures which Catholic and Protestant revivalists set up for the response to their call. At a Hennebery mission there was no walking forward to shake the revivalist's hand or verbal testimony. Instead the convert went to the confessional for the sacrament of penance – an intensely private act – and then joined with others at the altar to receive the sacrament of Holy Communion.

One of the highlights of a Hennebery mission was the temperance procession. During the late nineteenth century many of the Protestant evangelists from overseas had specialized in temperance preaching, a few of them so much so that they almost reduced the gospel to freedom from alcohol. From the late 1830s Father Mathew had given a powerful boost to a parallel campaign against drink within Irish Catholic communities both at home and abroad. Hennebery, like the Protestant campaigners, sought to administer a pledge not to indulge in spirituous liquors. The pledge cards issued by Hennebery were headed 'Catholic Total Abstinence Association' and this was stated at the bottom to have been founded by the Very Reverend Theobald Mathew.[85]

Here is how Michael Landers, a parishioner of St Francis's Church, Thames, described pledge night at Thames in December 1878. The temperance sermon to which Landers referred was once timed at two hours and 35 minutes.[86]

The rev. gentleman preached a most impressive sermon on the evil effects of intemperance, and proved how any person guilty of that sin violated the commandments of God, the precepts of His Church, and every law, moral and divine, and wound up a most brilliant discourse by exhorting the faithful to rise up as one man and take the pledge. About 400 rose to their feet, which did not altogether please the apostle of temperance, who requested them to be seated. He continued his exhortation, and after saying some very hard things about the chain that bound them, requested them again to arise and take the pledge, when a much larger number responded to his call. He then administered the pledge, the people holding up their right hands and repeating the words after him. Before dismissing the multitude he expressed his doubts whether a temperance procession would take place on Sunday and said it would rest with themselves, as unless a much larger number took the pledge he could not think of marching in procession.

Of course a much larger number did take the pledge. Hennebery did turn out. Agile onlookers clambered onto bare tufa rock overlooking the route to ensure a view.[87]

A Hennebery mission would close with an evening service that had been brought to the American frontier from Europe. In a church normally filled to overflowing the congregation would rise at Hennebery's bidding and light the wax tapers that he had asked them to bring. Then at his command the people would lift their lights into the darkness and repeat their baptismal vows after him.

When Hennebery was leaving New Zealand for further work in Queensland he claimed that during his New Zealand missions there had been 19 665 communions and that 23 000 people had taken the total abstinence pledge.[88] These figures are credible. In Auckland on a couple of nights he had capacity audiences in a marquee specially erected for him and holding 4000. At one service at five in the morning during the Auckland mission a newspaper reporter estimated there were 1100 present.[89]

Archbishop Redwood in his Lenten pastoral letter in February 1879 gave thanks for the wonderful effects of Hennebery's missions in his diocese, but also urged converts to guard against lapsing.[90] Hennebery was as concerned as Redwood about this and may even have been behind the warning. It was his practice to distribute Catholic literature and devotional aids and to begin devotional societies during his brief time in a parish so as to more effectively incorporate into church life the people who had been attracted to the mission.[91] He also promoted a wider sense of the church, urging Catholics to support their weekly newspaper and to get behind the bishops in building parish schools. In Auckland he raised sufficient money to build a Catholic boys' school and helped to begin the city's first successful Catholic newspaper.[92] Of course many of Hennebery's converts did lapse. Yet one priest reported in the 1920s that it was still possible to meet 'Father Hennebery's men' who had come off the drink during his missions.[93]

By the early twentieth century missions had become periodic events in the lives of many Australasian Catholics. In the Sydney archdiocese, for example, it was normal to have one about every two years in city parishes and about every three in the country.[94] The missioner who worked solo or in association with the local parish priest did not immediately pass from the scene in all dioceses[95] but the new frequency of missions was only made possible by episcopal employment of religious orders, who provided teams of men who went from parish to parish. To illustrate the periodic team mission I have chosen to concentrate upon the Redemptorists. They were prominent in this work and famous (or notorious) for their hell-fire sermons. Among the others were the Vincentians, the Passionists, the Jesuits and the Franciscans.

The Plenary Council of 1885 declared that regular parish missions were a necessity if the way to the sacraments were to be fully open to those who had lapsed.[96] The Council may well have been recognizing the success which the Redemptorists had already had in Australia and New Zealand and before that in Ireland and England. The order – the Congregation of the Sacred Society of the Redeemer – had come to the colonies in 1882 at the invitation of Bishop Murray of Maitland. Within months of their arrival in New South Wales the Redemptorists were at work in remote parts of Murray's diocese; within a year they were active outside it. In 1883 they conducted missions in New Zealand and thereafter returned annually, establishing a house in the archdiocese of Wellington in 1906. Their first monastery was Mount Saint Alphonsus at Mayfield near Newcastle, opened in 1887. Our Lady of Perpetual Help Monastery at Wendouree, Ballarat, was opened in 1893. Both were imposing buildings. By 1894 the Redemptorists had held over 700 missions in Australia and New Zealand.[97]

An article written by an anonymous Redemptorist and published in 1895 in the Australasian Catholic clerical periodical described how the Redemptorists conducted their missions.[98] The account was a detailed one, probably in part because the writer felt a need to defend the order from criticism that their missions were over-long and cost too much.[99] The writer's frankness about psychological techniques may have arisen from a wish to win full acceptance by parish priests. The latter were placed in a sensitive position since, by episcopal authority, for the duration of a mission control of the parish was handed over to the missioners. The emphasis of the article was on the methods the Redemptorists used, with the implication that they owed their success to these rather than to their personal abilities.

The writer explained that missioners were able to exercise such a large influence on the laity because in popular estimate they were holy men. Since they remained in a parish only a short time they did not lose their aura of mystery and power. The Redemptorists were also able, as the parish priest was not, to repeatedly preach the same sermon and perfect with practice both substance and delivery. There were also considerable advantages in the use of the confessional. One was experience. During a fortnight's mission a Redemptorist might hear about 500 confessions working about ten hours a day in the confessional. Another was the missioner's anonymity: many people experienced extreme difficulty in confessing 'certain more shameful sins' to a parish priest with whom they were acquainted and who they knew could not fail to recognize them in the confessional.[100] Experience had shown that many people's faith and morals had suffered because they made incomplete, invalid and even sacrilegious confessions. Missions had to be prolonged beyond a few days because a successful mission turned upon allowing everyone who attended to make his or her confession to one of the missioners. Normally a Redemptorist would seek from each penitent a general confession. A complete cleansing was required, not a little tidying.

The writer also explained that because the average parish mission lasted not less than ten days the Redemptorists were able to give systematic exposition of the central doctrines of the faith. The evening sermons, which were especially important in this respect, fitted in with the other elements of the mission and contributed to the total religious effect. Redemptorists liked to have a platform constructed at the front of the church to impress upon the people the exceptional nature of the mission and to allow preaching with 'abandon'. The evening's dramatic performance was balanced by a quiet morning instruction with an emphasis on intimacy and informality. The morning instructions were often given sitting down.

Father O'Farrell described for his provincial a mission held at Gunnedah during the first year of work in the Maitland diocese. Gunnedah was on the railway line and, though a small Catholic centre, was given a twelve-day mission. At the beginning only a few had come but the work in the confessional had prospered and lots of old scores had been cleared up. On the final Sunday, Bishop Murray, who had arrived on the ninth day of the mission, chose to have a show of the strength of the Catholic body of Gunnedah. A confirmation, a mass and the blessing of the cemetery were held on the one occasion. The people processed from the little wooden church led by those to be confirmed, the girls in white dresses and the boys and men in white coats. After the blessing of the cemetery, the mass, the confirmation, and a long sermon by the bishop, all in a broiling sun, a little doctor from Birmingham read an address to the bishop, assuring him that they would never forget the Rosary, the Daily Acts, the three Hail Marys and all that they had been taught during the mission. This address, according to O'Farrell, could not have been surpassed 'for earnest Catholic Loyalty and apostolic simplicity'.[101]

Another early mission was that at St Mary's, in the Melbourne suburb of St Kilda, in the winter of 1885. Many came each morning for the 5.30 mass and instruction, hundreds for the evening sermons. On a Friday evening of the mission Father O'Farrell preached to over 2000 people at a service of Reparation to the Sacred Heart of Jesus in the Blessed Sacrament, the altar dazzling with candlelight and massed with flowers. Father O'Farrell set forth the Catholic doctrine of the eucharist from a platform within the communion rail – he was a passionate, eloquent preacher – called on a priest to remove the veil that hung before the Blessed Sacrament and challenged the people: did they really believe that the same Christ who died on the cross was enthroned on the altar before them? They rose to their feet and cried: 'Yes, yes, we do believe it.'[102]

O'Farrell reported how the people at this St Kilda mission were often 'pitiful and at the same time amusing' in the appeals they would make at the beginning and end of each session.

'Father, I'm here since five o'clock this morning, fasting.' (This at 1 p.m.) 'Father, this is the sixth time I've had to go away after waiting all day.' 'Father, I have a cantankerous man to deal with, and I had to leave him without his dinner.' Next morning I said: 'Where is the woman with the cantankerous husband?' 'Here, your reverence', she cried out.[103]

Father Vaughan, the first leader of the Redemptorists in Australasia, gave particular attention to singing at revivalist services. Soon after the Redemptorists arrived, he produced for their colonial mission work a hymn book published in Sydney as the *Australian Catholic Hymnal*.[104] A journalist noted that during the St Kilda mission of 1885 the Redemptorists taught the children to sing 'I am a little Catholic' to a lively tune.[105] Hymn singing continued to be a feature of Redemptorist services.

At the opening of a mission at St Patrick's Cathedral, Melbourne, on 18 September 1886, both the Dean and Father O'Farrell explained that there were many indulgences to be gained during the mission. As was sometimes done a cross was erected at the close of this mission and in association with it indulgences were offered to those who remembered the mission worthily. The cross erected after this particular mission was one of white marble and had been brought from Rome by the late Archbishop Goold. A notice placed by the cross announced that to acquire a plenary indulgence a person who had been at the mission had to have made a worthy confession and communion, prayed for the intentions of the Pope, been present at the erection of the cross and then revisited it on certain specified days.[106] It would be surprising if some of those present had not understood that by doing as they were enjoined they ensured the removal of the soul of one they loved from the torment of the fires of purgatory into the bliss of heaven. This was not in fact the teaching of the theologians: according to them a plenary indulgence for the remission of the punishment attaching to sin was only totally effective where the disposition of the one praying on earth was perfect. But there was often much ignorance on the part of the laity about this, and either ignorance or silence on the part of many priests. One Catholic observed in 1922 that he had been 'amazed and a bit disappointed too' when informed that a plenary indulgence was hardly ever actually gained. 'I cannot understand why we are so often led to believe that we gain one when apparently we do not.'[107]

Redemptorists, like other Catholic missioners, were especially after men who were indifferent or casual about their religion. As one parish priest put it, male backsliders were 'the quality' among the penitents.[108] If these men could be got into the confessional in large numbers then a mission was judged a success. Certainly there were successful Redemptorist missions by this demanding criterion, especially when they were still a novelty. But it is unlikely that either the Redemptorists or the other orders succeeded to any large extent in revitalizing male religion. In the 1920s, as in the 1880s, it was a truism that Catholic men did not take their religion as seriously as women did.

In transatlantic Protestantism the doctrine of eternal punishment of the wicked in hell was increasingly questioned from the mid-1850s. By the 1890s the doctrine was defunct among the mainstream churches. Even in the mid-1870s Moody in Britain had not threatened hell-fire in his evangelistic addresses; no doubt he realized he would have cut a derisory figure among the educated if he had.[109] Similarly, during their interdenominational missions in Australia and New Zealand, Moody's imitators never drew vivid word pictures of the eternal punishment that awaited those who were unsaved. By contrast through to the 1920s and after Redemptorist missioners preached uncompromisingly about hell. They were perhaps to a degree curiosities in the Catholic world for placing so much emphasis on hell, but they were not laughed out of business. Today a Redemptorist who preached a hell-fire sermon in a parish church would be an embarrassment. This is a measure of how much closer Catholic culture has moved to the Protestant in recent years.

Many Catholic men were rendered immune to Redemptorist preaching about hell through coming under the influence of scepticism in the wider community. To a lesser degree this may also have been the case with Catholic women. Children were not so protected. Perhaps many children were like the young Vincent Buckley who was grateful for the drama and excitement that the Redemptorists introduced into the quiet tenor of parish life.[110]

Perhaps there were some children whom the Redemptorists hardly touched at all. But there were children who were deeply affected. Pat Lawlor, as an old man, attested that the Redemptorists softened their preaching when addressing children. Nevertheless he remembered being frightened when he was a boy in Wellington around the turn of the century. He was much troubled by an illustration that Redemptorists used time and again with small variations to make vivid the eternal nature of the punishment of the wicked. A bird made a single brushing stroke with its wing upon a steel ball the size of the earth. The touch was made only once every year. When the steel ball had been worn away in this fashion then eternity would not even have begun. The same would be true even if the brush of the wing on the iron ball occurred only once every billion years.[111]

In 1914 an eight year old, Kathleen Pitt, was taken to a Redemptorist mission at Portland, Victoria. Terrified by what she heard about hell, the thought preyed on her mind that she would die in her sleep while in a state of mortal sin. So she tried to stop herself going to sleep. She did this night after night. Even as an adult she did not succeed in going to sleep until some hours after going to bed.[112]

A Redemptorist sermon note book contains a story for use in a children's mission. Twelve-year-old Willie was liked by all and did well at school but he committed the mortal sin of not attending mass when he was able and so he went to hell. The preacher said to the children that he had to tell them what happened because of the risk they might sin like Willie. Four thousand miles below the surface of the earth there were the yawning gates of hell. Inside the gates fire came from the roof, the walls, the floor, yet there was also terrible darkness. Some years ago a child had been put in a dark room and had died of fright after two hours. Yet in hell there was not only eternal darkness, the shrieking of the damned, the noise of thunder, and the roaring of devils. In hell there were dungeons in which doors opened into little rooms.

> Let us go into one – the door is opened – what a sight – a little room but all fire – in the middle of the room – a bed of fire – boy lying on the bed fastened to it with chains – who is he? Boy who stayed in bed – [not] go [to] Mass. Now must stay in bed – chained to bed of pain – pillar of fire under head – bar of iron across forehead – red hot hands & feet chained – Beside bed 2 devils one beats – other laughs. Ha! bad boy not go to Mass – we kept you – will keep you now – no Mass now but bed of fire – burn for ever.[113]

The Redemptorists were concerned that any mission they held should effect a lasting improvement in parish life. The writer of the 1895 article explained that it was part of their strategy to return to a parish four or five months after a mission to attend to those who had been missed and to consolidate progress made.[114] They also formed and promoted confraternities and sodalities in order to strengthen the spirituality of the laity. At the end of the first Ballarat mission in 1886 they enrolled 700 men and 1000 women in the Confraternity of the Holy Family.[115] Bishop Moore commented five years later on the results of Redemptorist activity in the Ballarat diocese: 'Our congregations have been vastly improved. The Sacraments are more frequented; Sundays and holidays better observed; confraternities and similar associations established at the close of the missions serve to keep many from perilous paths; and altogether the tone both moral and religious is considerably raised.'[116]

In 1884 some people came from 70 miles away to be present at the first Redemptorist mission to be held in Oamaru.[117] A man walked 30 miles carrying his swag and slept each night in the churchyard to participate in the Gundagai mission of 1888.[118] During the month-long Melbourne mission at St Patrick's Cathedral in 1886 well over 7000 confessions were heard.[119] On the last Sunday of the Ballarat mission in the same year there were over 2000 communicants at the 7 a.m. mass, the bishop confirmed over 1000 in the afternoon, and more than 4000 came to the evening service.[120] The Redemptorists were new to Australia and New Zealand in the 1880s but it may also be that the early missions were especially successful because during this decade Catholics shared in a wider susceptibility to revivalistic religion. It was in the 1880s that the Wesleyan Methodist church recruited many new members and it was in ihe 1880s also that Salvation Army and Brethren membership expanded rapidly and that Protestant revivalists in the cities did well.

Even at the very beginning of Redemptorist work in Australasia regular churchgoers constituted a large share of their congregations. As time passed maintaining and reinforcing the faith of these people became an ever more important function of a Redemptorist mission. Probably the shift of emphasis from evangelization to maintenance occurred because of the very success of the early missions, for these depleted the pool of nominal Catholics who could be readily incorporated into parish life.[121]

The Redemptorists claimed 1854 Protestant conversions in Australia and New Zealand between 1882 and 1894.[122] Apart from the Redemptorists there were other preachers in the late nineteenth century who were instrumental in Protestants becoming converts to Catholicism. Cardinal Moran reported an estimate that no fewer than 300 Protestants were converted by Father

Hinterocker during his missions in South Australia in 1868 and 1869.[123] Bishop Reynolds of Adelaide claimed that in the first seven years of his episcopate, which began in 1873, 717 South Australian Protestants were received into the Catholic faith.[124] It was estimated that 40 Protestants were converted during just one mission of Father Hennebery in New Zealand.[125] Conversions of course continued thereafter, especially of Protestants who married Catholics, but the Catholic church became more inward-turned and conversions through revivalist missions declined. Geoffrey Webster was a New Zealand convert from the Church of England in the early 1930s. He remembered the church which he joined as having no interest in converting Protestants: indeed it 'seemed to be commonly accepted that Catholics never mentioned religion to non-Catholics.'[126] A Catholic layman, D. G. M. Jackson, charged in 1947 that the whole of the Catholic church's plant, organization and zeal was devoted to preserving the loyalty of those who were already its members.[127]

Both Protestant and Catholic revivalism had had their successes in Australasia, especially in the period from the 1860s to the 1880s. There were those for whom religion had come alive for the first time. There were others who had once been involved in church life, who had lapsed, and who through revivalism had returned to religious practice. Yet the Protestant revivalists had proved incapable of capturing and incorporating into the routines of church life the tens of thousands who were nominally Protestant and who laboured with their hands. Thus an old-world estrangement from organized religion had not been removed and was in time only likely to deepen and harden. Catholic revivalists may have done a little better in reaching labourers, but only those of Irish Catholic stock; no sustained Catholic effort was made to reach labourers in general. Revivalism in the 1920s was peripheral to colonial life as a whole, as it always had been.

Chapter Four

SEPARATION AND IDENTITY

An important aspect of the life of any group is its boundary lines. Not just relations with others are at stake here; relations within a group may be powerfully affected according to whether there is a shading from insiders to outsiders or a sharp line drawn between them. Joining with some in separation from others may generate a powerful sense of belonging; moving back towards others may diminish that sense. Separation and identity go together.

In this chapter three types of boundaries will be scrutinized for possible changes over time. The first concerns the local Protestant congregation and the distinction within it between members and non-members. The second type also concerns Protestants and deals with their propensity to stay within their denominational groups when choosing marriage partners. The third boundary is that between Catholics and Protestants. We have seen that in small settlements on the frontier friendly relations usually existed between Catholics and Protestants and that Catholics frequently had a weak sense of a distinctive religious identity. With the passage of time, and as Catholics increasingly resided in towns and cities, did separate Catholic sub-communities emerge and was there a strengthening of Catholic identity?

In Britain from around 1790 tens of thousands of individuals were converted. In consequence there was a re-affirmation of a distinction that had long been an important one within the Protestant world, the distinction between those who claimed personal religious experience of God's saving power and those who did not. In the English and Scottish dissenting bodies church membership was defined, and defined sharply, in terms of this same distinction. A line was drawn within the local congregation: on the one side 'members' and on the other mere 'hearers' or 'attenders'. Procedures for disciplining members were developed to ensure they displayed a high standard of moral and religious conduct. Members were supposed to be different from the hearers as well as from the completely worldly.

In the colonies the division between members and non-members was quickly effaced among Congregationalists. It was also being eroded at home during the nineteenth century, but in Australia and New Zealand the transformation may have been swifter, for the traditional view had not had time to become entrenched.[1] It is difficult to be precise about when the old exclusive conception of the church broke down in colonial Congregationalism. My strong impression is that it had occurred by 1880, if not earlier.[2] One reason for saying so is that I have not seen any instances of discipline being exercised after the 1860s.[3] Another is that from about 1880 ministers publicly expressed their concern that the purity of the church fellowships was in jeopardy.[4] A further piece of evidence is provided by the records of attendance at the Lord's Supper kept by one church fellowship in Melbourne. According to the traditional Congregational understanding, the Lord's Supper was a rite in which members enjoyed a high spiritual privilege of communion with one another and with their Lord. A shift from high to low attendance would therefore suggest an increasing distaste for involvement in the more intimate life of the church fellowship. If a high proportion of members made this withdrawal, this could be taken as a sign that the distinction between member and non-member was breaking down. At the Collins Street, Melbourne, Congregational fellowship there seems to have been a significant change in the religious attitudes of members during the 1870s. Between 1868 and 1880 the proportion of male members who participated in the monthly communion fewer than four times in a year, rose from 20 to 44 per cent. The corresponding increase for females was from 24 to 38 per cent.[5]

The same swing away from an exclusive understanding of church membership occurred among a large section of colonial Baptists. Baptist immigrants brought with them the rite of believer's baptism by immersion, something which the Congregational churches did not have. In the eyes of the world this rite was an oddity; thus to insist on immersion as a prerequisite of membership was to maintain a sect-like stance. In South Australia, where the Baptists were strongest in proportion to population, the churches rejected 'close' membership, and in some churches there by 1900 more than half of the new members each year were admitted without immersion.[6] By contrast in New South Wales by 1900 close membership was the rule of the Baptist churches.[7]

In early nineteenth-century British Methodism membership was not defined in terms of a local church fellowship as in the Congregational and Baptist traditions. But within the local Methodist congregation there was the same sharp line drawn between members and mere attenders at public worship. Being a member in the case of Methodism meant meeting in class along with ten or so others and joining with them to offer prayer and praise, to confess shortcomings and to receive support in living a

Australasian Wesleyan-Methodist Church.
FIRST CONFERENCE, JANUARY, 1855.

Quarterly Ticket for December, 1859.

But go thou thy way till the end *be* : for thou shalt rest, and stand in thy lot at the end of the days.—*Daniel* xii. 13

Walter McClelland

An early colonial Wesleyan Methodist class ticket. Wesleyan Methodism was both highly organized and uniform in its ecclesiastical arrangements and the quarterly ticket certifying membership of a class took a standard form.

truly Christian life. Only those attenders who held a quarterly class ticket and met weekly in class were Methodist members. This conception of membership was transplanted to Australasia and was unquestioned there among Methodists in the 1850s.

The Wesleyan Methodist church in Australasia kept an annual series of statistics on the numbers of class leaders as well as members in each circuit. In some city circuits the average number of members per class leader began to increase in the 1860s.[8] Here was an early sign of the growth of nominal membership and of the decay of the class meeting. In an issue of 1865 the *Wesleyan Chronicle*, published in Melbourne, carried an article which expressed concern about non-attendance at class. The writer reported that it was sometimes said that the number who stayed away was much on the increase.[9] A pastoral address following the Australasian Wesleyan conference of 1871 observed that some Methodists were now finding the class meeting irksome, whereas previously it had been a blessing to them.[10]

By the mid-1870s dissatisfaction in the colonies had become open, deep and widespread, just as it had at home and in North America.[11] In New Zealand in 1873 the Reverend W. Kirk said it was common knowledge that many Wesleyan stewards and trustees were only nominal class members.[12] In 1875 a Victorian minister claimed that in some circuits he knew there were as many professed members who had lapsed from class as those who continued to attend; another estimate in the same year put the ratio at two non-attenders for every attender.[13] The call for reform grew more insistent and lovers of the class meeting were passionate in its defence. It was not until the Wesleyan General Conference of 1890 that the younger men had the votes. This Conference resolved that attendance at a monthly meeting for 'testimony and fellowship' would be an acceptable alternative requirement of membership. In 1904 the General Conference of Australia dropped even this requirement.[14] It is highly doubtful whether it had ever been widely observed in practice.

One of the functions of the class meeting was to exercise discipline over erring members. Through to the 1860s members were admonished or even ejected from class for such things as card playing and drunkenness.[15] As reluctance to meet in class became more prevalent, the practice of discipline was abandoned. When the Reverend Robert Potter observed in 1876 that church discipline in Victoria in most of the Christian churches was practically non-existent,[16] Wesleyan Methodism provided no exception.

The defenders of the class meeting were inclined to idealize it.[17] The class books kept by Henry Dowty, a class leader in the Willunga circuit, South Australia, show that in his class average attendance between 1850 and 1874 more often than not was less than half the number enrolled.[18] For those who did turn up we have a picture of what it could be like from a minister who as a youth met in class in the Queanbeyan circuit in New South Wales in the 1860s and 1870s. This man remembered not spiritual enthusiasm but a pervasive sense of defeat as members repeated their shortcomings and failures week after week: 'As a growing lad I felt that it was extremely difficult to be good, at least after this model.'[19] Nevertheless the conservatives were sound in their instinct that Methodism, as John Wesley had founded it, stood or fell with the class meeting. Methodism from the beginning had been premised upon a sharp distinction between the godly and the ungodly. An obligatory class meeting was vital to maintaining a separation of the two. As a test of membership, wrote one Methodist defender of the class meeting in 1888, the class constituted an experience that 'few but those who really earnestly desire to lead a new life will care to stand'.[20]

As the line between members and non-members became ever more blurred there arose the problem of what to do with membership rolls. A possible response was simply to cease keeping them. This was not taken even in Methodism where membership had once seemed to be indissolubly tied to the class meeting.

Instead rolls were maintained and the meaning of membership was transformed: in effect, by the 1880s a member was someone who supported the local congregation and who did not object to being counted as a member. So completely was the exclusive understanding of membership rejected within large sections of Protestantism that it comes as a surprise to many of today's churchgoers to learn that it once existed.

Nobody has carefully examined what happened in the colonies to the different Presbyterian understandings of the church brought from Scotland. If the Presbyterian churches of Otago and Southland were at all typical, Presbyterian discipline relaxed substantially in the bulk of congregations. In the early days of Otago the elders of the Free Church had exercised quite strict surveillance.[21] In 1895 the Committee on Religion of the Otago and Southland Synod noted that not one case of discipline had been reported in returns from five presbyteries and 62 sessions. In its report the Committee added that the trend was towards dealing in private with cases that had previously been dealt with in open session.[22] In other words, it was no longer practicable to try to impose the earlier discipline.

Within the Church of England there was neither a tight understanding of the church nor a discipline over adherents to relax. Yet in the middle of the nineteenth century there was within the Church of England a *de facto* distinction between a general mass of adherents and a spiritual élite. Holy Communion was celebrated normally once a month, being tacked onto morning prayer, and most of those in the congregation would withdraw from the church at about the time the clergyman began the communion proper with the prayer for the church militant. From the 1870s an increasing proportion of the congregation received Holy Communion and Holy Communion was held more frequently, eventually replacing morning prayer in many dioceses.[23] The clergy sometimes hailed these changes as religious progress. This can only be maintained if progress is defined in terms of increased reception of Holy Communion. It is hard to see evidence of any general increase in Anglican piety; in fact, by the end of the century the proportion of all Anglicans who were regular churchgoers was declining. Thus the more general reception of Holy Communion may be interpreted as Anglican participation in the Protestant movement away from exclusiveness.

This review has made it clear that the various denominational traditions regarding church membership continued to exercise an influence in the new world. Developments took different paths because the inherited institutions governing membership were different. Nevertheless two generalizations are possible. The first is that, as in Britain and North America, there was a progressive erosion of the boundary between member and non-member in the local Protestant congregation. The second is that this erosion was already advanced by the late 1870s.

For the report on the New South Wales census of 1891 information was abstracted from the census schedules on the relative religions of husbands and wives. This information provides the first occasion on which we may learn from colonial census data how many Presbyterian men were married to Presbyterian women, to Church of England women, and so on.

Of special interest at the time was the extent to which Catholics chose to marry other Catholics. Thanks to a table in the census report we can state that precisely 81 in every 100 Catholics whose partners resided with them at the time of the census were married to fellow Catholics. This level of in-marriage was far above what would have been the case if chance alone had determined the selection of partners, for in New South Wales in 1891 Catholics were but 26 in every 100 of the total population. Nevertheless, the most striking feature of the table on the relative religions of husbands and wives concerns the different Protestant groups. Adherents of the Church of England, Methodists and Congregationalists were all married to their co-religionists to a greater extent than were Roman Catholics. Merely considering the percentage of married people who were in-married is, however, a treacherous way of comparing propensities to in-marry. Eighty-six per cent of Anglicans were in-married as against 81 per cent of Roman Catholics. But Anglicans were more than one and a half times more numerous than Roman Catholics. There is another factor to be considered. There was a substantial excess of Catholic married women over Catholic married men in New South Wales in 1891, an excess which had no parallel in the other denominations. This alone would have tended to produce a higher rate of Catholic out-marriage, all other things being equal. (A third difficulty can probably be overlooked. The figures pertain to the denominational affiliations of spouses at the time of the census. People who out-married but who transferred their denominational affiliation to that of their partners before the census were counted as in-marrieds. When a sociologist tested for this in Australia in the mid-1960s he found it happened only to a very limited degree.[24])

By using a statistical technique it is possible to estimate the *relative* rates of in-marriage once the size of the different groups

Table 3: In-marriage patterns by denomination, New South Wales, 1891

	Percentage of married persons who were in-married	*Standardized percentage of persons who were in-married*
Roman Catholic	81.2	82.9
Church of England	85.8	74.8
Presbyterian	78.7	84.7
Methodist	86.1	87.8
Congregational	84.1	95.3
Baptist	73.8	92.0

Source: N.S.W. Census, 1891

and the balance of husbands and wives have been controlled; that is, to give the patterns of in-marriage which would have resulted if there had been 1000 wives and 1000 husbands in each group.[25] Once the in-marriage figures have been standardized the Roman Catholics are still not seen to be exceptional in their propensity to marry co-religionists. Nor, incidentally, were the close-membership Baptists. It might have been expected that the New South Wales Baptists would have been much more likely to in-marry than the other Protestant groups. Congregationalists, however, had a higher rate of in-marriage than Baptists even when allowance has been made for the smaller number of Baptists.

How are we to account for the very high levels of in-marriage for all the denominations? There may have been a tendency for Scots to want to marry Scots and Irish to marry Irish, thus pushing up the rates of in-marriage of Presbyterians and Roman Catholics. But preference for a partner of the same nationality will not explain why the 'English' denominations – Congregationalists, Baptists, Methodists and Anglicans – all had high levels of in-marriage. The adherents of the different groups were not residentially segregated, so that will not do either. What about people being influenced in their choice of marriage partner by a desire to marry a co-religionist?

There were of course Protestants who were disinclined to marry Catholics. But this consideration aside, it is highly unlikely that Protestants in general gave any weight to denominational affiliation when deciding whom to marry. Doctrinal differences between the Protestant bodies were small and nearly all churchgoers were hazy about their nature. Denominational differences over church polity persisted but these were rarely taught in the local churches and there was widespread indifference to them.[26] With the exception of the Church of England, the hymns, the prayers and the general feel of services in the different Protestant denominations were very similar.[27]

When a person considered marriage what counted was the prospective partner's personal characteristics and circumstances. Consider a particular match. Fanny Bethune was the daughter of a Presbyterian minister, Fred Cato the son of a pious Wesleyan mother. They fell in love. Fanny was a true-blue Presbyterian, if ever there was one, and certainly would have preferred her partner to be one too. Yet Fanny accepted Fred's proposal of marriage. Fred was an active churchgoer and a man who prayed with his cousin about whether they should go into business together. Apparently Fred did not even begin to consider Fanny's Presbyterianism a difficulty.[28]

If we may eliminate Protestants seeking out co-religionists as a primary cause of the high levels of Protestant in-marriage, how are these to be explained? A factor of primary importance would seem to be that the local churches of each denomination provided social and religious activities through which young men and women could meet and get to know one another. Thus any particular denominational in-marriage rate was in large part a by-product of how far boy met girl in the local churches of that denomination. That Protestant in-marriages were so frequent suggests how little social contact many young people had outside their local church. This is not to say that always boy met girl through their mutual involvement in the life of the worshipping congregation. Often, perhaps, either or both were on the fringes of church life and first met at a church social gathering. Surely many a time a young man began attending church more regularly so as to spend more time with a girl to whom he had taken a fancy.

A Catholic writing to the 'Bachelors' Corner' column of the Melbourne *Advocate* complained in 1918 that he had attended one suburban church for over two years and that not one person had spoken to him the whole time.[29] Perhaps such an experience was more common at Catholic churches than at Methodist, Congregational or Baptist ones; the standardized Catholic in-marriage rate was significantly lower than the rates of these denominations.

It perhaps needs emphasizing that the in-marriage percentages which have been cited so far, both the unadjusted and the adjusted, summarize marriage patterns up to 1891 and for one colony only. They include marriages which were solemnized in the 1850s as well as those in the year of the census. They provide no information about change over time. Furthermore we have been discussing all adherents, not just those who were church members.

Table 4: In-marriage patterns by denomination, N.S.W., 1891 and 1921

	Number of persons in-married for every person out-married	
	1891	1921
Church of England	6.1	4.5
Presbyterian	3.7	2.2
Methodist	6.2	3.1
Congregational	5.3	2.1
Baptist	2.8	2.0

Source: N.S.W. Censuses, 1891, 1921

The evidence about membership considered earlier has suggested that by the 1870s the denominations with dissenting traditions were moving towards a more Anglican pattern. Since a breakdown in the practice of exclusiveness was involved we might expect the diminishing importance attached to membership to be associated with increasing interaction with those outside the local congregation. On this supposition we should expect a decrease in in-marriage. Information on the religion of spouses was collected again in New South Wales in 1901, an example which was followed in the Commonwealth censuses, which began in 1911. For the period after 1891 we may therefore test whether there was a decrease in the incidence of in-marriage. Table 4 sets out what in fact happened, comparing, for New South Wales, 1891 and 1921.[30] The rate of decline in the level of in-marriage was slowest in the case of the Church of England. The reason for this, of course, was that, taking into account denominational size, the Church of England in-marriage level in 1891 was already low. It is notable that the Baptist rate declined substantially. It did so, however, at a much slower rate than was the case with the Congregationalists, Presbyterians and Methodists.

What happened from the 1890s to the propensity of Roman Catholics to in-marry? The significance of developments here can not be understood unless the whole field of Catholic–Protestant relations is reviewed. This means going back to the old world and back to the man who was the single most influential figure in the history of Australasian Catholicism.

Paul Cullen was one of the most powerful Catholic ecclesiastics in the world during the nineteenth century. Rector of the Irish College, Rome, during the 1830s and 1840s, he gained the confidence of both Alessandro Barnabo, the secretary of Propaganda, and of Pope Pius IX. Appointed Archbishop of Armagh in 1849, he ultimately came to dominate the Irish hierarchy. In 1866 he was made Cardinal and given formal responsibilities in the oversight of Catholic mission fields.

In the 1850s the Catholic Church in Victoria and South Australia was already governed by Irish bishops but in New South Wales the English Benedictines were entrenched and in New Zealand the French Marists. From the mid-1860s Cullen in Dublin masterminded a virtual takeover of the Australian hierarchy. In New Zealand the Marists were able to hang on, principally through Francis Redwood, who became Archbishop of Wellington. (Redwood was born in England but spent nearly all his life in New Zealand.) Even so Cullen was responsible for two key New Zealand episcopal appointments, Patrick Moran to Dunedin in 1869 and Thomas Croke to Auckland in 1870.

The new Irish bishops were almost to a man protégés of Cullen. They moulded themselves upon him, they sought his advice, some had been his students at the Irish College in Rome.[31] At least three of the twelve Irishmen appointed to Australian sees between 1846 and Cullen's death in 1878 were related to him.[32] James Murray appointed to Maitland in 1865 had previously been Cullen's private secretary for eleven years. To this group of Cullen's men should be added two bishops actually appointed after his death. One was Patrick Francis Moran, who became archbishop of Sydney following the death of Roger Vaughan in 1883. The other was Michael Verdon, who became bishop of Dunedin in 1896. Both were nephews of Cullen. Patrick Francis Moran had also been Cullen's private secretary. So far as a celibate can, Cullen founded a colonial dynasty.

An able man, Cullen was dedicated to the reform of the Irish church. Apart from the correction of abuses and encouraging greater piety, he took this to mean a tightening and centralization of ecclesiastical authority and absolute obedience to Rome. Other bishops in late nineteenth-century Europe were reformers and had a sense of the Church under siege and the need to close ranks and follow Rome. The zeal of Cullen's ultramontanism had a specifically Irish side to it. In 1801 Ireland had been incorporated into a political union with England and Scotland, thus making Irish Catholics a minority within a Protestant state. A Catholic fear of being swamped or subverted was natural in the circumstances. And at no time was this fear more acute than during the first few years of Cullen's episcopal career, for then Protestant proselytizers, backed from England, appeared to be on the verge of major success. In February 1852 the Protestant *Dublin Evening Mail* crowed that of late 10 000 converts had been made in Connemara alone. This was a brag but the situation was sufficiently bad for Pius IX to express his personal concern at what was happening.[33]

Any protégé of Cullen was likely to detest schools that were controlled by the state. First, their master was a zealous ultramontanist, a Roman of the Romans. If the Pope spoke that was the final word. In the *Syllabus of Errors*, issued in 1864, the Pope had spoken, formally condemning the proposition that the state ought to have the entire direction of the formal education of the young. Secondly, Cullen's concern with proselytizing had a particular focus in education. When Cullen returned to Ireland in 1850 he found both Catholic and Protestant children in primary schools funded by the government and supervised by government-appointed commissioners. Cullen first struggled to impose unity on his fellow bishops in the formulation of a policy towards the national schools, then, from 1859, he led a campaign for the abolition of mixed schools.[34]

In Cullen's view the national schools were Protestant proselytizing agencies. They had not begun that way; Archbishop Murray, Catholic archbishop of Dublin, had approved them and even accepted a position on the Board of National Education. But from the late 1840s there were changes in the rules of the National Board which suggested a developing anti-Catholic bias on its part. Catholic fears in the matter came to a minor climax in 1866 when *The Life and Letters of Richard Whately* was published. Whately had been Church of Ireland Archbishop of Dublin and a Commissioner of the National Board. In the book, edited by a daughter, Whately was reported as having said in private conversation that the education supplied by the National Board was 'gradually undermining the vast fabric of the Irish Roman Catholic Church' and that the national schools were 'an instrument of conversion'. Read more than a hundred years later and making all due allowance for their context in the *Life*, the reported words look bad. How they appeared to Irish Catholics with a deep suspicion of all things British and Protestant may easily be imagined.[35]

James Murray and Matthew Quinn took up their appointments as bishops the same year Paul Cullen was made the first Irish cardinal. When Murray and Quinn arrived in Sydney on 22 October 1866 they were welcomed by the Sydney Catholic Guild. The address presented to them by the Guild spoke of 'the great progress of religion in Ireland' which had been 'directed by the zeal and defended by the vigilance of that devoted man by whose elevation to the purple the Catholics of Ireland and the Irish Catholics of every clime have lately been so honoured.' The address to the two Irish bishops went on: 'From your administrations here a like result is confidently expected.'[36]

It would have been strange if Murray and Quinn had not had the same high hopes. And it would have been strange also if they had not quickly involved themselves in the colonial debate on education, for education was the great issue of the day for the Catholic church in the colonies no less than in Ireland, and, moreover, primary education in New South Wales was largely modelled upon the Irish national schools. What remained to be seen was whether colonial experience would effect adjustments to the Cullenite set of their minds. The colonial tradition of co-operation and friendliness between Catholics and Protestants had been exemplified only the year before Murray and Quinn's arrival, when leading Sydney Protestants had rallied behind the Catholic community assailed by the disaster of the burning down of St Mary's Cathedral.[37] Protestants in the colonies did not have the evangelical fervour that marked the Protestants of Ireland; nor had they ever mounted proselytizing crusades; nor had they ever been energized by a major revival. Even more likely to warrant second thoughts was what the Cullenite bishops discovered about the existing state of Catholic education, or lack of it. A system of Catholic schools simply did not exist and the laity were apparently quite happy with the status quo, many sending their children to government schools.

In South Australia Bishop Geoghegan as early as 1860 had set about establishing Catholic schools, independent of government aid.[38] In the same colony in the late 1860s Julian Tenison Woods and Mary McKillop performed invaluable pioneering work for Catholic education. Later still, in the Sydney archdiocese, the English Benedictine, Roger Vaughan, was a prodigious worker to the same end. But without the Cullenites who arrived from the mid-1860s the issue would have been doubtful, so far as the Australasian church as a whole was concerned. In New South Wales, for example, Vaughan probably would not have moved so decisively if it had not been for pressure from Murray and the other suffragans.[39]

The first major contribution of Cullen's men on the educational question was at a provincial council of Australian bishops held in Melbourne in 1869. Here they secured a condemnation of the 'mixed' public schools more thoroughgoing than the Benedictine Polding would have liked.[40] From 1869 Matthew Quinn's Lenten Regulations forbade the sacraments to parents who sent their children to a public school when a Catholic school was convenient. Lanigan of Goulburn and Murray of Maitland were soon following suit in what was eventually to become a standard practice.[41] Moreover, and here the full extent of their uncompromising transfer of the Cullen mentality becomes evident, they wanted as a matter of highest priority an independent Catholic school system, and this at a time when the state was moving inexorably away from the public funding of denominational schools. The triumph of their policy within the Catholic church throughout Australasia was evident at the First Plenary Council of Australasian bishops in 1885. Henceforth each parish was obliged to have its primary school and each new parish was to have a school before a church if both could not be built together. By this time state support of denominational schools had ended.

Because of the episcopal stand on education, segregation from Protestants during school hours became the normal condition for Catholic children. This constituted a massive change in the social environment of young Catholics. In 1850 the proportion of Catholic children in Catholic schools was negligible; then, as a general rule, Catholic children attended mixed schools, or received no schooling at all. Either way they were in constant association with Protestants. By 1950 approximately four out of five Catholic school children were attending a Catholic school in Australia and a slightly smaller proportion in New Zealand.[42]

By the 1880s it was standard practice for the Catholic bishops to object to the public schools on the ground that they were 'godless' and purveyors of secular or pagan values. In a famous pastoral letter of 1879 the bishops of New South Wales went so far as to condemn the public schools as 'seedplots of future immorality'.[43] If concern with secularism had been the primary motivating force behind the episcopal demand that Catholic parents support an independent Catholic system, then the bishops would have carefully supervised the making of the curricula and what happened during the school day. Yet often the education actually given to Catholic children in the parish schools does not seem to have been one in which the religious and secular elements were so integrated as to continually impress upon young minds the reality of the supernatural. Religious instruction was tacked onto secular instruction, the very thing which Archbishop Polding had objected to in the public schools of New South Wales.[44] Whatever the rhetoric about secularism, anxiety about Protestant proselytizing seems to have been at least as powerful. As early as 1860 Bishop Geoghegan of Adelaide had asserted the need to combat 'a gigantic plan of proselytization ... put into action by the system of state-supported schools'.[45] Though most Catholic children were subsequently removed from the public schools in the various colonies there was an abiding concern about those who remained. Might not they go Protestant? For this reason when Protestants sought non-denominational religious teaching in the public schools the Catholic bishops opposed them. The bishops at once called the public schools godless and fought those who wanted to make the schools more Christian.[46]

The same anti-proselytizing preoccupation is also evident in the case of mixed marriages. Cullen in Ireland introduced harsh regulations against them.[47] At the 1869 Provincial Council in Melbourne his protégés forced through against Archbishop Polding twelve decrees severely tightening up on mixed marriages.[48] Henceforward consent to a mixed marriage was no longer virtually automatic and, when it was given, a normal Catholic wedding service was not to be allowed. At the 1885 Plenary Council this stand was reaffirmed. Normally, when a Catholic made a mixed marriage there was no nuptial mass, the solemnization was in the sacristy or some other room, and there were no flowers or candles. A Catholic who married in a Protestant church or in a civil registry was automatically thereafter barred from receiving Holy Communion. The non-Catholic had to undertake not to put any obstacle in the way of the children being brought up as Catholics. In 1908 the Papal *Ne Temere* decree declared a mixed marriage invalid in the eyes of the Catholic church unless celebrated before a Catholic priest. Before *Ne Temere*, though mixed marriages were prohibited, they were still recognized as valid even if they had been performed by a civil registrar.

Yet even after *Ne Temere* the stand taken by the Australasian bishops was not as strong as that on schools; the sacraments were never withheld from those who married outside the faith before a priest. Why were the bishops more lenient regarding marriages? The parish schools were extremely cheap and for very poor parents cost nothing at all. Therefore sending a child to a parish school may have required much less sacrifice than forgoing marriage to a Protestant whom one loved. If the bishops had asked for this greater sacrifice they may have conjectured that they would have been widely disobeyed. There may also have been worries about pre-marital pregnancies leading to illegitimate births: on a Catholic girl's part because she was keen to avoid the stigma of being an unmarried mother,[49] and would be prepared to defy the church if necessary; on the part of the bishops too because they wanted neither unmarried mothers nor defiance. Even regarding the schools the bishops could not elicit from their people a united front at parliamentary elections. Time and again an episcopal threat of a 'Catholic vote' proved hollow. One notable instance of this was when Bishop Moran of Dunedin seeking educational justice failed as a candidate for a parliamentary seat. From the returns it is obvious that many Catholics did not vote for him. In 1919 the Democratic party was formed in New South Wales with a view to exercising political pressure for the resumption of state aid to denominational schools. At the state elections the following year not more than one in six Catholic voters with an opportunity to do so voted Democratic.[50]

Cullen's men were convinced that mixed marriages, like mixed schools, were at once an expression and a cause of the feeble piety of colonial Catholics. Undoubtedly on many occasions a Catholic did marry a Protestant who was only nominally Christian and this did weaken the Catholic's own religious commitment. But to put the Protestant point of view, the Protestant partner might be a practising churchgoer and might even have a beneficent religious influence. Even from a Catholic point of view the stand on mixed marriages might be regarded as showing an obsession with proselytism which blinded Cullen's appointees to reality. In New South Wales in 1901 most children of mixed marriages were identified for the purpose of the census of that year as being Catholic: in 43 per cent of the cases where the father was a Catholic the children were themselves Catholic; where the mother was a Catholic, 70 per cent.[51] By the turn of the century some Catholic clergy were publicly acknowledging that there were benefits from mixed marriages. Bishop Delany of Hobart, for example, observed in 1900, that he had repeatedly tabulated the names of candidates for confirmation in many districts and been surprised at the large percentage of those of other than Irish origin. Delany found it 'very significant' that Catholicism was winning adherents from stock that had proved resistant in the past.[52]

To assist in drawing a line between Catholic and Protestant the Catholic bishops had much to say about Ireland. Their reasoning was simple: the church at home was identified with the national cause; therefore to heighten consciousness of being Irish would heighten consciousness of being Catholic.[53] Partly towards this end, it may be supposed, the Catholic cathedral in Melbourne was named after the patron saint of Ireland. In front of the cathedral was placed a statue of Daniel O'Connell, the 'Irish Liberator'.[54] In 1875 James Quinn, Catholic bishop of Brisbane, changed his name to O'Quinn to mark the centenary of O'Connell's birth.[55] Catholics who had never seen Ireland sang in 'Hail, Glorious St Patrick' of how their hearts burned for God, St Patrick and the land of shamrocks.[56] The Australasian Plenary Council of 1885 arranged for the celebration of the feasts of Irish saints: 'Fursey, Fintan, Cataldus, Frigidian, Rumbert, Kilian, Fiacre, Canice, Gall, Fridolin, Malachy, Livinus, Lawrence O'Toole, Columbanus, Virgilius, Brendan, Bridget, and Ita. Later, Carthage and Kieran were added to the list.'[57] When Henry William Cleary was consecrated (in Ireland) bishop of Auckland the invitations were in Gaelic and Cleary ensured that his episcopal robes were made in Ireland.[58] Norman Thomas Gilroy, who was Australian-born, arranged his episcopal consecration for 17 March, the feast of St Patrick.[59] Strings of churches were named after Irish saints. Instances of how variations were played on this theme of Catholic Ireland could easily be multiplied, for bishops and priests never tired of it. Even Roger Vaughan, an Englishman, boosted Irishness and linked it with zeal for religion, though in his case desire to make himself acceptable to his Irish people was undoubtedly also an element. He told a friend in 1877 that he had written more in favour of the Irish people than all the Irish bishops in Australia put together.[60] That reinforcing Catholic with Irish identity had become settled policy amongst the bishops as early as 1870 is suggested by a pastoral letter by Thomas Croke. Writing from Rome prior to taking up his appointment to the see of Auckland, Croke promised his people that he would often talk to them about Ireland, 'of its hopes and fears, of the wonders it has already achieved, and of all [it] is actually doing for the faith of Christ.' A lively young French nun who observed Croke in action in Auckland, summed up his message as 'the faith of Ireland and the Gospel of Erin'.[61]

For the link between Catholicism and Ireland to be fully effective, interest in Ireland had to remain strong, something which the bishops could not take for granted. As one Irish-New Zealander put it, many of his fellows did 'not trouble themselves very much about the affairs of the land of their fathers'.[62] Irish organizations were weak and evanescent because they were only supported by a small minority.[63] Once the Catholic education system was in place in New South Wales only a tiny minority of parents tried to insist that Irish history be taught in the schools; school readers which had Irish material were not introduced in New South Wales until 1908.[64]

Some did not want to remember Irish history, or at least not too vividly and in a fashion which perpetuated old resentments. There were those who did not want to commemorate the rising of 1798 at all, for fear of giving offence to friends and acquaintances of English stock.[65] The same pressures towards integration subtly affected the keeping of St Patrick's Day: in country centres, especially, a staple of the celebrations was the athletic sports meeting in which Irish and non-Irish participated.[66] So hegemonic were British values in these colonial societies that it was even possible for an Irish settler to gibe at Ireland's wrongs. One morning in the 1890s two Irishmen had a conversation in a tram in an Australian city. One was so upset by what his friend said that he recounted the exchange that night to his diary. The diary writer was a devout Catholic and a proud Irishman. He knew his friend to be 'weak when there is question of Ireland or, in fact, when there is question of Catholicity; but, of course, weak in one of these, weak in both, is a common observation.' The diary keeper, knowing that his friend had been reading Dante, asked him if he knew that the plan of the *Divine Comedy* had probably been borrowed from an Irish saint, who had had similar visions. The friend sneered his reply: 'Another injustice to Ireland'.[67]

Desire for acceptance was not the only factor which made the Irishness of the laity paler than their bishops would have liked. Through to the 1920s bishops and priests remained largely Irish-born and bred; the laity became ever less so. In 1914 at least 70 per cent of all Catholic clergy in Australian dioceses were Irishmen; by then the Irish-born were in a minority amongst Catholic adults living in both Australia and New Zealand.[68] The laity who had been born in the colonies could not feel for Ireland as they might have done if they had been Ireland's native-born.

The bishops would not have said so much about Ireland, the country, if they could have relied upon distinctively Irish folk ways to keep the laity apart from the Protestant majority. But these were already disappearing in the early nineteenth century. The triumph of the English language was all important here. At the census of Ireland in 1851 less than five per cent of the population were monoglot Irish-speakers.[69] No homogeneously Irish communities were formed in the colonies; therefore, what remnants of a distinctively Irish culture the immigrants brought with them could not be maintained into the second and third generations.

In the heat of the conflict during the making of the new education acts there were savage words from both sides. The bishops criticized the public schools in words that to Protestant ears were as offensive as they were untrue. When Catholic parents withdrew their children from public schools, Protestants described these parents as contemptible victims of priestcraft. The schools issue also engendered bitterness because the colonial governments not only withdrew financial assistance from denominational schools, they persistently refused Catholic pleas to re-introduce it. Thus if Catholics were to have their own schools they had to pay twice for education: once through taxes and once directly for the upkeep of their local parish school. Non-Catholic denominational schools were affected but these were relatively few in number and the parents of children attending these schools were on average much more affluent than Catholic parents. The state, therefore, seemed to discriminate against the Catholic poor.

The stand taken by the bishops upon mixed marriages exacerbated the tensions. To Protestant eyes Catholic 'principle' seemed a preposterous affront. Why should a Protestant be regarded as any less Christian than a Catholic when it came to choosing a partner? Why should a Protestant husband have to promise that his children would be brought up as Catholics? And then, with *Ne Temere* in 1908, how could any religious body have the nerve to declare that only marriages solemnized before one of its priests were valid in the eyes of almighty God?

Compounding these causes of friction came Ireland. It was not a running sore like education, and caused rather less trouble than might have been expected. Irish-Australians were never as fierce in their denunciations of Britain as Irish-Americans, or as active in the Irish revolutionary cause. But there were crises. One was the Fenian scare in the late 1860s, during which the second son of Queen Victoria was shot and wounded by an unbalanced Irish Catholic in Sydney. There was also trouble over Fenianism on New Zealand's west coast.[70] Another crisis was in the aftermath of the Easter Rising in Dublin in 1916. When the British government refused to allow Archbishop Mannix to land in Ireland in 1920 many Irish Catholics in Australasia were outraged.

The social divisiveness wrought by events of sixty and more years was symbolized on Sunday 9 December 1934. On that afternoon a hundred thousand and more Catholic men, women and children stood or knelt in homage as the sacred host was carried past them in the streets of Melbourne. It was the climax of a eucharistic congress, which Archbishop Mannix had chosen to make the chief Catholic contribution to the Victorian centenary celebrations of 1934. Mannix knew that many Protestants were offended by a religious procession in which the host was the centre of devotion. For him the Victorian centenary was an occasion for a display of Catholic strength, rather than for celebrating general togetherness and social cohesion.[71]

The growth of sectarianism from the 1850s undoubtedly did help to firm up the Catholic identity of many, but this truth needs to be qualified. Sectarian controversy, often dramatic in its mani-

The climax of the Eucharistic Congress in Melbourne, 1934. Under the canopy, the Papal Legate, bearing the Sacred Host, reaches the end of the processional route.

How the Loyalist League of Victoria saw Archbishop Mannix, *c.* 1919. According to the League, 'Mannix and Co.' constituted 'the bitterest and almost the only bigoted sectaries in our midst.' The caption of the cartoon read: 'Singed! "He that lighteth the flame shall burn his winglets in fire."'

festations, was only episodic. More prevalent was the ill-feeling fuelled by the controversies. Sectarianism in this second sense became a permanent background feature to the lives of many Catholics. They felt they belonged to the Catholic team and acted with suspicion towards the opposition.[72] On the other hand there continued to be many Catholics who had friendly dealings with Protestants. Writing to his fellow priests in Ireland, Father M. Long observed in 1883 that the noise made by Orangemen at elections was misleading. 'Perhaps there is no more telling evidence of the wholesome relations existing between Catholics and Protestants, than the fact, that, when a priest is on one of his long journeys, he often takes a Protestant squatter's residence as his stopping-place, rather than the neighbouring Catholic's hotel.'[73] Around the time of the First World War one Catholic in New South Wales protested at the behaviour of those whom he called 'jelly-fish Catholics' who both observed their religion and who were on the most amicable terms with Protestants, even to the extent of fraternizing with masons and donating for friendship's sake to Protestant churchbuilding funds.[74] At Hokitika on New Zealand's west coast in the 1950s the Catholic owner of the town's only hotel helped to erect a Protestant church.[75] Such instances could easily be multiplied. Protestant–Catholic relationships were relationships between human beings and therefore complex and many-sided. One further illustration may suffice. During H. W. Cleary's time as bishop of Auckland his coadjutor bishop was put on trial on a charge of sedition. This was in 1922. For Cleary's funeral in 1929 the life of the city of Auckland virtually came to a stop as Protestants as well as Catholics turned out to display the affectionate regard in which they had held him.[76]

Dr Herbert Moran went so far as to write that sectarian virulence had made his fellow Catholics 'a breed apart, firebranded like travelling stock in a strange country so that all might know whence they came.' Another Moran analogy was more apt because less dramatic: Catholics had become like a substance held in a flask, in suspension rather than in solution.[77]

There is one further aspect of Protestant–Catholic relations to examine before considering the question of what happened to Catholic marriage patterns from the 1880s. This is the policy of the Australasian bishops of providing a Catholic social and intellectual environment.

In the late nineteenth century the hierarchy in Ireland had sought to segregate Catholics over a wide range of activities. In

Europe and North America also there were attempts at segregation. Thus the Australasian Plenary Council of 1885 was only falling in with a wider trend when it evinced concern that young Catholics be surrounded by wholesome social as well as religious influences.[78] Archbishop Carr gave the matter further emphasis in 1904 when he addressed the Second Australasian Catholic Congress. Catholicism had entered a new phase, he declared, now that churches and schools had been largely supplied. It was the call of the hour to 'meet the intellectual and social requirements' of Catholics and to provide an environment that was as 'safe' as possible.[79]

From his arrival in Melbourne in 1887 Archbishop Carr had been especially concerned that lads who on leaving the protected environment of school and family too often lapsed into nominalism. He and the circle around him believed that much of the havoc was a consequence of bad friends being made. The answer was to provide clubrooms or a hall at the church under the eye of the parish priest. Carr revitalized the Catholic Young Men's Societies of Melbourne and provided the organization with its own organ, the *Catholic Magazine*, later known as *Austral Light*. This activity was impressive compared with the preceding apathy, but even in Victoria, where the movement was so much stronger than elsewhere, not more than 2500 were enrolled in 1904. This was estimated to be one in twenty of those who were eligible. The emphasis on debating and literature appealed to clerks and tradesmen eager for self-improvement, not to unskilled labourers.[80]

Concern with the school leaver was persistent. In 1907 one writer identified the source of the poor church attendance of men as being the drift out of church life by boys as soon as they left school.[81] In 1920 Father Eustace Boylan S. J. observed: 'I think it is no exaggeration to say that nothing gives more anxiety to pastors and others who have the welfare of souls at heart than this question of perseverance on leaving school.'[82] Boylan was an advocate of clubs and communion guilds. Another priest who discussed 'the problem of leakage' thought that special instruction for school leavers might help.[83]

Much less concern was shown about protecting girls and holding them within the church. It seems many priests believed that providing sodalities for girls to join was sufficient. Certainly sodalities and other kinds of devotional associations were more popular with girls than boys, yet girls were by no means immune to the world's allurements. Membership of Children of Mary sodalities in the schools may often have been large only because

Children of Mary in the annual eucharistic procession for the Feast of Christ the King at Sacred Heart College, Richmond Road, Auckland, during the 1930s.

there the girls had no real choice: Father Boylan thought it rare for more than one girl in four who left school to continue to belong to the Children of Mary.[84] To judge from reports made by Children of Mary sodality members in 1920 girls often stayed away from meetings if something more attractive turned up. A typical parish sodality of the Children of Mary was composed almost entirely of older school girls and those who had paid employment. It met weekly or fortnightly on a Sunday afternoon or week night. Members would say together the Little Office of the Immaculate Conception; receive spiritual instruction from their director; after this there might be Benediction of the Blessed Sacrament with Hymns and Act of Consecration to the Most Glorious Queen of Heaven. Once a month a parish association of the Children would take Holy Communion as a body, wearing their cloak, white veil, blue ribbon and silver medal. Children of Mary were usually active about the parish in providing stalls at bazaars and fêtes, organizing communion breakfasts, caring for altar linen, helping with church socials. One New Zealand girl reported that, after the director retired, the girls talked about fashions or admired a new hat or costume. 'We are just very ordinary girls, who do not soar to any wonderful heights. To the best of us our Sodality means a lot, and to the worst of us – who knows but that it may mean even more.'[85]

By the Second World War there was a bewildering variety of Catholic associations, clubs and guilds for adults to join: medical and funeral benefit associations, such as the Hibernians; for social work, the St Vincent de Paul Society; a range of sodalities and other devotional societies, including the Holy Name Society, popular with men; the Catholic Women's League; a plethora of sporting and recreational clubs and occupational associations; there was even a male secret society, the Knights of the Southern Cross, to counter the Masons. If a city Catholic wanted to be surrounded entirely by other Catholics in spare hours he or she could be. Within the one parish of Ashfield, Sydney, in 1944 there were no less than 26 different societies.[86]

In the last quarter of the nineteenth century, in the colonies as elsewhere in the Western world, there was an enormous increase in the volume and variety of popular literature: newspapers, magazines and books of fiction and non-fiction. The Catholic bishops became ever more active in warning their people about the possible harm that might result if they were not highly selective about what they allowed into their homes. (Very little was said by Protestant leaders.) Bishop Corbett of Sale wanted parents to collect all the bad books in their houses and burn them.[87]

Bishop Cleary of Auckland, a gifted journalist, was especially indefatigable in campaigning to ensure a 'merciless barrier of moral quarantine' against unsuitable newspapers and books. Amongst the material he was keen to keep from Catholic eyes was information on birth control.[88]

Included in the class of undesirable literature were novels deemed sexually suggestive – Bishop Corbett urged parents to absolutely prohibit the works of Zola, books by atheist or agnostic thinkers, and books by Protestants offering anti-Catholic interpretations of the Christian faith or Christian history. Municipal or other public libraries that made available such books could not be closed, but a partial answer was to set up Catholic libraries, both in the parishes and in central locations. The first, second and third plenary councils of bishops got behind the movement. Central libraries were established in the cities but it is doubtful that they modified Catholic reading habits substantially. The Melbourne Central Catholic Library established in 1924 was judged especially successful, having by 1937 more than 2000 borrowers.[89] Yet there were close to 200000 Catholics living in Melbourne on the eve of the Second World War.

There was considerable progress in providing a Catholic press. To illustrate this we may compare the position in Victoria in the 1860s and in the 1920s. For approximately half the 1860s there was no Catholic paper at all in Victoria. In the 1920s there were two Catholic weeklies. The *Tribune*, founded by Archbishop Carr and the official paper of the Melbourne archdiocese, was subsidized to cost only one penny to achieve as wide a circulation as possible. The *Advocate* was run on commercial lines. Founded in 1868 and initially a paper for the Irish colonist with little religious intelligence, by the 1920s the *Advocate* had long had a heavy content of denominational news. Also being published in Melbourne in the 1920s were the *Austral Light* and two Jesuit devotional monthlies, the *Australian Messenger of the Sacred Heart* and *Madonna*. But a daily had not emerged in Melbourne, or even in Sydney, which by 1930 had a Catholic population of around a quarter of a million. Many of the laity just would not support the Catholic press, as Catholic journalists frequently lamented.[90] Father T. A. Fitzgerald commented in 1900 that there were Catholics who boasted about their ignorance of religious affairs and who professed not to want a Catholic paper because Protestant visitors might see it on the table and they wanted to appear broadminded.[91]

Anything that marked Catholics as different had the potential to segregate them from Protestants and so place them in a safer environment. On this principle Bishop Murray told Cardinal Cullen in 1870 that he opposed the use of the vernacular in the mass. Murray also declared that Protestant bigotry could have a good effect in reducing social intercourse between Protestants and Catholics.[92] Rules about abstinence from meat on Fridays, if complied with, tended to serve a similar function. But there were Catholics ready to 'forget' this rule.[93] Legalism too was a resort. In the Korumburra district in Victoria during the late 1940s balls were held on a Friday night, Protestants and Catholics attending each other's functions. Catholics who got the early sittings for the ball suppers were accustomed to swap with their Protestant friends so that they could have the sausage rolls after midnight.[94]

Priestly fear of contagion was at its most acute in the matter of Protestant religious services. Attendance at ordinary Sunday services was out of the question. More difficult was drawing the line about weddings and funerals. In 1920 Father Boylan told an inquirer that it was not permitted for a Catholic to be a member of the wedding party in a Protestant service, but he did not think it forbidden for a Catholic to attend so long as he or she sat away from the wedding party.[95] In 1922 Boylan told another inquirer that a Catholic could walk to the graveside for the funeral of a Protestant friend but ought to withdraw a little when the religious rite began.[96] Father Rumble of Sydney, always a man for sharp lines, declared that it would be a sin for a Catholic convert to attend the funeral service of his Protestant mother.[97] How much notice did the laity take of these restrictions? Father M. D. Forrest remarked in 1928 that Australian Catholics abstained from any form of common worship with Protestants.[98] This was certainly not true of all lapsed Catholics. And there were even some among those practising their faith who quietly broke what they regarded as a taboo against attending Protestant weddings.[99]

Now, finally, let us take up the subject of Catholic marriage patterns from the 1880s. Was there a fall in the proportion of Catholic mixed marriages such as to indicate a movement towards a self-contained Catholic community? Such a tendency would not be unexpected given the harsh Cullenite line on mixed marriages, the episodes of sectarian controversy, the formation of a Catholic school system, *Ne Temere*, and the formation of many Catholic associations. Yet in New South Wales the proportion of married Catholics who were in mixed marriages *increased* steadily from 1891, including the years after *Ne Temere*. In 1891 in New South Wales there were slightly over four Catholics married within their denomination for every one in a mixed marriage; thirty years later there were slightly under three in-married Catholics for every one in a mixed marriage.[100] There was never a Catholic ghetto in the nineteenth century and this century did not see one come into being.

The bishops and priests did not cease to strive for a laity that was compliant to their rules and wholly identified with the Catholic body. Total success was always impossible. There was always a lurking anxiety that even 'good' Catholics would defect or compromise themselves in some way. As Vincent Buckley remembered his Catholic boyhood in the 1930s and 1940s, insecurity was pervasive in gatherings of practising Catholics.

> There was a highly formalized and constant sense of crisis in little things, a pressure to join, not to abandon the lifeline. Sermon after sermon was devoted to this kind of thing. . . . Most of the signs by which a Catholic was defined and might be recognized were presented as matters of conscientious conviction related to very sacred beliefs.[101]

Chapter Five

SUNDAY

Among the many statistics collected by the colonial governments in the nineteenth century were some that pertained to Sunday worship. These included series on the numbers of seats available for public worship and the numbers of people usually attending. These Sunday statistics were seen as means of measuring social, moral and religious progress.

In 1850 the churches were better supported than they had been twenty years before when large-scale free settlement was just beginning.[1] But a concerned Christian who analysed the religious statistics at mid-century would have found little to cheer about. The flow of immigrants in the 1830s and 1840s had outstripped the provision of buildings and preachers for religious services. In 1850 there were sufficient seats in places of public worship for only one European in four living in Australia and New Zealand and only about one person in five was usually at public worship on a Sunday.[2]

For the next forty or so years statistics pertaining to Sunday tell of substantial progress. To take the especially dramatic case of Victoria to illustrate the improvement regarding religious accommodation, in that colony the proportion of the total population provided with a seat in a place of worship increased from 14 per cent in 1851 to 54 per cent in 1890.[3] In Britain, providing services and religious accommodation for town dwellers became an obsession with ecclesiastical authorities in the early nineteenth century. Too seldom they asked themselves whether the working classes wanted to attend. But in the colonies many potential churchgoers were to be found in virtually every area of settlement. To the end of the century, increasing the provision for public worship was almost always rewarded by attendance. In Victoria the proportion of the total population usually attending church increased from around 14 per cent in 1851 to around 34 per cent in 1881.[4]

The Wesleyans often beat the other denominations in providing the first services of worship in the gold fields and in newly settled agricultural districts. For months or even years Anglicans, Presbyterians and others would be obliged to attend Wesleyan services, sometimes turning Methodist in the process. In part the Wesleyan church got the jump on the other denominations because the Wesleyan system of church organization combined flexibility with central control; in part the Wesleyans were better at

Table 5:   Social class and church attendance, Melbourne, 1887

	Mean attendance in each group of municipalities (attendances as a percentage of adherents)	
	Northern	Southern
Church of England	12.0	23.1
Presbyterian	26.5	30.0
Wesleyans and other Methodists	78.0	63.7

Source: *Daily Telegraph*, 11 May 1887[6]

providing services because of their use of lay local preachers. In both Victoria and South Australia during the 1850s and 1860s more colonists attended Wesleyan services than the services of any other religious body.[5]

The Wesleyans also surpassed the other principal denominations in reaching down the social scale to attract people to worship. Gold and copper miners performed hard physical labour and many of them were Wesleyans. A difference could also be observed in the cities between the Wesleyans on the one hand and the Anglicans and the Presbyterians on the other. In 1887 the *Daily Telegraph* conducted a census of churchgoing in Melbourne, a city in which the well-to-do tended to reside in the southern suburbs. In Melbourne in 1887 Methodist religious practice was less clearly distributed along class lines than was the case with the Anglicans and the Presbyterians (see Table 5). The Wesleyan superiority here, however, was very much a relative one. Some Wesleyan congregations were sufficiently wealthy to erect imposing churches. Some charged pew rents, in the old world a telltale sign of estrangement from the working classes.[7] So far nobody has identified any urban Wesleyan congregation that included significant numbers of unskilled labourers.[8]

In the 1880s approximately six in every ten adults were normally at public worship on a Sunday in Victoria.[9] Probably at least seven in every ten adults in Victoria then went to church on at least some occasions during the year. This was religious practice of at least as high a level as was reached in England at any time during the nineteenth century.[10] South Australian colonists probably went to church as much as the Victorians, those of New Zealand and New South Wales rather less. The different mixes of denominational and social groups amongst the immigrants to the four colonies go a long way towards explaining these variations in attendance levels.[11]

Sunday was a subject of passionate public controversy in the late

Sunday school children, Reefton, New Zealand. This group is likely to have included children whose parents seldom observed Sunday by any form of religious practice for themselves.

nineteenth century. At times, for many people the 'Sunday question' counted more than the latest political crisis or who won the Melbourne Cup.

The issue was not whether people should go to church; few public figures were prepared to question the desirability of that. The differences were over how people should spend their time on a Sunday when they were not at public worship. God himself had commanded 'Six days shalt thou labour, and do all thy work: but the seventh day is the sabbath of the Lord thy God.'[12] Nearly all colonial churchgoers agreed that Sunday ought to be kept as the Sabbath and that therefore all should rest on Sunday. But what constituted resting?

Before about 1880 there existed a large group of churchgoers whose desire was a rest kept in the spirit of a religious retreat. They included Presbyterians, Methodists, adherents of the smaller Protestant denominations, and a wing of the Church of England as well. Their leaders were adamant that on the seventh day all 'worldly' activities and amusements, not just paid employment,

Sunday afternoon in the Botanical Gardens. Elements of restraint and relaxation are both present in this depiction from the *Sydney Punch*, 1866.

must cease. It was 'a happier Sabbath', a Presbyterian elder was convinced, when it was 'pretty closely confined to religious duties, privileges, conversation and reading, than when spent, even only in part, in social but not religious conversation.'[13] A Methodist minister counselled in 1860 that if a working man had no opportunity for fresh air and exercise during the other six days, because of his work, a family walk to enjoy the beauties of God's creation would not be wrong. But, he added, the walk had to be genuinely to the glory of God since pleasure-taking on a Sunday was always wrong.[14] Charles Perry, Church of England Bishop of Melbourne, declared in 1870 that children should be asked to put aside their 'usual occupations' and practise 'special self-denial', though he professed to be concerned that Sundays should not be gloomy.[15] In South Australia swings in children's playgrounds were padlocked on Saturday evenings.[16] In line with this Old Testament strictness the word 'Sabbath' was often preferred to 'Sunday'. These Protestants by-passed as best they could the liberalism regarding the fourth commandment of that Jew whom they called their Lord.

According to the spokesmen of the colonial Sabbatarians, that God himself had rested on the seventh day after his acts of creation showed that the command to keep holy the Sabbath was part of the eternal moral law valid for all times and places. Therefore society should so order itself that even those who were outside the churches should be compelled to keep a day of rest. What people might prefer to do was irrelevant; the issue was whether men and women were or were not subject to the divine authority. The way of obedience, however, was the way to the soul's true good. To keep the Sabbath well was in fact to anticipate the rest which would be the reward of the faithful in heaven. The Reverend Dr Robert Steel described the Sabbath as 'one of the few memorials which remain of Eden, and one of the most interesting types of the saints' everlasting rest.'[17] This comparison of the Sabbath with heaven was no mere literary figure. The Reverend Dr Adam Cairns, another colonial Presbyterian divine, told Christian parents to use and enjoy the Sabbath well for thus they would prepare themselves and their children for 'the blissful rest, the ecstatic joy, the unfading glory of the Sabbath above'. Not to cherish 'the holiness, the peace, the saintly communion' which was the privilege of the Christian family on the Sabbath was to jeopardize the promise of heaven.[18]

But was it possible to persuade or hector or compel the common stock of humanity to live in even outward conformity with this ideal? To the very end of the nineteenth century and into this century lovers of the Sabbath continued to bewail (and exaggerate) the amount of Sabbath desecration on the frontier.[19] But the frontier aside, observance does seem to have improved in the colonies through to the 1870s. The Reverend Robert Sutherland was a Presbyterian minister who arrived in Victoria in 1854. In the late 1870s he looked back over his years in the colony as a time in which 'public opinion' had built up against Sabbath desecration: public houses had been closed by law, rail traffic had been curtailed, P and O boats had ceased departing Port Phillip Bay on the Sunday; in the pastoral districts tradesmen and merchants had ceased soliciting orders or collecting their accounts, for 'respectability of character' regarding the observance of the Sabbath had become 'even necessary to the success of their temporal affairs'.[20] Vigilant Presbyterians in the Otago province of New Zealand in the early 1870s took similar satisfaction in progress made.[21] Yet even as these advances were being made the Sabbatarian position was being undermined ideologically and popular opposition to it was forming.

In 1860 an Anglican divine, Dr J. A. Hessey delivered the Bampton lectures at Oxford on the subject of the religious history of Sunday.[22] Hessey marshalled an impressive body of evidence that in the early church the Lord's Day had been an institution entirely separate from the Jewish Sabbath and that therefore all arguments as to the proper observance of the Christian Sunday which proceeded from an Old Testament basis were invalid. In any case, if the Old Testament was binding in this matter, then Christians ought to keep Saturday as their Sabbath as the Jews did, and they also should observe all the practices required by the Jewish law, such as not lighting fires for cooking. He also struck hard against the argument that God had instituted the Sabbath at the creation; there was, he said, no evidence that the Jews themselves had observed the Sabbath before the giving of the law to Moses. Perhaps hardest of all for the evangelical clergy to bear was Hessey's documentation that the Continental heroes of the Reformation had condemned Sabbatarianism as an offence against the gospel. Hessey's work was quickly noted by some newspaper editors in the colonies who had liberal views and his book was increasingly mined in the 1870s and 1880s.[23] In Scotland in the mid-1860s the Reverend Dr Norman MacLeod, a prominent Church of Scotland minister, caused an enormous stir by defending the running of trains on Sunday. He called the Sabbatarian position 'Judaizing'.[24] Reports of his views caused Free Kirk Presbyterians in the colonies to worry.[25] There was also the precedent provided by a famous Church of England preacher, F. W. Robertson of Brighton. Robertson's sermon on 'the religious non-observance' of Sunday was reprinted a number of times in the colonies.[26]

Popular opposition to the Sabbatarians became evident in the early 1870s. In 1871 the government of Victoria considered a proposal that once alterations to the warship *Cerberus* were completed, it should be opened to the public for inspection on Sundays. Immediately they learned of the idea in July a group of church leaders organized meetings and petitions to protest. In a circular to the ministers of religion in Victoria, the Reverend H. B. Macartney, the Church of England Dean of Melbourne, the Reverend John C. Symons, a Wesleyan Methodist, and Mr James Balfour, a Presbyterian, claimed that the campaign over the *Cerberus* was 'specially important, because of its being the probable commencement of efforts which may be made for opening places of amusement in general.' In October 1871 a deputation of liberalizers waited upon the Chief Secretary. Led by Mr Frank Walsh, a member of the Victorian Legislative Assembly, this group pressed both for Sunday visits to the *Cerberus* and for the opening of the Melbourne museum and public library.[27]

The clash of opinion in Melbourne in 1871 mirrored what was happening at home. For those in the Puritan tradition Sunday observance was a test of vital religion, almost a sacrament.[28] As the middle and upper classes in Britain came increasingly under evangelical influence from the 1790s so there was a build-up of social pressures circumscribing Sunday and protecting it from 'desecration'. By about 1850 Sunday observance was a fetish.[29] In Scotland it was a common practice to pull down window blinds and it is said that women used wire to fasten buttons on gloves to be worn at church rather than use needle and thread on the Sabbath.[30] But by the early 1870s there was increasing dissent. Within the House of Commons Mr Peter Taylor pressed for liberalization of the legislation governing behaviour on a Sunday. Outside it there were campaigns to open museums and galleries; in 1872 the free libraries and art galleries of Birmingham were in fact opened on a Sunday after much public controversy.[31] It would not be surprising if a future researcher discovered evidence that a few of the colonial liberalizers corresponded with their counterparts at home. In any case, press reports made both the liberalizers and their opponents aware of what was happening in Britain regarding the Sunday question.

The Sabbatarians prevailed in Victoria in 1871. Three years later a more ambitious attempt to open all publicly-owned museums, parks and picture galleries in Victoria also failed.[32] Those who wanted to liberalize Sunday observance achieved their first considerable victory in the colonies in Dunedin, chief centre of Otago, the leading New Zealand province of the time. The breakthrough in Otago is a little curious, considering that the province was a major Free Church stronghold. Perhaps the liberalizers won because their forces had been so recently strengthened by the influx of non-Presbyterian blood during the gold rushes of the 1860s. The Athenaeum in Dunedin was not a public institute but it was in receipt of public money and therefore the move in January 1874 to open its library on a Sunday was seen on all sides as an important test case. After a struggle within the committee of the Athenaeum's subscribers a special general meeting was held on 11 February, and in a scene of confusion, hooting and footstamping, the decision to open was made, 252 votes to 242.[33] A visitor to Dunedin wrote how the result created a commotion in both town and country.[34]

Quickly thereafter public institutions elsewhere in the colonies were thrown open and some restrictions withdrawn on the running of public transport.[35] In 1882 a New Zealand Methodist commented: 'Stake by stake the fences are being pulled down. Inch by inch the public reverence for the day is being undermined. First the trains are run, then museums and libraries are opened, then tramways run.'[36] In Sydney in 1886 even Sunday newspapers were introduced. Melbourne held out longest over the museum

Premier Murray proposes to put the fire out. Victoria has had a long history of politicians siding with those who wished to retain a Sunday free of public entertainments and newspapers. Here Premier Murray aided by a wowser clergyman seeks to put out the fire of Sabbath desecration.

and art gallery – right through to 1904. There the confrontation between openers and closers was at its fiercest. In early 1883 there were mass meetings in Melbourne, Sunday school children went door knocking for signatures against opening, newspapers carried column after column of correspondence, the *Melbourne Review* ran a symposium on the theology of Sunday, politicians worried about the way they should jump. Passions ran high in Melbourne partly because the openers met so much resistance from embattled Presbyterians and Methodists who together made up a large share of Victoria's population. Another reason was that Melbourne was the leading intellectual centre in the colonies in the late nineteenth century and so the thrust of the liberals there was especially forceful.[37]

The pronounced shift in attitudes towards Sunday was reflected in the popularity of a new word, 'wowser', meaning kill-joy or censorious person. An early, if not the earliest, use was on 8 October 1899 in John Norton's *Truth*.[38] 'Wowser' was adopted and exploited by the *Bulletin*, also published in Sydney, and the cartoon figure of a man in black with a brolly and a censorious face, became a stock figure of fun. The wowser was against anything enjoyable according to his enemies, including a little amusement on Sunday. It was no new thing to ridicule Sabbatarians. For example, an 1860 issue of *Melbourne Punch* carried a cartoon of the doughty Presbyterian Sabbatarian the Reverend Dr Adam Cairns, his hands sanctimoniously clasped, his eyes cast down in prayer, a brolly handle over his right arm.[39] The difference was that by the time of the First World War the Sabbatarians were far more on the defensive. The old-style strict Sabbatarian had, in fact, become a marginal figure.

The period through to the early 1880s was distinguished by an intense emotional commitment to a strict Sunday observance on the part of large numbers of Protestant churchgoers. Many of them worried about the thin end of the wedge: allow amusements and it was only a matter of time before shops would open and the churches be empty. Another concern was morality. Comments about this were seldom explicit but some seem to have believed that, for the unchurched especially, subjection to the restraints of a quiet Sunday checked inclinations to sexual immorality and drunkenness.[40] The Reverend J. L. Rentoul, a leading Victorian Presbyterian, was one of the more enthusiastic proponents of this argument from morality. In an article for the *Melbourne Review* in 1883 Rentoul claimed the British Sunday had put iron in the nation's moral blood and saved it from 'a nameless lust'.[41]

Some churchgoers may have opposed liberalization partly because, consciously or unconsciously, they desired to protect family and patriarchy. Sabbatarians were wont to eulogize Sunday as the day at home, the one day of the week on which the father was free to be with his family and provide uninterrupted moral and spiritual leadership. To desecrate the Sabbath was therefore indirectly to attack the sanctity of the Christian home.[42] Strict observance may also have had a hidden connection with the cleavage which existed for evangelical Protestants between grace and nature. Evangelicals tended to have an aversion to the life of the senses: the body was in an obscure way corrupt and a chief means of sin. The created world generally was seen as remote from God's purposes.[43] As God was set apart from the world so Sunday was set apart from the other six days. On Sunday nature was driven from the field and grace reigned supreme; therefore worldly pleasures were interdicted. Growing up in the 1910s Brian Lewis received the impression of one Melbourne Presbyterian congregation that there were couples in it who abstained from sexual intercourse on Sunday.[44] If so they would have been in accord with the symbolism of Sunday as a day of grace, not nature.[45]

Instinctively, those who sought to revalue the world of the senses began to treat Sunday more like other days. Some of these were Christian believers, some were not. From one point of view, opening the Melbourne art gallery was a secularization of Sunday; from another it was an affirmation of the worth of Monday to Saturday.

By the early 1880s the defence of the Sabbath had an hysterical edge. This was not just because the Sabbatarians realized that public opinion was moving inexorably against them regarding public institutions; there was also the hidden fear of defections within their own ranks. In 1883, for example, the Reverend Charles Strong, minister of Melbourne's leading Presbyterian congregation, was much criticized for speaking at a large public meeting organized by the Sunday Liberation Society.[46] His ideas regarding Sunday could only have been regarded as such a threat if it were believed that many erstwhile staunch Sabbatarians were weakening in their convictions.

And indeed they were. In a love letter written in 1882 a young Wesleyan pointed out that he was writing on a Sunday evening and asked if his fiancée did not think he was being wicked. A pious Presbyterian, she replied that to make a habit of writing on a Sunday would be sinful but that a few loving thoughts could not be wrong.[47] Also in 1882 a New Zealand Presbyterian committee, referring in particular to sightseeing, visiting and holidaying, commented that a 'secularisation of the Sabbath' seemed to be slowly but surely creeping over the colony.[48]

In the 1880s the Saturday half-holiday started to become common.[49] As Professor K. S. Inglis has pointed out, a new division of time was born, the week of five days and two, instead of the six days and one of the book of Genesis. A new word entered the English language from the late 1870s: 'week-end'. Probably it was not coined in the colonies but there the 'week-end habit' was to flourish more than in England.[50]

By the mid-1890s the popularity of Sunday 'amusements' had grown appreciably, with concerts, picnics, excursions, balloon ascents, cycling, tennis and cricket all occurring.[51] In 1895 the Presbyterian General Assembly of New South Wales received a report on Sabbath observance based on returns from every presbytery in the colony. This report noted that a change had 'swept over the religious spirit of the age, and the views of even Christian people have altered considerably.'[52] In 1904 a leading article in the *Australian Christian World* commented that many church people if they were honest would have to admit that they used Sunday for activities that had nothing to do with 'private soul culture'.[53] In 1912 Bishop Sprott of Wellington declared that people were demonstrating their devotion to the god of pleasure by choosing as their chief day of amusement the day immemorially consecrated to the Christian god.[54]

There was a further pronounced relaxation of Sunday observance by churchgoers after the First World War. Assisted by the introduction of the motor car, weekends and holidays away and Sunday day trips became more common. So did the playing of Sunday golf and tennis by churchgoers. By 1937 the process of liberalization had gone so far in New South Wales that when a Methodist minister brought a prosecution under the Sunday observance act of 1781 against a gatekeeper at a Sunday rugby match there was dissension in Protestant church circles about whether he had done the right thing.[55] When Protestant ministers now defended the Sunday rest it was often not in terms of what God had commanded but that a rest was physically and spiritually beneficial. Methodist and Presbyterian leaders referred less to Sunday as the Sabbath.

In 1897 a writer for the Sydney *Churchman* stated that the change that had come over Sunday observance was more evident in the cities than in the country.[56] The difference was a persistent one it seems. During his study of a New Zealand rural community conducted in the 1930s H. C. D. Somerset noted that the farmers were by city standards strict about their observance of Sunday. There was no teamwork with horses or harvesting or shearing, and mustering of stock was only done when it was unavoidable. The farmers voted down a proposal that the tennis club be allowed Sunday play on the community's courts out of church time. The few who played on Sunday on Littledene's six hole golf course were 'looked upon as being almost beyond the pale of civilization'.[57]

Protestant ministers who from the early 1870s had resisted Sunday leisure activities had done so in large part because they believed that these would lead in the short or long run to thinner congregations. Did their fears turn out to be justified?

In New Zealand between 1874 and 1926 at every census of the population and housing there was also a census of religious practice.[58] Any person who had charge of a place of worship was compelled by law to provide details on the number of persons usually attending church services at that place in the month of the census. There were eleven such censuses between 1874 and 1926 for which the results were published. For all of the eleven we have available in the census reports the total number of attenders by denomination and by province. From 1891 we also have available a breakdown of attendance by county, a sufficiently small unit to allow us to distinguish between attendance in rural and urban areas.

This New Zealand series is probably unique in the English-speaking world. It takes us well into the twentieth century. The number of places of worship that failed to make a return in any census year was insignificant; under the Census Act the superintendent of a church who failed to make such a return faced a fine. More importantly, the attendance series of the major Protestant bodies correlate so closely that they must be assumed to be reflecting similar movements in attendance levels. There is no reason why the superintendents of the places of worship belonging to the other denominations should have been any less accurate in their counting. This does not mean that we have in the statistics a precise guide to how much churchgoing there was in New Zealand at any one time. Not all superintendents were equally careful and not all defined 'usual attenders' in the same way. It does mean, nevertheless, that we have in these statistics an invaluable guide to broad trends in churchgoing over time and by denomination.

Analysis of the statistics suggests that the level of churchgoing in New Zealand rose during the late 1870s and 1880s to a peak sometime in the 1890s. By 1900 the trend of attendances was

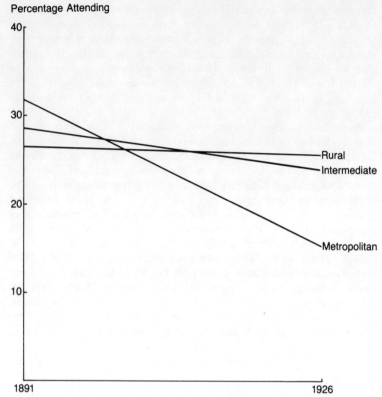

Graph 2:   Trends in church attendance in selected New Zealand counties, 1891–1926 (percentage of total population attending). (Source: NZ censuses)

downwards and for decades the decline was primarily in the metropolitan centres of Auckland, Wellington, Christchurch and Dunedin.

It is possible that an easing of attendances at public worship might have occurred in the cities before it registered in a decline of usual attenders according to the statistics: perhaps people dropped from being twicers to oncers or from four times a month to twice a month and were still counted as usual attenders. If the New Zealand statistics provide only a crude measure of attendance, then they would seem to be consistent with the supposition that an erosion of attendance at public worship began within a few years of the opening of museums and art galleries in the mid-1870s. If the statistics provide a sensitive indicator, then there was a lag of well over a decade between liberalization regarding open-

Table 6:   Protestant churchgoing in New Zealand, 1891–1926

| | *Usual attenders as a percentage of adherents 15 years and over by denomination* | |
	1891	*1926*
Church of England	24.5	15.2
Presbyterian	48.0	28.0
Methodist	93.5	40.7
Congregational	92.3	64.7

Source: New Zealand censuses

ing and a decline of church attendance. In neither case should we assume that a liberalization of Sunday observance caused a decline of churchgoing in any simple way. The two may have interacted. Both changes may also have been manifestations of some deeper cultural shift.

The magnitude of the decline can be fixed within certain limits. A principal uncertainty about the statistics is whether in analysing them it should or should not be assumed that those making returns of attenders at public worship included Sunday-school children in their count. Practice seems to have varied between denominations and even within particular denominations over time. Yet however the statistics are analysed they indicate a substantial decline. Assuming that Sunday-school children were not included, then the level of adult attendance was 43 per cent lower in 1926 than it had been in 1891. (For the purpose of this calculation usual attenders were expressed as a proportion of the population fifteen years and over in the two relevant years.) Assuming that Sunday-school children were included then the level of usual attendance on the part of the European population as a whole (men, women, and children of all ages) was 33 per cent lower in 1926 than in 1891. In absolute terms the decline was least in the Church of England, the least evangelical of the principal Protestant denominations.

After 'a careful study' a New Zealand Methodist committee reported in 1931 that the actual number of Methodists who never went to church was small; rather there was an increasing number of 'intermittent and most irregular' churchgoers. This seems to have been a general Protestant pattern.[59] The sense of duty about being in church each Sunday largely disappeared.[60] According to some ministers there was even a tendency to think one could have Christianity without the church. E. S. Kiek in the mid-1920s discerned a new breed who sought to practise what he called 'Private Christianity'.[61]

It was primarily males who drifted to the margins of church life through irregular attendance. A census of churchgoing was held in Auckland in 1882 which distinguished between men and

CONSOLATION
Methodist Parson. '*Ah, brother, it's sad to see such a small congregation!*'
Brother Spadger. '*Yes, but, thank the Lord, the Presbyterian one is smaller!*'

Lionel Lindsay comments on the trend towards small congregations in *The Bulletin* in 1910.

women. At this census, if we exclude the Anglicans, Protestant men equalled women in their attendance at church.[62] But not many years later people were asking 'Why don't men go to church?' A journalist who surveyed Adelaide churches in 1894 found that generally women much outnumbered men. At an evening service at Pirie Street Methodist church he counted about

400 males and 1100 females.[63] Going to church remained socially important to many married women because their opportunities for meeting people outside the home were so restricted.

Despite the decline of churchgoing amongst Protestants and despite the increasing 'desecration' of the Sabbath, colonial cities and towns early this century were by today's standards very quiet places on a Sunday. Few trains ran; few shops opened. In Camberwell, in Melbourne's 'bible belt', it was not until 1959 that ratepayers voted to allow non-commercialized games on municipal reserves.[64] In churchgoing homes it was only imperceptibly that special ceremonies surrounding Sunday ceased to be practised. In one devout Church of England family in the Tasmanian countryside early this century the children were not required to eat porridge for breakfast and at dinner got a pudding they specially liked: a round of Victoria sandwich soaked in fruit juice or wine, underneath a little jam with fruit arranged around, jelly poured over, then the top decorated with whipped cream and jelly pieces.[65] The Lewis family was liberal Presbyterian and around the time of the First World War their Sunday rituals were self-indulgent by the standards of strict Sabbatarians of an earlier generation. For the children the day began with a lie-in-bed and no weekday cold shower. After morning church this Melbourne family sat down at a table covered with a starched damask cloth and all ten places with a clean napkin: usually there was a roast joint, a special dessert such as tapioca with meringue on top, and always as well, for those who could fit it in, a goblet of jelly (two colours) and a goblet of custard. Mr and Mrs Lewis and the older children took claret. For the evening meal there were scones from the Sunday oven and sponges and lamingtons cooked on Friday and saved for Sunday. Then the family would gather to hear Mr Lewis read stories such as *Nights with Uncle Remus*. One of the boys remembered into his old age the still and happy Sundays of his childhood.[66]

Protestants threatened by the erosion of Sunday observance in the wider community were prone to single out Catholics as desecrators-in-chief.[67] There were many Catholics who did conform to this Protestant stereotype of treating Sunday just like any other day by playing sport, drinking, gambling and the like. But there were also many Catholics who willingly fell in with the ideal of Sunday as a day apart and kept the day decorously.[68] In many Catholic families the ritual of Saturday tasks to prepare for the coming of Sunday persisted well into this century just as it did in Protestant ones. A priest, remembering Catholic rural life in

New Zealand in the 1930s, has described Saturday as 'spit-and-polish day': 'the house was thoroughly cleaned, the lino waxed and polished (usually by the younger children who skated up and down with rag dusters tied like giant slippers on their feet). In the evening, best clothes which were also school clothes, were sponged, pressed and ironed ready for Sunday Mass.'[69]

For their part the Catholic bishops were far from wanting to abandon all discipline about what happened on a Sunday. Cardinal Moran even suggested on one occasion that Sunday observance should be a subject for Catholic and Protestant co-operation.[70] Though the bishops regarded Sunday recreation as legitimate they also believed that labour should cease in conformity with the fourth commandment.

According to the catechism endorsed by the Australasian bishops, hearing mass on Sundays was a matter of obligation binding under the penalty of mortal sin. And according to the same catechism a person who was in a state of mortal sin at the time of death would be consigned eternally to hell. Giving advice in 1923 in the semi-official *Australian Messenger of the Sacred Heart* Father Eustace Boylan stated that a mass would only be too far away to attend if a person in average health could not walk to it in an hour and a quarter.[71] Back in the 1850s many colonial Catholics would have had to walk a very long way indeed if they had been determined to get to mass. But by the 1870s two changes were in progress that were to allow most Australasian Catholics to be at mass on a Sunday, if they so desired. The first was a slowing in the rate of Irish Catholic immigration. Only half as many Irish immigrants arrived in Australia and New Zealand in 1866–80 as arrived in 1851–65.[72] In the 1890s the flow almost ceased. And when the volume of total emigration from England and Scotland picked up rapidly after about 1905 emigration from Ireland did not. Although the Catholic population continued to grow through natural increase the problem of supplying clergy was therefore less severe for the Roman Catholic church by the 1910s and 1920s than that faced by the major Protestant churches.

The second change was that increasingly Ireland had more priests to give. In 1858 Bishop Goold reported gloomily on the results of his recruiting trip home. 'It is with the greatest difficulty that priests can be obtained. There are not enough for the Home Missions.'[73] It was not that the church in Ireland was then turned in on itself. When Goold made his comment Carlow College had about as many priests training for overseas as for work at home and All Hallows College was a purely missionary establishment.[74]

But the Australian and New Zealand missions had to compete with those in Britain, India, South Africa, Canada and above all the United States. By the 1870s, Australia and New Zealand had displaced Great Britain as the most popular destination after the United States.[75] By the 1890s the continuing decline of the population in Ireland combined with an extraordinary increase in vocations from the 1850s,[76] meant that hundreds of priests could be freed for overseas work. In 1880–81 32 priests went from Carlow College to Irish parishes, 46 to the missions; in 1907–08 twelve stayed in Ireland, 112 went overseas.[77]

South Australia and New Zealand having smaller Catholic populations were more easily supplied with priests than New South Wales and Victoria. As early as 1870 there was one priest for every 750 Catholics in New Zealand, one for every 950 in South Australia. In Victoria as late as 1880 there was still only one priest for every 2000 Catholics. By 1930 the bishops in Victoria and New South Wales had closed the gap. In all four there was one priest for between 700 and 800 Catholics. Taking Australia and New Zealand as a whole, the Roman Catholic population was twice as well supplied with priests in 1930 as in 1870.[78]

The obligation to be at mass on Sunday did not extend to receiving communion. But when communion was taken, and this was required at least once a year, a fast had to be observed beforehand. Not even a cup of water was permissible. This was a tough rule for priests since they took communion every time they celebrated mass. A country priest might have to travel many miles in severe heat before he could say his final mass on Sunday. A Frenchman, who observed Catholic life in the diocese of Ballarat in the 1880s, noted that the country priest often had his tongue so dried out by the time of the second mass late on Sunday morning he often delayed the sermon until the end of the service and before going into the pulpit slipped into the sacristy for a quick cup of tea.[79] For the laity also, in the country fasting could be a tough discipline. Dairy farmers might rise at five or earlier, then milk, do the separating, put the cans at the gate for pickup, give the skim milk to the pigs and do the cleaning up. Mass might not be until eleven, so that the first thing to eat or drink would not come until after noon.[80] Protestants worried about the legitimacy of church trains or Sunday afternoon walks; Catholics of a scrupulous turn worried about what constituted the prohibited 'sup'. Was it necessary to dry the mouth after cleaning the teeth? Would a small boy who swallowed a wad of paper be able to receive communion? Was ingesting saliva permissible? What about perspiration that had hair oil in it? One boy living in Wellington around the turn of the century would not receive communion if he had got a drop of rain on his lips.[81]

Among the laity at mass Sunday by Sunday there were some who sought only to satisfy the letter of the church's law. Technically you could assist at mass without being present for the sermon. One dodge was to always go to an early mass when no sermon was preached.[82] Another was to arrive late at a service and to leave early, on the grounds that one was indeed at mass so long as one was present from the offertory to the priest's communion.[83] Bishop Luck in 1888 admonished Catholics who absented themselves from preaching at Sunday services, declaring with undue tact that this was 'almost indicative of a disrelish for the Word of God'.[84] A New Zealand Catholic complained in 1923 that he had seen many quick getaways in various churches over the years. 'As soon as a lad finishes his schooling and begins to "grow up" he begins to develop a tendency to remain near the church entrance, and even to kneel in the passage-way – so much so that latecomers often think the church is packed.'[85]

In city and suburban parishes there were very many Catholics who never went to mass at all. The magnitude of this non-practising body in any district could only be gauged once account was taken of the total Catholic population from which practising Catholics were drawn. Because this was but seldom done, there flourished a stereotype of Catholics as a people who always went to mass. Even priests could be ignorant about the true state of affairs in their parishes. An unusually statistically aware priest, Father J. M. Cusack, examined two parishes in Sydney in 1933. In the first parish there were two Sunday masses and accommodation for 400. Total attendances in this parish on three consecutive Sundays were 751, 693, 702. But the parish roll contained the names of 1633 baptized Catholics. In a second parish there was accommodation for 800, three masses on a Sunday and total attendances on three consecutive Sundays of 2300, 2194, and 2410. Here there were 6323 baptized Catholics. In both cases the parish priest had claimed that nearly all his flock performed their Sunday obligation.[86] The position might have been even worse than Cusack himself believed because Catholics who had long abandoned practice of their religion might never get onto a church roll. According to Catholic parish rolls there were 15 291 Catholics in the diocese of Auckland about the time of the 1906 government census; the census itself revealed 30 956. Priests' estimates of the Catholic population of the archdiocese of Sydney in the early 1930s were below the actual number by almost a third. The error

A Catholic rural congregation with their bishop, 1912. Bishop John Norton of Port Augusta flanked by the parishioners of St Canute's, Streaky Bay, South Australia. Streaky Bay was known for the number of 'good' Catholics living there and the usual Sunday congregation was much the same size as the group here.

in parish rolls in Melbourne seems to have been about the same.[87]

The non-attenders in the two parishes examined by Cusack almost certainly included a disproportionate number of men. At the newspaper census of church attendance in Auckland in 1882 there were recorded at Catholic places of worship 1154 separate attendances by men and 1496 by women.[88] For priests it was axiomatic that women were better churchgoers. The Plenary Council of Bishops in 1885 protested against the notion that religion was fine for women but not something to be taken seriously by men.[89] In 1907 a Catholic discussing a Protestant question of the day – why men did not go to church – was clear that while Catholic men went to church more than Protestant men, they were not as good as Catholic women.[90]

There seems to be no evidence which would allow a rigorous comparison for any time before the Second World War between the religious practice of Catholics who had gone to parish schools with the religious practice of Catholics who had not. Thus a school influence independent of the home may never be proved for this period. But a survey conducted in Australia in 1966 showed that where the home background was one of practising Catholicism attendance at a Catholic school had a reinforcing effect on adult attendance at mass. There does not seem to be any reason why the same should not have been true earlier.[91]

According to returns made to the government statistician, usual attenders at Catholic places of worship in New Zealand in 1886 constituted 55 per cent of the Catholic population fifteen years and over. Between 1886 and 1926 this level was maintained in New Zealand with but minor fluctuations. Judged against the Methodists, in the 1860s and 1870s Catholics were mediocre church attenders; by the 1930s the Catholics were better attenders than the adherents of all the principal Protestant denominations and the gap was steadily widening. If the trends in churchgoing continued indefinitely, the preservation of the religious significance of Sunday was going to depend upon the Catholics.

Chapter Six

DOCTRINE

By the 1920s Protestants who attended church regularly in Australia and New Zealand had crossed the threshold into a post-doctrinal age. They had become more like those outside the churches in the indefiniteness of their religious ideas. Doctrine continued to exist in the sense that ministers were still required to subscribe to doctrinal standards and that no denomination formally repudiated an early Christian creed. But, speaking generally, standards and creeds now provided at most a feeling of continuity with the past; the actual thinking of churchgoing Protestants about religion had become inexact, formless, and diverse.

Preaching was one area in which the supersession of dogma was manifest in the 1920s. 'One of the cant phrases which has gained currency in the churches for some years', commented a Victorian Presbyterian in 1920, 'is "that the age we live in has outgrown doctrine", and that, therefore, it is well that the preaching of all Christian doctrines should be avoided, the more especially as such preaching is sure to be dry, unattractive, uninteresting, and calculated to drive people away from the church.'[1] Many wanted to work out for themselves what to believe. In *Khaki and Cassock*, the Reverend K. T. Henderson gave evidence about this revolt against dogma which is especially valuable; as one of the chaplains to Australian soldiers during the First World War, Henderson was thrown closer to ordinary Australian men than ministers in general had ever been before. In his book Henderson depicted a scene which he said typified many conversations he had with soldiers. A soldier with an educated voice asks the padre whether he does not think 'the day of the churches is over.' In the soldier's view men are now thinking for themselves and 'religion has become a matter for the individual.' The padre replies that there is 'an awful lot' in what the soldier has said and that 'There's an all-round hankering for intellectual adventure, for originality, and men have got the idea that they're tied to certain things in the Church, and have got to go outside it to be free.'[2]

It was not true, however, that 'freedom' of belief was only to be found outside the churches. Regular churchgoers were exercising it. 'Each individual to-day claims to pick and choose his Christian doctrine, irrespective of higher authority than his own intellect and reason', declared an Anglican clergyman in 1904.[3] Some of those in official positions in the Protestant churches openly did the same. The most publicized case before the Second World War was that of Samuel Angus, a professor at the Presbyterian Theological Hall in Sydney. Angus saw close parallels between primitive Christianity and contemporaneous mystery religions; he disputed the Westminster Confession on human depravity; he was unwilling to assert that following the crucifixion Jesus was raised physically from the dead. Angus did become the centre of theological controversy, but an extraordinary feature of his Australian career was the effort made by moderators, clerks and procurators to bend the rules to keep him in his chair. No formal charge of heresy was ever laid against him.[4]

Some research has already been done on how Australasian Protestants came to enter the post-doctrinal age. One important finding by Professor Michael Roe is that liberal views regarding doctrine had already gained a foothold in the colonies by the middle of the nineteenth century. In an essay first published in 1847 a native-born colonist, Charles Harpur, claimed that there was an 'Individualizing process' at work in religion which could not be stopped and which he approved as leading towards full personal freedom. Harpur believed that with the right education men might become more and more 'Governments in themselves'.[5] Here, palpably, was the 'anti-dogmatic principle' which John Henry Newman abhorred and regarded as the essence of religious liberalism.

We also know, thanks to some high quality research, that overt public protest against evangelical doctrines went through a decisive stage in the 1880s. In the colonial cities generally, but in Melbourne especially, there was an unprecedented public debate about science and the Bible, about the atonement, about the status of creeds. Mr Justice Higinbotham undoubtedly caught the mood of many educated colonists in a famous address he gave in Melbourne in 1883. It was, he said, the layman's duty to throw off dogmas which science had shown to be untrue and then 'set out alone and unaided on the perilous path of inquiry'.[6]

It is easy to see that there is a more or less straight line from Harpur to Higinbotham and on to the soldiers to whom Henderson talked. But we need to know to what extent and how fast ordinary men and women in the pew abandoned evangelical doctrines. Ideally we would be able to graph over time the increase of the individualizing spirit, discriminating between men and women, young and old, city and country. Since this is at present impossible, I offer a case study of one religious group within Protestantism.

The Congregational churches were in theory autonomous in all matters, including the correction and discipline of doctrinal error. This may have meant that in Congregationalism there was less of a brake on the spread of heterodox ideas than in more centralized denominations. Congregationalists were better educated on the whole than Presbyterians, Methodists and Anglicans.[7] They were also a much more urban group than were the Methodists, the Anglicans or the Presbyterians. But study of them does provide a rough guide to what was happening to Protestant doctrine in the cities, especially as most Congregational churchgoers were not Congregationalists by conviction but Protestants who joined a Congregational church because it happened to be the most accessible place of worship to their home.[8]

My method in making this case study was to work through the Congregational periodicals and year books, together with any other relevant published material I could find. I made no strenuous efforts to locate diaries and letters and what I found did not provide significant material. The denominational newspapers and year books only became an established feature from about 1870 which makes the reconstruction of earlier doctrinal change hazardous. The significance of another fact about the nature of our evidence is difficult to assess. Most of the comment is from ministers. They were more given to theological reflection than their people and thus in attending to their comments we risk exaggerating the pace of doctrinal change in the denomination as a whole. On the other hand ministers saw themselves as pastors. Because of this they may have been discreet in their public discussions of doctrinal change. In tempering the wind to the shorn lambs they may have played down how much change was in progress.

Speaking to his fellow Congregationalists in the mid-1870s the Reverend John Legge warned that though the ark of the church had been sailing in smooth waters, a 'protracted storm' was looming.[9] In fact the storm was already breaking. A minister in New South Wales reported in 1872 that some youths who had been attending Sunday school had not graduated to church membership because they had come under the influence of doubt.[10] The editor of the *Victorian Independent* remarked in 1874 that 'an entire revolution' in many important aspects of theology was in progress.[11] Legge himself, as chairman of the Victorian Congregational Union in 1874–75, gave two addresses in defence of Christian doctrine. He was especially concerned to refute *Supernatural Religion* which had recently been published in a colonial edition.[12] Plainly, some Congregationalists had read the book and been worried by its argument that the four Gospels were worthless historical evidence because they post-dated the death of Jesus by a century and a half. It also seems that there was questioning in colonial Congregationalism in the early 1870s regarding the eternal punishment of the wicked, for in 1873 the *Victorian Independent* published four closely argued sermons by the Reverend A. M. Henderson defending the traditional doctrine of the afterlife, including the eternal punishment of the wicked.[13] In 1876 the Reverend T. J. Pepper declared that patterns of religious thought had already changed so far that it was 'not difficult to trace outlines of belief and tentative conclusions, which are essential departures from the old standards of orthodoxy.' He had in mind particularly the Christian's understanding of creation, the doctrine of the inspiration of the Scriptures and the doctrine of the eternal punishment of the wicked.[14]

I know of no firm evidence that significant numbers of colonial Congregationalists were becoming restive about evangelical dogma at any time before the early 1870s. But my guess is that in the late 1860s some were experiencing doctrinal constraints as irksome. There are two reasons. First, the groundswell against dogma evident in the early 1870s was so strong then that it is hard to believe that it had not taken a number of years to build up. Secondly, in the late 1860s heterodox religious ideas, even anti-religious ideas, began to circulate, especially in Melbourne.[15] The Reverend William Roby Fletcher remarked in 1866 that while it 'used to be a matter of common remark' in Victoria that 'whatever might be the amount of religious indifference, avowed infidelity had but little foothold; but during the last three years there has been wrought a most manifest change.'[16] It is highly likely that some Congregationalists in the late 1860s attended to heterodox ideas and began to question their own beliefs in consequence.

For years before this at least one Congregationalist in the colonies had been accustomed to exercising his own judgement to reach novel religious conclusions. Richard Hanson as a young man in London had sat under the famous Reverend Thomas Binney, at the Kings Weigh House chapel. After spells in Canada and New Zealand, he had migrated to South Australia in 1846, becoming attorney-general of that colony in 1856 and chief justice in 1861. In 1849 he gave his first public lecture on religion in Adelaide, and so insisted on the necessity for reading the Bible in a spirit of inquiry that his hearers had been shocked. When he gave a paper on 'Science and Theology' to the Adelaide Philosophical Society, some members were disturbed because they understood him to be seeking to establish the impossibility of miracles. This was not his intention but there was plenty in the paper to show that for him rational investigation should be followed wherever it led, unhindered by fear of the consequences for religion. In the same paper, published in 1864, he asserted that if evolution had occurred, as he believed it had, then the doctrine of the fall 'as represented in our systems of theology' was 'obviously erroneous'. In 1869 Hanson completed *The Jesus of History*, a book which he had been working on since 1866. In it he announced the necessity of sifting documents, of weighing probabilities and of getting behind church dogma to the real Jesus of Nazareth. Through long and painful questioning Hanson had come to disbelieve in the divinity of Christ. His belief in God remained but he rested it on neither the authority of the Bible nor of the Church but his own and other people's experience. The individual had to decide what to believe for himself: 'a slavish submission to the dogmas of a self-styled infallible Church' was inadmissible.[17]

Richard Hanson was remarkable for his intelligence, his independence of mind, and his interest in overseas theological developments. He departed so far from the piety of his circle in Adelaide that he felt obliged to publish *The Jesus of History* anonymously. Six years later, in 1875, a work on Paul and the primitive Church appeared over his own name. Since this book was even more radical, the disclosure of his identity is an indication of how rapidly the religious climate was changing.

In 1876 the Reverend Thomas Roseby declared that evolution by natural selection was not inconsistent with Christian belief: for Roseby how the species had come into existence was simply a question of which method God chose to use.[18] Roseby, who was a minister in Dunedin at the time, was in perfectly good standing in the denomination. In 1882 the chairman of the New South Wales Congregational Union, the Reverend J. F. Cullen, adopted a similarly positive attitude to evolution.[19] By the turn of the century there were many Congregationalists who had abandoned the old literal interpretation of the Genesis account of creation. But those who referred approvingly to evolution usually did so vaguely. Only a small proportion of those who adjusted their thinking had read and understood Darwin.

In the late 1870s also, the limits of permissible belief were being vastly expanded in relation to the afterlife. In 1878 a debate about eternal punishment of the wicked was conducted through letters and articles in the *New South Wales Independent*. Ten years later two speakers at a denominational intercolonial gathering were

Richard Davies Hanson.

agreed that the doctrine had been largely abandoned in the Congregational churches.[20] More was involved in the change than a
revision of theological speculation. Over the generations tens of
thousands of Protestant children had been badly frightened by
vigorous and vivid preaching about hell. Grown men and women
had been oppressed as they dwelt upon the interminable and
unspeakable torments in hell of millions upon millions of souls.

Now, quite suddenly, the doctrine was defunct. Yet Congregational ministers do not seem to have candidly confessed that a grievous error had been made.[21]

The penal substitutionary theory of the atonement was as much a part of the earlier evangelical religion as belief in the eternal punishment of the wicked. Both presupposed a conviction that the deity was a god of wrath as well as mercy. According to the penal theory God visited upon His only Son the suffering which would otherwise have been meted out to sinful men and women. Only through the vicarious punishment of the innocent Christ on the cross was there forgiveness of the guilty. A pseudonymous letter-writer to the *Australian Independent* in 1889 asked whether the time had not come, if men were moral, for the doctrine to be reconsidered. This person's intercourse with businessmen had convinced him that this doctrine more than any other cause had led honest and thoughtful men to hold aloof from the churches. He believed there were many ministers as well as lay persons who accepted the substitutionary doctrine 'nominally, because of the "it is written"'.[22]

The Reverend James Hill was one of a small number of Congregational ministers in the 1880s who did not like what they saw happening to evangelical doctrines and said so publicly. In his chairman's address to the New South Wales Congregational Union in 1886 he said that though he had not lost faith in liberty it was his duty to protest against 'the chaotic condition' into which religious belief had fallen. The nebulousness of current beliefs, as well as the laxity of discipline regarding conduct, he found to be ill-suited to the practical needs of human nature. The contemporary distaste for doctrine Hill regarded as a symptom of a decline of interest in the theological profundities of the faith.[23]

By the early 1890s few Congregationalists had gained first-hand knowledge of the 'higher' criticism of the New Testament which had long been developing in Germany. But there were many who had read sufficient about the historical approach to become troubled. When the Reverend John Fordyce lectured to Congregational Sunday-school teachers on higher criticism in 1893, he gave as his reason that some of the teachers had already been exposed to higher criticism and become half-believers as a result.[24] In the same year the Reverend William Roby Fletcher commented that many Congregationalists had been deeply disturbed by higher criticism and singled out young men, the old, women and Sunday-school teachers as especially affected.[25]

A pamphlet published in Hobart in 1889 vividly illustrates just what the difficulties were. In 1888 the novel *Robert Elsmere* had been published in London. Its hero was a clergyman of the Church of England, living in Westmorland, who resigns his orders, after coming to doubt the miracles of the New Testament. Elsmere's loss of faith occurs after he comes under the influence of a free-thinking, highly intelligent squire who is conversant with German biblical criticism. The Reverend George Clarke of Hobart gave a lecture discussing the novel and claiming against its author, Mrs Humphry Ward, that the evidence of the New Testament was historically trustworthy. Clarke's lecture drew an anonymous reply. This pamphlet would certainly have been read by some Congregationalists since Clarke was the doyen of Congregational ministers in Tasmania. The rejoinder to Clarke may even have been written by a Congregationalist, who, because of his church association, did not wish to disclose his identity.

Clarke's adversary did not claim to be a biblical expert, but just such a person of education and culture whom the minister tried to persuade in his lecture. This defender of *Robert Elsmere* did not take as his premise the impossibility of the New Testament miracles. Instead he wanted to know why they should be regarded as true, while those outside the Bible were not. Saint Ambrose's story about the butcher of Milan, who received his sight after he touched the bodies of two dead martyrs, was better attested than anything in the New Testament. Clarke considered that the apocryphal miracles were 'grotesque and absurd' but how did they differ from the Gospel stories of the cursing of the fig-tree or the Gadarene swine? Clarke appealed to Paul's testimony that Jesus had worked miracles but he was challenged to cite a single passage from Paul to support his claim. Paul, indeed, provided evidence to the contrary. If Paul believed Jesus to have been a miracle worker, why had he not told the Jews about it? Instead, although the Jews had sought miracles, Paul had told them about Christ crucified. And why did Jesus refuse to work a miracle when the Jews had sought one? Perhaps it was because he did not know how. And if Paul knew of the virgin birth, why did he not mention it and why had he affirmed that Jesus was 'born of a woman', the very phrase which Jesus is recorded to have used of John the Baptist, who presumably had not been born of a virgin? Why, when rehearsing the tradition which he had received of Christ's resurrection, had Paul not said anything of the appearance to Mary Magdalene or the rolling away of the stone? Why did Paul speak of the resurrected body as a spiritual body, when, in another place in the New Testament it was narrated that the risen Christ walked along the Emmaus road and that he ate bread and fish? And what about the discrepancy between the Paul of Paul's own letters and the portrait of him in the *Acts of the Apostles*? And if the early Christians had misrepresented Paul, why could they not have misrepresented Jesus, whom they understood even less? Clarke had said that the issue was simple: either Jesus was what he said he was – divine – or he was not deserving great respect as a religious teacher. Yet, the anonymous author said, this begged the question of what Jesus in fact claimed to be. The answer could be arrived at only through a 'sifting of documents'.[26]

The problems created by higher criticism were not quickly faced and quickly overcome. The reverence for the Bible in the Protestant tradition went too deep for that. New ideas about the dating and authorship of documents progressed fastest amongst ministers, yet even here there was considerable resistance. Dr Bevan, no reactionary, as late as 1892 defended the Mosaic authorship of the Pentateuch.[27] There seem to have been large differences among the laity as to when and how much they were exposed to biblical criticism. Reports of confusion continued for more than two decades. In 1907 a leader in the *South Australian Congregationalist* lamented that though many of the Biblical critics were Christian believers 'the doubts they have suggested and the negative beliefs they have proclaimed have entered as an armed force into a multitude of hearts, destroying their peace and producing confusion and dismay.'[28] Speaking as chairman of the Victorian Union in 1910, Dr Bevan said that the consequences of higher criticism for church life had to be recognized:

> Our congregations listen with inquiring mind and doubting heart. Many old standards are deposed; the very conditions of belief have changed. A spirit of often fierce antagonism is abroad. Men grow impatient with ideas, and demand facts. The scientific spirit paralyses our faith. No man believes because of the fathers.[29]

Theological uncertainty by this time affected even the citadel of evangelical faith – the atonement. There were some forthright attacks on the substitutionary theory.[30] Even more disturbing for older ministers there was a tendency to reduce the emphasis which evangelicals had been accustomed to place on the cross of Christ. In South Australia the so-called 'New Theology' of R. J. Campbell, minister of the City Temple, London, was an important influence. The Reverend Alfred Depledge Sykes, a leader amongst the liberals in Adelaide, had spent some time with Campbell at the City Temple when on a trip to London in 1906 and 1907.[31]

The New Theology, colonial style, did not go uncontested within the South Australian Union. In defence of what he called

'The Theology of the Glorious Blood', the indefatigable J. C. Kirby moved at the October 1909 meetings of the South Australian Union 'That Congregationalists have and ought to have a common creed.' Feelings ran high. An amendment 'That Congregationalists have a common faith' was accepted and a split avoided.[32] Nevertheless, when a visiting English Congregationalist reported in 1914 on the denomination in South Australia he commented on the damage that had been done.[33] Though Kirby professed otherwise, for the conservatives it had been a defeat. The spread of extreme theological liberalism had not been checked. Mr F. G. Scammett, speaking against Kirby during the debate, said that the only creed to which he could subscribe 'would have to be as wide as the heavens'.[34]

In 1896 the *Australasian Independent* published a poem by J. H. Palmer of the Sydney suburb of Burwood. It was called 'Perplexing Questions'. Palmer asked whether he was only 'an evanescent spark'

> Struck from the void – to scintillate and die –
> To be extinguished in th'eternal dark?
> A question merely, with no sure reply?

and concluded that he had to grope his way in 'silence and in darkness'.[35] A year later the Reverend Joseph Robertson of Adelaide's Stow church preached a sermon on the death of T. H. Huxley and spoke in respectful terms of the great agnostic. Robertson told his congregation that he knew there were some of them troubled by doubt.[36]

Young men were especially unsettled. A pastor put the matter simply at a meeting of the Melbourne Congregational Ministers' Association; one of the reasons why young men were not committing their lives to Christ was their uncertainty whether the Christian faith was true.[37] Mr Joseph Vardon explained the leakage of Congregational young people between Sunday school and church in terms of this same unsettlement. A boy, he said, could not help being affected by the ideas of those with whom he worked upon leaving school; too often these workmates were unbelievers and critical of what they alleged were the inconsistencies between the theory and practice of the Christian faith.[38]

Some ministers probably exacerbated unsettlement in the pew by saying things that suggested that nothing was certain any more. For example, Alexander Gosman, a professor of the Victorian Congregational College, told an assembly of his Union that no person should be excluded from a church fellowship because he did not believe in the virgin birth or the resurrection of

Christic.[39] Alfred Depledge Sykes spoke of the duty of Congregationalists to take the lead in 'a new religious synthesis, expressed in a church which will dare to stand or fall by its acceptance of truth from whatever quarter it may come.' Congregationalists must not shrink from the task, he said, though the way was 'through certain storm, tumult, and confusion'. According to Sykes, the process of adjusting Christianity to modern thought had to go further than expressing traditional doctrines in new ways. Christians had to abandon their traditional division between the natural and the supernatural (God did not break into the natural course of events to work miracles), the idea of a fall at the beginning of history, the traditional understanding of the atonement, belief in punishment or bliss after death. They also had to realize that other religions had their contribution to make to the new synthesis.[40]

Once in a sermon the Reverend Dr Llewelyn Bevan imagined himself doubting as perhaps his hearers had. First he rejected the infallibility of the Bible. Then he gave up belief in the infallible Christ because Jesus may have been a simple Galilean who never performed a miracle and never claimed to be Son of God. Dr Bevan included the resurrection in this hypothetical jettisoning of dogma: either Jesus never came back to life or he only seemingly died on Good Friday. Yet, declared the preacher, even when these beliefs had been abandoned, faith, hope and love abided and by abiding somehow guaranteed the existence of God. It was a message of Christianity without Christ. What were they thinking and feeling as they listened to him, those people in Pitt Street church, Sydney, that Sunday evening 25 October 1896?[41]

The situation in Congregational fellowships on the other side of the Tasman seems to have been little different. In a paper delivered to the Congregational Union of New Zealand in 1904 the Reverend David Hird contrasted the definiteness about belief in the previous generation with the contemporary attitude which he described as 'essentially non-committal'. 'We have found a place – perhaps a larger one than we think – for such a thing as Christian Agnosticism.'[42]

References to doubt concerning the divinity of Christ became more frequent in the denominational literature of the 1900s. In April 1902 the *Victorian Independent* carried an article quoting a student who said he felt estranged from Christianity, although he still attended the Congregational church with which so many happy memories were associated. His reading and thinking had led him to doubt the divinity of Christ. When the denominational paper in New South Wales reprinted this article a comment was added that there were many like this student in the Congregational churches.[43] In 1913 the New South Wales Union held a symposium on 'The Divinity of Christ' in an attempt to answer people's uncertainties. From the three papers which were delivered, it is clear that many Congregationalists were coming to think of Jesus as a great and good man, a God-inspired man, but a man nonetheless.[44]

The reports of unsettlement are thickest in the years immediately before the First World War. It would be wrong to assume that all or even most of the Congregational churches were deeply affected at this time – some ministers were conservatives who sought to shield their people and we may guess that many churchgoers had no taste for theological speculation – yet there was an unprecedented unrest. Congregationalists who assembled in conference during these years frequently told one another the same thing: 'There is in our hearts much doubt, and in the Churches great anxiety', 'there is much anxious inquiry as to what is most surely believed amongst us', 'a faith that is hardly to be called faith – it is so hesitant and faltering'.[45]

Presumably the First World War tested the faith of many Australasian Congregationalists. As much as other Christians they were asked to reconcile the suffering of the War with the God of love and they too had prayers go unanswered. But these problems hardly ever surfaced in the Congregational press. In the 1920s we have a similar silence about unsettlement regarding science and biblical criticism, not a complete absence of comment but minimal relative to that around 1910. Probably the same thing happened here as occurred with the emergence of a more superficial style of church involvement: neither problem had disappeared; it was more that ministers had learned to live with them.

'Every preacher knows' said one Congregational minister in 1925, 'that doctrinal preaching is at a discount.'[46] Speaking about the problems of the preacher in 1926, the Reverend J. E. James remarked that the demand was 'for shorter sermons, for services without sermons, for ceremonies which we may interpret as we like, rather than sermons with their doctrines and decisions.'[47] A distaste for serious thought associated with a faster life style may also have contributed to this restlessness in the pew. The Reverend W. T. Kench called it 'an age of intellectual tit-bits' and declared that people came to church 'in about the same frame of mind as they attend a popular lecture.'[48] Many Congregational ministers capitulated to this pressure to give what one critic called 'topical talks'.[49] Edward Kiek, the principal of Parkin Theological College, told the 1929 annual assembly of the South Australian

Union that it was not good enough for ministers to offer their people 'essays on Biblical criticism, discussions of moral virtues and counsel on social problems'.[50] Kiek advocated that ministers put the atonement back at the centre of their preaching. Yet this was difficult if the preacher did not possess a credible theology of the atonement. As Kiek himself pointed out, the traditional soteriology was difficult to preach and modern theories were generally unsatisfactory.[51]

Addressing a Camden College gathering in 1930 the Reverend W. J. Ashford criticized the current 'theological anaemia' and advocated the 'new Calvinism' of Karl Barth. After a quarter of a century of preaching, Ashford was totally dissatisfied with the purely immanent God of liberal theology. The need, he claimed, was for theological reconstruction which did not burke metaphysical questions, not even the question of the person of Christ. 'I have found personally more or less humanitarian or semi-pantheistic interpretations of the Person of our Lord unsatisfying to myself, and, as a Gospel for preaching to the multitude, quite hopeless.'[52]

For Ashford the wheel had turned almost full circle, but in following Barth's lead he was a self-conscious exception amongst the ministers of 1930. Barth's work had only just begun to be translated into English.[53] So far as the sources allow us to tell, the theology of those in the pew was predominantly a formless liberalism.

Reflecting on the doctrinal developments in colonial Congregationalism over seventy or so years, consider three points. First, by the early 1870s there were many individual Congregationalists who were dissenting from particular doctrines which were previously regarded as vital to evangelical religion. Second, in time the questioning of Congregational doctrine pushed far beyond dissent from particular doctrines and involved the repudiation of the authority of the church in any shape or form to regulate what an individual Congregationalist should believe. Whereas before church authority had a role, now the only authority acknowledged was the heart and mind of the individual believer. Third, what we have been looking at is a process of change, the progressive working out of that individualizing spirit which Charles Harpur praised in 1847.

The Catholic bishops condemned the doctrinal adjustments that were occurring in Protestantism. The image they sought to project was of the unchanging church, set upon a rock. Nor was this disingenuous; at the official level there was remarkably little change in Catholic teaching about the faith. Thus while Protestant teaching about hell turned nebulous and then disappeared, Catholic teaching kept its sharp, hard lines – even though insistence that God punishes had to many Australians and New Zealanders come to seem an affront to common decency. In 1904 the Anglican bishops in England were considering what to do with the embarrassing references in the Athanasian creed to the everlasting punishment of the wicked. The Anglican archbishop of Melbourne, referring to this question, denied that there was a material hell. Thomas Carr, his Catholic counterpart, insisted that there was a material hell and that punishment there was eternal.[54] Thirty years on the Reverend Dr Rumble was still making no concessions in his Catholic radio programme: though the fire of hell did not depend upon fuel or combustion yet it was a real fire that would burn the body.[55]

Traditional Catholic teaching on faith and morals was not exhaustive. Even when it did cover the ground it could be re-expressed in contemporary language. There were therefore opportunities for intellectual effort, even exploration. These were seldom taken. Partly this was because the bishops and priests were faced with the practical tasks of establishing a church in a new land. But so were Protestant ministers and some of them found time for inquiry and reflection. Speaking generally, compared with Presbyterian and Congregational ministers Irish Catholic bishops and priests were ignorant of advances in science and biblical scholarship. They were also intellectually timid.

In 1907 by decree and encyclical Pope Pius X condemned modernism, a European Catholic intellectual movement whose leaders were influenced by a critical historical approach to the New Testament. Naturally, after the Pope's condemnation there was not a whiff of modernism amongst the clergy of the church in Australasia.[56] But there had been little before. Thomas Hayden, a professor at Manly theological seminary, is perhaps the only Catholic priest who could be regarded as tending in a 'modernist' direction before 1907 – he kept his head down thereafter – and what do we find constituted his advanced views on the New Testament? So far as his published opinions are concerned the most radical thing of Hayden's we can point to is an article in the *Australasian Catholic Record* in 1905. In this he suggested that the words of Jesus as reported in the Fourth Gospel were not always historically accurate. Compared with Hanson's *The Jesus of History* published almost 40 years before, Hayden's position was very conservative.[57]

There were some signs of movement in Catholic teaching in the colonies in at least two areas. One concerned the Old Testament. Cardinal Moran in 1898 declared that God had created the sun on the fourth day, just as was stated in the book of Genesis.[58] But in 1929 addressing the Catholic Evidence Guild in Sydney, the Reverend Dr P. J. Sheehy said that Genesis ought not to be taken as providing scientific truths; rather, behind the narrative one should look for the theological truth that God created all things. In the same address Sheehy said it was not against Catholic teaching to hold that there had been an evolution of plant and animal species. Though Sheehy still stopped short of a personal belief that man's physical body had evolved, his position regarding Darwin's theory was far more liberal than Catholic apologists in the 1860s and 1870s.[59] As late as 1890 the Reverend Dr Slattery had devoted only one paragraph to Darwinism in an article on humankind. 'I only introduce it', he explained, 'to dismiss it with a laugh.'[60]

A second instance of minimal adjustment in the absence of dogma or papal direction concerns purgatory. There are signs that at least some priests wanted to play down the intensity and physical nature of the suffering of the souls in purgatory. One Irish priest who migrated to Victoria in 1924 used to say when preaching on the subject that the suffering of a soul in purgatory was like that intense remorse a man might suffer when first greeted by his family after a spell in prison. This priest taught that the fire sometimes spoken of in connection with purgatory was a figure to describe a spiritual state.[61] Father Eustace Boylan S. J. also 'spiritualized' the suffering of the souls in purgatory and in an article in 1928 even went so far as to say that it was 'a good place, and despite the anguish of pain and remorse, there is happiness also, because there is complete conformity with the holy will of God.'[62] But there were other priests who maintained a more literal understanding. For example, in one of his radio replies, Father Rumble of Sydney insisted that the souls in purgatory experienced 'unspeakable suffering'.[63]

In their dealings with the laity the bishops and priests strongly emphasized the importance of following the teachings of the true church. They were imbued with the spirit of the Vatican Council of 1870, which in a declaration on papal infallibility had given new force and precision to the principle of church authority over the individual believer. (Cardinal Cullen helped to formulate this declaration.) Children were drilled in correct Catholic beliefs by the rote learning of the penny catechism. Sermons presented the truth as defined by the Council of Trent.

This priestly pressure had a substantial effect. At Catholic gatherings and in the Catholic press the laity, in so far as they expressed themselves at all, invariably followed the official line. Privately, too, Catholics tended to be guided by official teaching: in no other way is it possible to explain why 64 per cent of Catholic respondents to a Gallup poll in Australia in 1969 said that they believed in hell; the comparable figures for Methodists, Anglicans and Presbyterians were respectively 28, 26 and 17 per cent.[64] Yet there were other pressures, as well, on Catholic beliefs.

In discussing in an earlier chapter how immigrants were affected by the environment of the colonies, I cited evidence that some Catholics came to see good in Protestantism and even to think it did not matter to which church a person belonged. Implicit in this attitude was disregard for the teaching authority of the Catholic church. For the laity to believe that one church was as good as another was to believe what their bishops and priests said should not be believed. The practice of seeing good in the Protestant religion continued amongst native-born Catholics, despite the growth of sectarianism. According to Father Patrick Dowling a sectarian episode could even lead Catholics to play down their doctrinal differences with Protestants. When a religious controversy occurred, Dowling told the third Australasian Catholic Congress in 1909, the Catholic wanted to keep in with his Protestant friends, declared that he hated bigotry, and told himself that it was what the Catholic and Protestant faiths had in common that counted most. Seeking to justify this new attitude he contrasted to himself the lives of his Protestant friends with those of bad Catholics. This undermined for him the superiority and authority of the Catholic church, whereupon he was less likely to be a regular attender at Sunday mass.[65]

Fathers Hurley and Phelan were two priests who compared the religious climate in Ireland with that in the colonies at the end of the nineteenth century. Both commented on the severe testing of their faith which poorly instructed Catholic immigrants had to endure. 'Passive credulity is not a gift of colonial youth', wrote Hurley. To Father Phelan it seemed that everywhere there was restless intellectual activity: every town had its library and its local paper, everyone had opinions, and people on the whole were better informed than at home; even a priest could have his head sent spinning on arrival, so unprepared was he for the intellectual challenges which he met at every turn.[66]

Father Hurley specified the intellectual challenge as one of the reasons why Catholics in New Zealand lost their faith. Loss of faith in the strict sense did happen although it was perhaps not usual. Christopher Brennan, a native-born son of devout Irish

Catholic parents, began attending the University of Sydney in 1888. During his second year he attended some classes of Francis Anderson, a philosopher who used the Socratic method and was a foe of dogma. In February 1890 the young Brennan purchased a Greek New Testament and began comparing the gospels. His diary entry for 5 March 1890 announced 'Agnosticism AGNOSTICISM'.[67]

Priests who commented on the dangers of the anti-Catholic environment in which their people were set often distinguished between men and women. Men were more at risk because they moved more amongst sceptics and Protestants. A writer for the *Australasian Catholic Record* in 1907 also singled out young males.

> Even the ordinary man of the world does not deem religion a topic too sacred to speak about in his daily conversation, or a subject on which he cannot pose as an authority. And by a little ridicule and banter he can set thinking the young lad, only lately released from the discipline of school life, and persuading himself that he has had a surfeit of religion already. There is also the common danger of our Catholic young men cultivating the friendship of persons who themselves have little respect for religion in any form, and making them their companions. If this friendship is to last, it often necessitates for the Catholic an attitude of compromise in regard to his religious principles, and the whittling down of many of his former cherished beliefs. We have all met some time or other the omnivorous reader, who in due course becomes omniscient, and who cannot brook any dictation from the priest on the question of religion and its obligations. His faith has been sapped by the reading of poisonous literature, and his pride of intellect will not allow him to submit to any authority, ecclesiastical or divine.[68]

In his views the omniscient young man was far from being a representative Catholic. But such were the social pressures and intellectual influences of the environment that encompassed them, there were many Catholics who privately moved some of the way down the road to heterodoxy. This inference may be reinforced by referring again to the 1969 Gallup poll. Sixty-four per cent of the Catholic respondents said they believed in hell. The other side of the coin is the 36 per cent who said they did not.

Chapter Seven

THE FAMILY

There are many ways by which we might judge the effectiveness of the churches in reaching into the family. In a religion as ethical as Christianity how family members deal with one another is a good test – by their fruits ye shall know them. Another guide is the extent to which parents mediate to their children values promoted in the churches such as thrift, sobriety and sexual self-control. Another is whether objects about the house reflect church influence: for Protestants framed texts, photos of famous preachers, a Bible prominently displayed; for Catholics holy-water fonts, crucifixes, statuettes of the Virgin and the like. From the wide range of possible subjects, I have chosen to examine contraception, family worship and authority within the family.

The colonies were places of children. Colonial homes were full of them. In the late nineteenth century it would have been hard to walk down the street of any town, small or large, without seeing a pregnant woman or a baby. The censuses held in 1871 revealed that slightly over four persons in every ten in the colonies were then aged under fifteen.[1]

Many families were large. A group of 58 women who married in Western Australia in the early 1850s have been traced to the end of the child-bearing period. The median number of births to these wives was 8.9.[2] In another study 99 women who had the birth of their first child registered in the Castlemaine district in Victoria in 1861 were traced to the registration of the birth of their final child. Of the 99, there were 69 who had at least one child after their 35th birthday. In this group of 69 the median number of issue was 9.0.[3] The number of births in particular families went much higher. In the late nineteenth century on the Darling Downs of Queensland there were three couples with 49 progeny between them.[4]

By the early 1880s family sizes were beginning to dwindle in colonial cities.[5] The long, slow, momentous shift had begun towards the one- and two-child family and to couples who are childless by choice. In the process church leaders came to face a difficult problem. Moral standards are not supposed to vary according to time and circumstance. Traditional religious teaching in the West was that measures to prevent conception were morally wrong.[6] Yet by around 1900 advertisements for contraceptives were all too visible and chemists were selling sheaths, sprays, pessaries and the like. Furthermore substantial declines in the colonial birth rates had become apparent. It was too much to believe that many churchgoers were innocent of using preventive measures, even if they were not procuring abortions.[7] But these men and women might not take kindly to criticism, and they paid the ministers' stipends.

In 1903 the New South Wales government appointed a Royal Commission into the decline of the birth rate. Official representatives of the principal denominations were invited to provide witnesses to appear before the commission. The verbatim report of what was said by the eight clerical witnesses allows us to probe the attitudes of those who were in effect accredited spokesmen of their churches. The hearings were not open to the public.[8]

The ministers who gave evidence to the Commission condemned contraception. They were happy to agree with those who questioned them that there were secular reasons why small families were undesirable. For instance, they thought having small families unpatriotic: a rapidly growing population was needed to ward off the yellow myriads of Asia. The religious men had religious arguments as well. God had told Adam to be fruitful and multiply; to use an artificial check on conception was to violate this natural order instituted by God. It also compounded the amount of selfishness in the world, for children from small families tended only to think of themselves. Another worry about the prevalence of contraception was that it suggested a weakening of religious sentiment in the community. According to the Reverend N. M. Hennessy, 'where the religious sense is profound, that will carry with it a belief that God has some care for offspring, and there would be no desire to adopt these artificial methods for the limitation of the family.'[9]

Protestant ministers, however, did not speak out against family limitation when they stood before their local congregation. J. Howell Price, a Church of England clergyman, told the Commission that the laity were touchy on the subject, and, as they exercised the power of the purse without compunction, the clergy were afraid to cause what they knew would be a certain offence. Price testified that he had once condemned birth control in a sermon and he had experienced trouble.[10] Though Price did not say so it was an evasion for Protestant church leaders to make generalized condemnations of birth control at denominational gatherings, given that churchgoers were not being confronted where it mattered – face to face from the pulpit at Sunday worship.

The adjustment of the official line within the various Protestant churches was managed about as quickly as was decent. From the early 1920s there was a major revision in Anglican official attitudes. The colonial leaders of the Church of England regarded as authoritative resolutions of the Lambeth Conferences in England. In 1920 the bishops at Lambeth had condemned family planning; in 1930 a large majority was prepared to condone it. Methodist spokesmen began adjusting their views earlier. By the 1950s the mainstream Protestant churches had abandoned their earlier condemnations of birth control.[11]

There were good churchgoers who were evangelists of family limitation. Most were women. A few of the witnesses before the Royal Commission had themselves come under pressure from these ladies. The Reverend Dr Dill Macky's wife had been urged again and again by her friends to limit her child bearing.[12] The Reverend J. Howell Price's wife had received a visit from a lady who was a propagandist for birth control not long after the Prices had had another child. This woman, a churchgoer and a communicant, though not apparently one of Price's parishioners, told Mrs Price how the birth of further children might be prevented. Mrs Price referred the lady to her husband. A little later when Price was making a parish visit, this lady happened to be present. As soon as the clergyman entered the room she challenged him: 'Before the hostess and the two daughters of the hostess she informed me that I was a brute because I allowed my wife to have children, and that God had given reason and that we ought to use it; that my wife was a slave to the home and a slave to the children. I suggested to her that if she would send her husband to me I would argue with him, but not with her; but she would not have it.'[13]

Appearing before the New South Wales Royal Commission Cardinal Moran was asked whether he believed there had been of recent years a decline in the religious sentiments of the community. Behind the question was the assumption that a principal cause of the decline in the birth rate was the decline of religion. Though quite happy with the idea of a general religious decay, the Cardinal wished it to be understood that there had been a heightening of piety in the Catholic community of recent years. Though he did not say so outright, Moran may have been aware that there were Catholics who were using preventive measures. Some statistics he quoted implied as much.[14] In 1901 in an article in the *Australasian Catholic Record* Father T. A. Fitzgerald had stated that there were Catholic wives who were 'easy victims of that indolence which rejects the sacred duties of motherhood.'[15] If Moran had been ignorant about this matter in December 1903 when he appeared before the Commission he would have been disabused the following year by Dr J. B. Nash. Speaking at the Second Australasian Catholic Congress Nash told how his experience as a member of the New South Wales Royal Commission had opened his eyes to what was going on.[16] Of all religious leaders in Australia at the turn of the century only the Lutheran ones would have had much of a basis for claiming that their people were continuing to increase and multiply without artificial checks. And by the First World War even the Lutherans had begun the shift towards smaller families.[17]

In Australia both Catholic and Protestant wives who completed their families in the 1880s had on average around seven live births. Catholic and Protestant wives in Australia who completed their families in the 1950s both had on average between two and three live births, with the Catholic women at the higher end of the range.[18] Protestant and Catholic fertility declines in New Zealand were similar to those in Australia and therefore to one another.[19] Catholic family sizes began to grow again slightly in the 1950s, once more in correspondence with Protestant developments.[20]

The adoption of contraceptive methods by Catholics was slower in country than city.[21] Another difference within the total Catholic population seems to have been that Catholics who had been born in Ireland and migrated to Australasia were slower to practise contraception than Catholics of Irish stock who had been born in the colonies. Table 7 is taken from statistics supplied to the New South Wales Royal Commission by Timothy Coghlan, the government statistician of that colony.[22] The statistics themselves were drawn from the New South Wales census of 1901. There is no reason for believing that the picture in the other

Table 7: Average issue of native-born wives of all denominations and Irish-born wives of all denominations in N.S.W. in 1901

| | Average issue of women born in: | | | | | |
| | New South Wales | | | Ireland | | |
	Marriages prior to 1881	Marriages 1881–1901	Difference	Marriages prior to 1881	Marriages 1881–1901	Difference
Age of wife at marriage						
20–24	8.23	4.82	3.41	7.66	6.40	1.26
25–29	6.10	3.27	2.83	5.70	4.12	1.58
30–34	4.09	2.06	2.03	3.66	2.24	1.42
35–39	2.04	1.07	.97	1.70	.92	.78
40–44	.60	.29	.31	.61	.17	.44

Source: See endnote 22

colonies was significantly different. The table refers to wives born in Ireland not Catholic wives born in Ireland but the two may be regarded as roughly equivalent. We may also take it as certain that the fertility of native-born Catholic women stayed very close to that of all native-born women in New South Wales. At the 1911 census the average issue of native-born wives of all denominations was 3.80 and of all Roman Catholic wives, including the more fertile Irish-born wives, not much higher at 4.12.[23]

In 1870 the level of marital fertility of the population of Ireland was slightly below that of England and Wales.[24] As marital fertility began to fall in England and many other parts of the western world from around 1870, Irish families started to become exceptional for their size. Between 1881 and 1911 in Ireland the annual average number of legitimate births per 1000 married women aged 15–44 years rose from 274.6 to 306.9.[25] A decline in Catholic family sizes in Ireland did begin after 1911, but a wide difference between Catholic and Protestant fertility was maintained in Ireland and the decline in Catholic fertility in Ireland was very slow compared with the Catholic decline in Australia and New Zealand. Around 1950 wives with five or more children were twice as common among the Catholic wives of Ireland aged 40–45 as they were among Australian Catholic wives aged 40–45.[26] Throughout this century the fertility of Catholic wives in Australasia has been close to what is normal in western countries, the fertility of Catholic wives in Ireland outstandingly high.

Thus, if the New South Wales statistics provide a reliable guide, there was a gradation in the pace of fertility decline among those of Irish stock: fastest among the colonial born, more slowly among the Irish-born who migrated to Australasia, slowest of all among those who remained in Ireland. In Australasia, as in Ireland, the Catholic bishops and priests taught that it was a mortal sin to practise preventive measures. Catholics in Australasia by and large accepted the dominant values of the wider culture and sought the regard of non-Catholics. As the prevailing ethos favoured birth control Catholics tended to comply. Individual Catholics in Ireland, by contrast, were exposed to powerful pressures in favour of large families. The Irish-born who had families in Australia fell in between these two groups in their fertility because they had been subjected to two, not one, sets of influences.

One of the reasons for the sharp contrast between the fertility of colonial-born Catholic women and those resident in Ireland is that such a large proportion of the Catholic women of Australia and New Zealand have been involved in mixed marriages. But even for Catholic women married to Catholic husbands the rate of fertility decline has not been that much slower than for Protestants. At the 1961 Australian census Church of England women married to Church of England men had on average 2.33 children; the average of Catholic in-marriages was 2.65 children.[27]

The period before 1930 was distinguished not only by a severe decline in Catholic fertility but also by the ignorance of Catholic couples of the 'safe period' for intercourse without conception.[28] Abstention from sexual intercourse is hardly likely to have been practised on a scale sufficient to effect such a large reduction in Catholic fertility. Thus many regular attenders at mass must have begun to practise some form of contraception from the 1880s. It seems likely that many Catholics did not divulge in the confessional what they were doing. It may be, in addition, that some priests heard penitents confess to the practice and decided not to take a strong stand against it.[29]

Daily or near daily common worship in some form is vital if a group is to practise a religion which deeply penetrates the lives of its adherents. Private worship is too demanding for the average person to sustain. Unless there is some form of religious community such as a monastery or a seminary then this common worship will have to be in the family.

Family worship was fashionable among middle and upper class Protestant churchgoers of mid-Victorian Britain. It is impossible to be precise but it seems that amongst the wealthy who had come under evangelical influences, prayer with the servants and children was almost *de rigueur* by the 1840s and 1850s. This was so both for those who belonged to the established churches and those who stood outside them. The practice of family worship seems to have been especially strong amongst Presbyterians. Robert Burns's poem 'The Cotter's Saturday Night' was for them an inspiration as to what family piety ought to be.

> The chearfu' Supper done, wi' serious face,
>   They, round the ingle, form a circle wide;
> The Sire turns o'er, with patriarchal grace,
>   The big *ha' Bible*, ance his *Father's* pride:
> . . .
> Then kneeling down to HEAVEN's ETERNAL KING,
>   The *Saint*, the *Father*, and the *Husband* prays:
> Hope 'springs exulting on triumphant wing,'
>   That *thus* they all shall meet in future days.

The Free Church of Scotland took up this tradition and promoted it with fervour. Manuals of family worship, sometimes big and costly volumes, were aimed at adherents of a particular denomination or the general evangelical market. But the centre of family worship for evangelical Protestants was the family Bible.[30]

In the colonies in the mid-Victorian period Presbyterian ministers were active promoters of family worship. They frequently discussed the subject at meetings of presbytery or in annual assembly. As a guide to their views we may take *Family Religion*. Published in the *Christian Review and Messenger* in 1866 and then re-issued under separate cover, this was an address which the Reverend Dr Adam Cairns had been commissioned to give by the General Assembly of the Presbyterian Church of Victoria.

For Cairns the family stood at the centre of the purposes of God.

> We speak of the Church as the grand ordinance of grace; but the Church in its largest form is just an aggregation of families. The great household of faith known as the Church is composed of those lesser circles known as the households of believers. The quiet, simple, unostentatious family is the true nursery of the Church below and of Jerusalem above. Let such houses disappear, and the Church will be at once extinguished.... That there may be a church there must first be a family. That Heaven may be filled with the redeemed from the earth there must be holy families on earth.

Every believer was a priest but parents were priests *par excellence*. It was their obligation and their privilege to lead their children in daily worship and to ensure they learnt the catechism. The priority that Cairns gave to family religion is evident in his treatment of the Sabbath. Before going off to church the family should have their own act of worship. Cairns deprecated the colonial practice of a church service on a Sunday evening because it interfered with the time parents and children should have at home for intimate converse about spiritual things.[31]

In the mid-Victorian period colonial Methodist leaders shared the strong belief of the Presbyterians in the desirability of family prayers and bible reading. The Methodist ideal was a church in every member's house. It was standard practice for Methodist leaders to refer to parents as priests and to the family altar. No doubt Anglican colonial leaders in the 1850s and 1860s also saw family prayers as desirable, but they had much less to say about it. References to family worship in Anglican official sources during these years are few and far between.

It is almost impossible to determine how much family worship was actually practised in the colonies during the mid-Victorian period. The evidence is fragmentary and where a report does try to generalize it is invariably vague. There were Anglicans in the colonies who regarded themselves as belonging to a social élite and who did observe family worship as one of the proprieties of

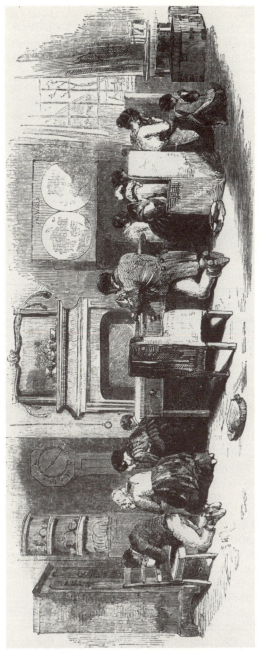

The paterfamilias leads his household at prayer. Almost certainly from a British publication, this was found as a cutting in a colonial clergyman's letter-book.

their position. In Canterbury, New Zealand, some Anglican station houses had private chapels. In Victoria's Western District Jane Henty saw to it that daily prayers were held in her remote bush home with servants attending. She once got the outworkers of the Henty run to come to Sunday services by giving them a slice of plum cake and a tot of rum.[32] But the typical Anglican in the colonies was of humble origins and not accustomed to the practice in the old country. 'Omicron', writing to the Adelaide *Church Chronicle* in 1865, declared that fewer than one in twenty of Anglican churchgoers was habitual in family worship.[33] 'Churchman' writing to the *Melbourne Church News* in 1866 stated that, with few exceptions, only in clergymen's families were family devotions practised. 'A.B.C.' in a follow-up letter agreed, noting that he had had ten years experience in Victoria in both town and country districts.[34]

There was also considerable neglect of family worship in the homes of non-Anglican churchgoers, even of those who were church members. The Victorian Presbyterian Assembly commissioned Cairns to deliver an address on family religion as one step towards remedying its neglect. Cairns observed that in many 'respectable' families there was but occasional family prayer and bible reading.[35] *The South Australian Wesleyan Magazine* for October 1869 contained a long article on family prayer which complained that it was 'no uncommon objection in the minds of many, that family prayer is too great a consumption of time, and proves an impediment to their temporal concerns.'[36] A writer for the Congregational *Southern Spectator* in October 1858 referred to neglect of family worship by those who were zealous Christians.[37] In 1873 the Reverend C.S.Y. Price declared in his chairman's address to the Victorian Congregational Union 'our family religion is very little in quantity and very poor in quality; from some Christian households it is absent, in many others no special time is set apart ... such trivial things as a friend's call, or a friend staying rather long make a prayerless day. In other houses prayer is so cold, formal, and ungenial, that many vote it a bore, and some try curious arts to avoid it.'[38]

Yet in the mid-Victorian period at least some effort was made in a sizeable minority of Protestant households. And there were families, and not just ministers' ones, where daily worship was an absolute rule.[39] Perhaps the common prayer and bible reading often constituted an irksome routine forced on the children and observed by the parents because it was the custom of their kind. But not always. The Smaills and the Darlings were early settlers at Inchclutha in Otago. William Smaill recollected that the practice the two families had of joining in worship each night in one group brought and held them together more than anything else. 'Everything seemed to straighten out here. Father lead the singing, Mr Darling read the chapter and Father lead in prayer.... All the rejoicings and family unions and reunions were always closed with combined family worship. However short it was always warm and appreciated by all.'[40]

It is interesting to speculate on the possible consequences for domestic relations of the widespread neglect of family prayer. Frank Fowler wrote in the late 1850s that one of the reasons why mistresses and servants were frequently at enmity in the colonies was that they were but seldom combined in family prayer 'that most beautiful of all domestic customs – at once the most conservative and the most levelling'.[41]

In 1877 a pastoral address to the Wesleyan Methodists of New South Wales admonished heads of families about 'a growing tendency' to hand over to the Sunday school teacher the duties of the parent in providing worship and discipline for the child.[42] A pastoral address to the South Australian Wesleyans the following year warned: 'Maintain with regularity family worship. We fear there is with some a growing laxity in this matter.'[43] In 1882 the Committee on Religion of the Otago and Southland Presbyterian Synod, in a pastoral address issued at the command of the Synod, declared that family religion was 'falling into oblivion and neglect' as parents sought to transfer to Sunday school teachers and pastors responsibility for the religious upbringing of children. The excuses of these parents were summarized: 'We cannot read and explain the Bible to them. We cannot unfold to them religious truth, we cannot preach, we cannot summon courage, as we have no ability, to pray to God in words of our own among them.' This, thought the committee, was nonsense.[44]

It therefore appears that evangelical Protestant church members were less assiduous in the practice of family worship by the late 1870s than they had been in the 1850s and 1860s. In the 1880s and 1890s there was further decay of the practice to judge by the growing numbers of complaints and admonitions from evangelical church leaders. The Presbyterian leaders made the most consistent effort to ascertain what was occurring. Almost every year a committee charged with reviewing the spiritual condition of the congregations would try to gather reports about family worship along with other items of interest. But the returns from the congregations were nearly always very incomplete and the responses often hazy. The report made by the Committee on Religion to the Otago and Southland Synod for 1896 was an exception.

A Protestant family, *c.* 1921. The Merritts of Auckland were accustomed to have a Bible reading and prayers in the drawing-room of 'Hartsholme' before leaving for worship at the Beresford Street Congregational church. Mr H. T. Merritt was a successful wholesale merchant.

The Committee devoted their attention that year entirely to the family and obtained returns from almost all the charges. Over 500 elders assisted in the making of the returns. To quote the report on family worship, 'In the great majority of the returns it is said to be not generally observed, sadly neglected, and so on.'[45] A return made for the 1900 report by the same committee reported on developments with only a touch of exaggeration: 'Rapidly passing into oblivion and in another generation will probably be defunct.'[46] There was, however, still a sufficient number of Presbyterians willing to practise family worship to make possible colonial collections of family prayers, such as *The Church at Home* published by the Australian Presbyterian Church in 1907 and *Prayers for the Home Circle* published by the New Zealand Presbyterian Church in 1917.[47]

There could be no comparable Church of England decline since there was no comparable level from which to decline. Bishops and clergy continued to show almost no concern about promoting family worship. Was it that they believed the Sunday school was adequate as a means of introducing children to religion? Or did they despair of motivating parents to bring religion into their own homes? They were certainly aware of how puny were religious influences in Church of England homes. 'Any clergyman who has worked among the lower middle and lower classes', observed one senior clergyman in 1888, 'knows that the theory of a religion generally home-taught is a breath from fairyland.'[48] The Reverend H. L. Jackson, incumbent at St James's Sydney in the late 1880s, was an Anglican oddity in rejecting the Sunday school. He believed it would be preferable to establish agencies to assist parents in discharge of their duties. But religious education more than family worship was his concern.[49]

The Mothers' Union movement which began in Australasia in the 1890s was the first substantial attempt made within the Church of England to get worship into the colonial home. Every member of the Mothers' Union was supposed to do her best to be a regular church attender and develop her spiritual life. She had daily to say her Mothers' Union prayer with its commitment to strengthening religion in the family. Regular meetings of her local branch provided support and practical information about the spiritual side of a mother's life and work. *Mothers in Australasia*, the Mothers' Union magazine, in the 1920s ran numerous articles on religion and the child.[50] All this work probably increased the number of Anglican children who said their prayers at the bedside. Yet the Mothers' Union did not promote genuinely family religious exercises, because it was tacitly recognized that fathers would not allow it. The movement sought to reach children only through mothers, and however inevitable this limitation was, given the attitude to religion of Anglican men, nevertheless the Mothers' Union thereby severely circumscribed its influence. Anglican boys and girls were in effect being taught that prayers were not for men and not for the family as a whole. Also limiting the influence of the Mothers' Union movement upon Anglican families was the relatively small size of its membership – fewer than ten thousand members in Australia and New Zealand in the mid-1920s in a total Anglican population of nearly three million.[51]

In the mid-nineteenth century few Catholic homes in the colonies practised family worship. When indifference to the sacramental life of the church was rife, the average Catholic couple did not take the trouble to lead their children in prayers. Many would probably not have known what prayers to say. It was difficult enough for Catholic priests and teachers to get parents to take any interest in the religious welfare of their children.

The very first Catholic bishop appointed to a see in Australasia composed two pastoral letters on religion in the family which constitute the finest statement of the ideal I know made by any Christian, Catholic or Protestant, at any time since the European arrived in Australasia.[52] Even as John Bede Polding was writing these pastorals in 1862 the schools question was starting to become pressing. The two matters – religion in the schools and religion in the home – were in theory complementary, not antithetical, but in the 1860s and 1870s the former monopolized episcopal attention. Initially it seems the Irish bishops decided that nothing should be allowed to divert attention from the colossal task of creating an independent Catholic school system. The bishops certainly believed that it was futile to rely upon Catholic parents to teach their children about religion. They may have believed that to stress the role of parents in the religious formation of children risked setting parents thinking whether parish schools needed to be established.

The pastoral letter issued by the Plenary Council of 1885 enjoined Catholic parents to practise family prayer morning and evening; the evening rosary was especially recommended.[53] From about this time a new emphasis on family worship is apparent. The parish school continued to be the prime episcopal concern but frequently the laity were reminded that the schools were not ends in themselves but aids to the Catholic home in the moulding of young lives and that religion provided in the parish school should not be used as an excuse by Catholic parents for evading their personal spiritual responsibilities.

It was no easy task to school parents in a new habit which required considerable motivation. And many Catholics as working class people lived under conditions which were unfavourable to family devotions. Their houses were cramped. The parents often led irregular lives. Fathers were frequently drunk. There was often domestic violence. Mothers and fathers were often exhausted at the end of the day and it required energy to marshal recalcitrant children for prayer.[54] But there is no doubt that by the early years of this century the incidence of Catholic family worship was increasing as that of the Protestants was declining. Moreover, the Catholic church was succeeding in reaching working class people, even though the practice was probably more popular with middle class Catholic families. Progress was probably assisted by the arrival from Ireland of men and women whose religion had been affected by the heightening of Catholic piety following the Famine. For these folk it was simply a matter of continuing to say the rosary.

Missioners and parish priests as well as bishops promoted religion in the home. The parish school was also important, for there children got accustomed to daily devotions and became more susceptible to leading family worship when they became parents. Another agency to promote family worship was the *Australian Messenger of the Sacred Heart*, a monthly magazine run by the Jesuits. Initially the *Messenger* concentrated upon promoting individual piety through an Apostleship of Prayer dedicated to the Sacred Heart of Jesus. From 1918 the *Messenger* got behind an international Catholic movement, originating in France in the 1880s, to recruit Catholic families who would consecrate themselves to the Sacred Heart.[55] The editor recommended that the first Friday in the month be chosen for the consecration, that the family go off to early mass and receive Holy Communion, and that later in the day the priest be present with all the members to bless a picture of the Sacred Heart using holy water. This became the family shrine. In the Act of Consecration, which was to be said by father or mother, the Sacred Heart was invoked, the family declared itself to belong to it, offered up all its joys and sufferings and entreated the Sacred Heart to lavish its blessings upon all members of the family whether present or absent, living or dead. This Act of Consecration was to be renewed every first Friday of the month and the picture of the Sacred Heart kept as a little shrine where all could see it, honoured by lights and flowers.[56] The editor of the *Messenger* announced in July 1923 that 2117 names had already been inscribed in a volume to be forwarded to France and placed in the chapel at Paray-le-Monial, the spiritual centre of the movement. These names included convents and schools as well as families but the editor asserted families accounted for at least ten thousand individuals.[57] Many families had forwarded their names independently, before this special effort.

The shrine of the Sacred Heart often meant a lot. One family in Sumner, New Zealand, used a picture of the Sacred Heart which for many years had been owned by the wife's mother. In another the husband made it a practice to send in by one of the children 'any extra nice flower' from the garden to put in a vase before the Sacred Heart. A Melbourne family had the picture placed before a lamp which was always kept burning, and the shrine placed in the bedroom of one invalid member in constant pain. One woman in North Queensland wrote the editor of the *Messenger* how she had

For Catholic homes. These items, which were probably imported, reflected old-world taste in Catholic requisites.

got a large picture of the Sacred Heart and a souvenir Act of Consecration from W. P. Lineham, Catholic suppliers of Melbourne. When the priest came, which he did about once a year, he had blessed these. For the service she had read the Act of Consecration printed in the *Messenger*: 'we recited five paters and aves in honour of the Sacred Heart, and then we said the rosary of our Blessed Mother. We remembered in our prayers my mother, who is dead, and my sister who is absent. We keep flowers before the picture every day, and every night we light two candles and say five paters and aves in honour of our Divine Lord, and then we say the Rosary. This is our custom.'[58]

In 1909 Father Patrick Dowling, parish priest in Botany Bay, Sydney, claimed that family prayer was the exception in the city. For Dowling this lack of family prayer reflected a general weakness of the Catholic family as a religious force. According to him, in many Catholic homes there were few Catholic pictures or emblems and frequently these were restricted to bedrooms for fear of offending Protestant friends. In 'many instances' Catholic homes were 'so many avenues through which the inmates pass, and in which they rest for a while in the intervals of work and amusement.'[59]

In the country all members of the family were more likely to be present for the rosary, if only because there was less to draw them off than in the city. The famous poem by 'John O'Brien', 'The Trimmin's on the Rosary', describes a country family. It would be unwise to assume that country Catholic mothers were all like the mother of the poem adding her prayers to the rosary:

> She would pray for all our little needs, and every shade of care
> That might darken o'er The Sugarloaf, she'd meet it with a prayer.
> She would pray for this one's 'sore complaint', or that one's
>   'hurted hand',
> Or that someone else might make a deal and get 'that bit of land';
> Or that Dad might sell the cattle well, and seasons good might rule,
> So that little John, the weakly one, might go away to school.

O'Brien, in real life Father P. J. Hartigan, may have been drawing on memories of his own childhood in the 1880s as much as what he observed in his parish, and Hartigan's family was exceptionally devout. Of the nine children, two became priests and four entered Mercy convents.[60] The bishop of Ballarat, a country diocese, lamented in 1904 that the neglect of morning and evening prayer in Catholic homes, was 'sadly general'.[61] Nevertheless by the early years of this century there were many Catholic homes in the country where family life was strong and the rosary at night second nature. Such was the New Zealand Irish Catholic family portrayed in Dan Davin's novel, *No Remittance*. Norah makes the mistake of marrying Kane, a Protestant. Nevertheless saying the rosary is ingrained in her. As Kane and Norah live with her parents after the marriage she kneels with them night after night at the rosary. Kane dismisses it as play-acting that does no good. When he finds the old people bear up well under the tragedy of losing a son in the First World War he decides it is because of the rosary: there has never been a day in the year that they haven't taken time off to tell themselves that there is no true happiness on this earth.[62]

In November 1865 the Sydney *Presbyterian Magazine* carried an article, 'Maxims for Parents', apparently written by the editor, the Reverend Dr Robert Steel. The maxims included such things as teaching the children to be clean and tidy, to tell the truth, never to encourage by 'amusement' 'an immodest action', never to give children anything because they cried for it. Six of the seventeen maxims dealt with obedience. Parents ought never to punish in a temper but disobedience should never go unpunished: 'Be calm as a clock, yet decisive.' Maxim number one was that from earliest infancy parents should inculcate '*instant, unhesitating* obedience'.[63]

Others who wrote for the religious public of the colonies in the late nineteenth century now and again gave similar advice about exacting obedience from children. Concern with the proper training of children was a powerful tradition among evangelical Protestants, stretching back to the seventeenth-century Puritans and beyond. By the mid-Victorian period the insistence on obedience had been softened and we hear little about breaking the will. When Bishop Perry of Melbourne gave an address on 'Parents and Children' in 1870 he said care ought to be taken not to arouse in children a spirit of opposition and not to give the impression of being arbitrary.[64] Nevertheless, in the colonies in the mid-Victorian period, churchgoing Protestant parents were left in no doubt that they ought to aim for obedient children. Perry (who had no children) himself said that the authority of parents should be 'perfectly absolute'. 'Presbyter', writing for the evangelical Protestant *Testimony* in 1866, argued that self-will was so deeply rooted in human nature that at a very early age the child ought to be 'brought into subjection and trained to the habit of immediate and thorough compliance with the parents' commands.'[65] In 1861 a Wesleyan Methodist exhorted that the parent was a king as well as a priest in his own home, and, as one appointed by God in both spheres, had a duty to command his children.[66] This same tradition was reasserted in 1896 in New Zealand by 'Pastor' writing for a Presbyterian periodical, *Christian Outlook*.

> What is home training? Obedience! OBEDIENCE! OBEDIENCE! Obedience is the first and most important lesson that the child needs to learn – obedience instant and uncompromising. It should be taught this lesson in unconscious years, and have formed the habit of obedience to the will of father or mother long before it can understand the reason. It should be taught so early that it would become almost instinctive, and as second nature.

Only thus could the 'evil tendencies and weaknesses' innate in children be overcome.[67]

For some churchmen who wrote about the obedience of children there was a deeper end than achieving a well-regulated family. Their professed ultimate objective was an adult who obeyed his or her God. It was impossible to teach an infant to obey God but the youngest child could be taught to obey its parent, and the habit of obedience could easily be transferred later to God himself. Bishop Perry explained the principle succinctly. 'The parent stands towards it [the child] in the place of God; and if the authority of the earthly father be not, that of the Heavenly Father cannot be enforced. A child who habitually disobeys its parents cannot render obedience to God.'[68] As the obedience to God tended to be cast in terms of unquestioning submission to a higher will, so also with the obedience owed to the parent. 'Pastor' told parents in 1896 that the child 'having formed the habit of submission instantly and trustfully to the stronger human will' 'would all the more readily in after years submit instantly, trustfully, and lovingly to the higher and more perfect Divine Will.'[69]

It may be that teaching of the sort that has been quoted was infrequent in Protestant colonial church circles in the 1850s and 1860s. Yet it is significant that strong statements about the obedience of children were made then by at least some ministers in good repute. To this extent an ideology of obedience was intact in the mid-Victorian period. By the 1920s, however, no Protestant denominational periodical ever carried teaching about obedience remotely like that of Bishop Perry or 'Pastor'. We are therefore compelled to ask whether there was an associated decline in authoritarian *practice* within the families of Protestant churchgoers. If there was such a decline we have another question to explore, namely whether the change in behaviour within Protestant families worked against the churches by facilitating a decrease in church involvement by young people. Put simply, if they became less subject to their parents did they decide to go to church less?

The discussion which follows is necessarily to a large extent tentative and provisional. Research on parent-child relationships in the Australasian past has hardly begun. There are also formidable difficulties in trying to reconstruct anything of what happened within the colonial family. First, relationships within the family constitute a largely hidden world and specific evidence is both limited and hard to locate. Secondly, comment of a general kind about the family was often motivated by fear or social prejudice, so that people's beliefs about what ought to have been the case often distorted their perceptions of what was the case. Thirdly, the family is an endlessly variegated institution, with so many different kinds of families in so many different types of circumstances that any person wishing to speak with authority must make an attempt at a systematic, comprehensive investigation. So far as I know, no such investigation was made either in Australia or New Zealand before the Second World War.

A writer for the *Christian Advocate*, published in Adelaide, complained in 1859 that colonial parents too often indulged their children and that evangelical parents were no exception; the faults of 'pettishness, deceit, equivocation, sullenness, indolence, vanity, prodigality, &c.' pervaded every stratum.[70] In the 1870s and 1880s there was a flood of such comment about colonial children. Most of this criticism seems to have been prompted by the 'larrikin' as the colonial street rough was called. The word, apparently coined in Australia in 1870 or slightly earlier, helped to focus concern.[71] Almost everyone who tried to explain larrikinism declared that the chief cause was lack of discipline in the colonial family. R.E.N. Twopeny believed that because colonial parents refused to restrict their children 'Young Australia' was so assertive as to be obnoxious. For Twopeny, writing in the early 1880s, the relationship between parents and children was 'undeniably the weak point of family life in the colonies'.[72] Another typical comment was published in the Sydney *Bulletin*: 'It is the mother and father who are to blame, first, last and always. The licence that is allowed children in this country is simply scandalous. From high to low, in all households, the children seem to be the first and the parents nowhere.'[73]

Bishop Perry complained in 1870 that 'many pious parents' made a 'manifest failure' of training their children.[74] It was in fact quite usual for colonial commentators to assume that Protestant churchgoing families lacked discipline. Nor were Catholic families exempted from criticism by Catholic leaders. In 1862 Archbishop Polding spoke of his grief at seeing children 'indulged in all that they craved; permitted, unpunished and uncorrected, to fly off into passion, or to become sulky and pettish when refused what

they have pettishly asked.'[75] Bishop James Moore in 1903 considered it necessary to remind Catholics in the Ballarat diocese to
'strive energetically' against the 'spirit of independence' so characteristic of life in Australia by cultivating reverence for authority
and 'by enforcing a noble and generous docility that so well
becomes young people.'[76] Father Linus, C. P., giving a Catholic
Evidence Guild lecture on the family in Sydney in 1927, ex-
claimed, 'What strikes with astonishment a stranger coming to
this country is the attitude adopted by children to their parents.
They talk to them in a bold and disrespectful manner, which
would not be tolerated in the home countries.' In Linus's view a
spirit of independence from lawful authority was thus developed
and this led on to wilful disobedience.[77]

All this criticism is insufficient to establish that family life in the
colonies was peculiarly weak. Jessie Ackermann, an American
who travelled widely in Australia before the First World War,
stressed the strength of family feeling that she found and thought
it hardly equalled among the Scots.[78] A researcher who interviewed a small group of Australians who were growing up before
the First World War uncovered a similar picture.[79] The mistake
made by those who talked about the decay of the colonial family
was to equate a strong family with tight discipline and submissive
children. Children were more independent and self-confident but
not necessarily at the expense of family cohesion. Edward
Wakefield, writing of New Zealand, perspicaciously observed that
'the alleged want of respect of children towards their parents is
more in appearance than in reality. Children in the colony are at
once more companions of their parents than at home, and more
independent of them. They learn from an early age to think for
themselves and to do a great many things for themselves which
their parents would do for them in old countries.'[80] It seems that
the same thing happened with children as with women: in the
new colonies where everything had to be created from scratch, a
premium was put on resourcefulness and capacity to help with the
manifold tasks of pioneering. Need both brought forward ability
irrespective of age or sex and led to a higher valuation of the
proven helper.[81]

As life became more settled in the colonies, however, authoritarianism within the family was not re-established. The explanation seems to be that Australia and New Zealand shared in a
movement occurring in many parts of the Western world towards
a democratization of the family. This second factor was superim-
posed upon the effect produced by specifically colonial pioneering
conditions. Few nineteenth-century colonial commentators could

see this because they were unable to observe the family free from an urge to make simple-minded and moralistic contrasts between the colonies and home. One of the exceptions was Charles Strong. He remarked in 1877 how the mighty movement towards untrammelled liberty and independence in many spheres of life was affecting family cohesion. According to Strong, in new countries this 'democratic wave' was 'more marked, though not, perhaps, on the whole, more remarkable, than in the old world'.[82]

The important point, though, for the present discussion is not the explanation for the continuing democratization of family relationships in Australia and New Zealand; it is the fact of democratization itself. The testimony of the Reverend Professor A. P. Elkin is especially powerful in this regard, since Elkin was an anthropologist with a special interest in the family and a keen observer of Australian life. Elkin wrote in the 1950s: 'If the grandparents of today compare the attitude and behaviour of the members of their grandparents' and parents' generations with their own attitudes and behaviour and with that of their children, they will realize generally a decrease of the authoritarian approach.'[83]

The discussion so far has reached the conclusion that there was probably a long-term decline of parental authoritarianism within Australasian families, and this as a matter of practice, as well as theory. Thus the second question becomes a real one: did the decline of the authoritarian approach within the family adversely affect the churches?

The more authoritarian parental style of the mid-Victorian period benefited the Protestant churches. In one respect the benefit was quite direct and straightforward: pious parents who had tight control over their children would ensure that they attended church and Sunday school and could be relied upon to powerfully influence their children towards church membership as they grew older. More speculatively, a strong parental authority also aided church authority indirectly, for the two reinforced each other in subterranean fashion, intuited rather than analysed by contemporaries.[84] A parent who laid down the law for his child mirrored the church which laid down the law for its members. The child was told to be punctual and clean; the church member was told that drunkenness or profanity was inconsistent with a Christian walk or that those who knew not Christ would perish in eternal torment. Congruence between the two kinds of authority is hinted at in terms used of the church and its clergy. Catholics talked of 'mother' church and of the priest as 'father'. Protestants too could refer to their church leaders as 'fathers'. Protestants sometimes referred to fathers leading family prayers as priests.

The deep, hidden affinity between the two kinds of authority nearly broke the surface when the theological justification for a child learning to obey was given. Mother and father were said to stand in the place of God for the child. This was very close to saying that the parents mediated the authority of the church, for it was the church which claimed to disclose the will and presence of God in the preaching of the Word and the administration of the sacraments. Of course in Protestantism there has always been a lively tradition that the church could fail to declare the will of God or even oppose it. Nevertheless in the early and mid-Victorian periods the evangelical denominations did exercise considerable discipline over their members and did claim to define true doctrine. Both claims were premised on the assumption that for practical purposes the church stood in the place of God or mediated God, just as the parent was supposed to do for the child. Since church and parent were so bound together it was only natural that churchmen should magnify parental authority.

A decline of authoritarianism within Protestant families helped to erode the hold of Protestant churches over their adherents. Young people came to exercise increasing control over their own lives. Of course this did not necessarily always work against the churches. Young people might freely choose to throw themselves into some form of church life, and this notably did occur in the Bible Class movement. But for many, increasing autonomy facilitated a withdrawal from church influence that had not been possible before. To say the same thing from the point of view of the Protestant churches, freedom issued in licence.

By the 1890s there were numerous complaints that young males were shying away from assuming the responsibilities of church membership.[85] The Reverend Dr Michael Watt was adamant that a decline of parental authority had fostered this new and disturbing trend. In a report to the Otago and Southland Presbyterian Synod he urged that parents 'should grasp the reins of family government more tightly'.

A wretched individualism has crept into modern religious life, in virtue of which the father thinks he ought to leave his children to decide for themselves points of duty which he, as the father, ought to decide for them. Many parents who are religious people themselves, consider it too great an interference with the liberty of conscience of their children to bring pressure to bear upon them when they have come to mature years to complete their church-membership, and thereby take over upon themselves the responsibilities their parents assumed on their behalf when they were infants. We have heard of parents allowing their children to select the Sabbath school they attend, and even the congregation with which they unite in worship, a different congregation from that to which the parents themselves belong. Nothing but evil can come from domestic anarchy of this kind. The solidarity of the family, its unity of action ought to be maintained in its worship of God as well as in all its secular relations.[86]

Another Presbyterian minister charged in 1896 that many children attended church and Sabbath school and Bible class 'just as they please, and when they please'.[87] A few years later a Presbyterian committee reported that some young people were passing out of church life altogether after their parents had allowed them to become irregular in church attendance.[88]

The trend was towards self-regulation of belief as well as of behaviour. As early as 1877 Charles Strong in Melbourne detected an unwillingness on the part of Christian parents to teach their children doctrine. For Strong it was not a simple matter of parents abdicating in the face of their children's self-assertion. Parents were less confident in this area because they were losing certitude about what was religious truth. Also, Strong charged, parents wanted to give up their erstwhile feudal dominance out of selfishness; it was easier for them not to assume the responsibility. Nevertheless, Strong contended that there was strong pressure from the children themselves: parents could not prevent them from thinking and reading and could not even if they had wished dictate their creeds.[89]

Until very recent years girls seem to have been less affected than boys by this long process. Nevertheless, it would seem impossible that girls too were not powerfully influenced, and it is up to future researchers to show how. It may be that the 1920s were especially critical. At an address at a New Zealand Bible Class conference in the mid-1920s, Mrs Thomson emphasized the growing self-assertiveness of girls with whom Bible Class leaders had to deal, something she associated with 'the slackening of parental control and the loss of conventions'. She thought the adolescent girl of the day freer even than the girl of a few years before. The change could, she said, be seen in fashion; the girl had burnt the trammels of her flannel petticoat both physically and mentally. The response which Mrs Thomson recommended indicates just how far in her view had been the inroads made by the individualizing spirit. It could not be stamped out, only assisted so that when it was given free play the truth might authenticate itself.

> We must learn to respect the individuality of the girl. What is truth for us may not necessarily be truth for her yet. We cannot give our experience to her. We cannot say, 'We have a rule for our life, and it must be your rule, too.' We should plead with her to test all things for herself, and when she has found the truth to hold by it. This is the only way that will tell now. It is a free age.[90]

In 1922 Father J. M. Cusack remarked that what he regarded as the good old-fashioned home was 'going, or gone'.[91] Yet my impression is that Catholic spokespeople like Cusack still had more to say about the authority of father and mother within the home than their Protestant counterparts. Gone were the days when any Protestant or Catholic churchman could ask for absolute obedience within the home, but the Catholic commentators retained more of the old spirit in their injunctions. Cusack, for instance, while conceding that the father should use discretion – some children responded best to encouragement and to small acts of kindness – also insisted that when the father gave orders they were to be respected without discussion. This difference of emphasis and tone in the public statements may well have mirrored differences in Catholic and Protestant parental attitudes. In a survey conducted in 1966 a large sample of Australians was asked whether they agreed or disagreed with the statement that the most important thing for a child to learn is to obey rather than to think for himself. To judge by the responses Protestant parents were substantially less authoritarian in their approach to child-rearing. Sixty-two per cent of Catholics who had primary or some secondary education agreed that it was more important for a child to learn to obey. Forty-seven per cent of non-Catholics who had primary or some secondary education agreed that it was more important for a child to learn to obey.[92]

The material we have been looking at in this chapter has been diffuse and rather complicated. It may help to summarise. So far as contraception is concerned there was a demonstrable and revolutionary change in both Protestant and Catholic *behaviour*. Protestant official *teaching* against contraception was passing away by 1930, the Catholic line held firm. Regarding family worship the evidence is good enough to allow us to claim a measure of decline in Methodist and Presbyterian homes between 1860 and 1930: amongst Catholics there was a substantial improvement from a very low level about 1860 – just how substantial that improvement was is anybody's guess. Protestant ministers in the 1920s were no longer talking at all about the authority of the parent as being near-absolute as some had around 1860; nor was the earlier link being made between the authority of God and the authority of the parent. This change in Protestant teaching was associated with a shift towards a less authoritarian approach by churchgoing parents within the home. Among the Catholics change may have been less pronounced both in ideas regarding authority in the home and in actual behaviour.

So taking together the three areas we have some large questions. How is it that the Catholic population managed to a degree to be different? Or to look at the evidence another way, why were Catholics not *more* different, either in teaching or behaviour? Regarding the Protestants there is above all perhaps the puzzle of how so much change occurred in sixty or so years. These are of course questions which might well be asked of Sunday observance, of revivalism and of doctrine. It is time to see if it is possible to make sense of the whole.

CONCLUSION

The changes in Protestant religion that have been discussed were gradual and cumulative. The chapter on Sunday provides the best documented and clearest example of this. From the late 1860s there was a spread of liberal attitudes to Sunday observance and a deepening of the intensity with which these liberal attitudes were held. Churchgoers moved from accepting to questioning strict observance, then to an ever greater readiness to engage in leisure activities on a Sunday. By the late 1890s many churchgoers had begun to make the shift from regular to intermittent attendance at Sunday worship, a trend which became more pronounced in the following decades. It was not possible to provide so comprehensive a picture of the development of changes in doctrine. Nevertheless, the case study of one denomination did show an ever more thoroughgoing and more widespread rejection of dogma. The democratization of Protestant family relationships was a long process, as was the shift towards smaller families. There was a gradual breakdown in the distinction in the Protestant 'dissenting' churches between members and non-members. To judge by the waning success of the revivalists among the Methodists, the revival impulse weakened steadily in the Protestant churches from the late 1880s. Even in the 1860s it was not as strong as it had been in England between about 1790 and 1840. It cannot be claimed that there was a substantial decline over many years in the practice of family worship by Protestant churchgoers – probably they never practised family worship on a large scale at any time in the colonies. Yet even family worship represents only a partial exception to the rule of gradual change, since there was a waning emphasis by Protestant church leaders on the ideal.

Each process of change involved a weakening of some kind of corporate control over individual Protestants. The individual's opportunities for self-regulation were thereby increased (and, equally, opportunities for receiving support from the religious group were thereby diminished). To be specific, the waning of local revivals diminished the Protestant churches' control over their young people. This was so because the revival meeting was *par excellence* an opportunity for group pressure to be exercised over the children of members and to integrate them into the life of the group. This is not to gainsay the deep personal assent to the Christian faith which a conversion at a revivalist meeting sometimes brought. But from the point of view of a local church, conversion into its membership was all the more effective because

167

it was so personal. The blurring of the line between members and non-members in the Protestant churches helped to diminish the responsibilities of members and the effectiveness of group discipline of the individual member. The relaxation of expectations regarding the observance of the Sunday rest, both within the local churches and within society at large, increased the individual's opportunities for leisure. The disintegration of dogma marked the eclipse of corporate control over what individual churchgoers believed about God and his ways with man. The lifting of the Protestant denominations' condemnation of birth control made it easier for churchgoers to decide for themselves how many children they were going to have.

The anthropological notion of the cultural pattern may help to deepen understanding of what happened. Professor William H. McNeill has defined a cultural pattern as 'a cluster of repeatable forms of behaviour that complement one another in mutually supportive ways and give definition and a limited predictability to aspects of human conduct caught up in and conforming to such a pattern.'[1] Strict Sunday observance, acceptance of the dogma of eternal punishment, stress on parental authority and so on were mutually supportive. As the different corporate controls over the religion of the individual were weakened at least some of the different changes reinforced and accelerated one another. Religious change was systemic.

But why did the religious changes occur? And to what extent were they dependent upon wider social changes? It should be evident by now that these natural and important questions cannot be answered solely or even mainly by reference to the history of Australia and New Zealand. For colonial religion was derivative through and through. Even the propellants of religious change were generated in the old world. As surely as starlings on the perimeter of a flock wheel under the influence of mysterious pulls from the centre, so the colonists moved in accord with religious signals from London, Edinburgh and Dublin. Contact between the colonies and these metropolitan centres was continuous through migration, through visits both ways and above all through the written word – letters, newspapers, books, periodicals. Virtually instantaneous cultural transmission from the British Isles to the antipodes occurred on 10 December 1934 with the first airmail service between Britain and Australia. But the time lag had always been negligible since the introduction during the 1850s of clipper ships sailing the Great Circle route.[2] In England on 6 March 1861 the Reverend Dr Pusey wrote a letter to the *Guardian* about a controversial religious book *Essays and Reviews*. Pusey's letter was given in full in the issue of 20 June 1861 of the Adelaide *Church Chronicle*.[3] Thus behind the decline of colonial Protestantism lies what one historian has called 'the making of post-Christian Britain'.[4]

Cultural diffusion from the metropolitan centres does not explain every aspect of colonial religion. Religious innovations spread unevenly in the new world – fastest in the cities and among the well educated and often slowly among women and farmers. It is therefore necessary to call upon local circumstances to explain variations in the degree and speed of religious change.[5] In remote and sparsely settled districts religious behaviour continued to be almost wholly shaped by local circumstances.

The Catholic experience was both like and unlike the Protestant one. Catholic institutions – churches, schools, devotional associations, and so forth – remained well supported by the laity long after Protestant church attendances began to decline. Yet, a covert Catholic individualism was displayed. Against the rules of the Catholic body, there were Catholics who married Protestants, Catholics who practised birth control, Catholics who did not go to mass, Catholics who disbelieved in hell.

These two Catholic features of support for corporate life and a flouting of its norms are easily reconciled if it is remembered that the Catholic church in Australia and New Zealand was on the one hand cast in an Irish and Roman mould and on the other operating in a pluralist setting. The old-world inheritance was hostile to the exercise of personal autonomy. The Cullenite bishops brought with them an authoritarian style and their practice of it had an inhibiting effect upon the laity. Even more important was that most of the nineteenth-century immigrants were from peasant families. These people were poorly educated and poorly equipped for publicly disputing the rulings of their priests and bishops. In the view of Horace Plunkett, the religion of the Irish peasant was characterized by a 'repression of individuality'.[6] In the new world, however, these Irish influences were offset by others. Catholics were surrounded by Protestants of every degree of church involvement and none at all. By the last quarter of the nineteenth century unsettlement of belief was in the air that everyone breathed. Non-Catholics also decided for Catholics, especially Catholic men, the standards by which self-worth was defined. Religious orthodoxy in behaviour and belief rated very lowly. In consequence, many colonial Catholics came to make in some way or degree a covert rejection of the standards and teachings of their church.

Today the Catholic church in Australia and New Zealand is in ferment. There are many voices. It all seems so different to the monolithic front that the Catholic church in Australia and New Zealand presented to the world in the days before the Second Vatican Council. And it is different. But the public questioning of today is no surprise in the light of what has long been the case in private.

This is not to say that in the years before the Second Vatican Council every Catholic in Australia was a crypto-Protestant. Some Catholics did behave as though their church never existed; some gave unquestioning obedience to what their bishops and priests asked of them; many, perhaps most, fell in between. A related point is that not all Catholics were equally involved in the life of the Catholic church. In 1932 Father J. M. Cusack distinguished three concentric spheres of involvement in parish life which, he claimed, were 'easily enough recognized almost everywhere'. Those of the inner sphere came to mass, frequented the sacraments, joined the parish societies and took the Catholic papers. The tendency with these persons was to increasing involvement and fervour. The second sphere, that of the half-hearted, was also large. Those who belonged to it went to mass regularly and would almost never eat meat on Friday. But these people would have nothing to do with the Catholic societies and never took a Catholic paper or read a Catholic book. They did not follow the church's teaching about birth control and some held privately that there was no hell. With them the tendency was centrifugal towards the third sphere. This was composed, went on Cusack, of those who hardly ever went to mass and who hardly even knew about the Catholic societies. They kept the name Catholic and would perhaps fight for their church if it were attacked, but for all other purposes they had ceased to belong. The same Catholics would say that any form of belief was as good as another so long as a person led a good life. Still further out were Catholics who had dropped even nominal allegiance.[7]

Addressing a meeting of South Australian students in the mid-1920s, an English-born Congregationalist, the Reverend E. S. Kiek, expressed his anxiety about the morality of those who put themselves outside the churches. There were decent people who did not go to church, Kiek agreed, but these people were living on Christian capital accumulated down the ages. The first generation outside the Church remembered much of what they had been taught so there was still a good deal of 'diffused Christian sentiment' and a good deal of Christian practice. The second generation would remember less. The third generation would be pagan.[8] Few Australians and New Zealanders were as articulate as Kiek but the feeling that morality was dependent upon the churches seems to have been widely shared. The McIntyres, as a result of a sociological investigation in the early 1940s, formed the impression that in Victorian country towns, the majority considered the church to be part of the established order of things and the thought of it not being there frightened them. They frequently encountered the feeling expressed by the man who said to them that it was just as well others were better at supporting the church than he was because 'if we had no church we'd have no morals' and 'be just like wild beasts'.[9] Kenneth Dempsey's findings from his study of one rural community in New South Wales are similar. Dempsey interviewed 109 Methodists in 1966 and found that they understood the role of the church 'in fundamentally moralistic terms'. Fewer than a dozen ascribed to the church a theological role. The bulk thought of it as a useful agency for teaching the young 'the importance of such things as kindness, courtesy, frugality, and honesty, and the virtues of participation in family life'.[10]

This moral emphasis might be interpreted as valuing the churches just for their social utility. This consideration has certainly been a powerful one from the time that the early governors tried to render convicts docile by mustering them for Sunday services. Yet it is a curious tribute to religion on the part of the worldly-minded that the churches should be thought to have this power. Furthermore, attachment to the churches has gone deeper than this. During the 'Religion in Australia' survey in 1966 respondents were presented with six statements about the Church, one of which they were asked to choose as most nearly expressing their own attitude. Not surprisingly only a minority of Protestant respondents, both regular and irregular attenders, chose the description of the Church as the home and refuge of all mankind. A more interesting finding was that the most popular description of the Church amongst Protestant respondents was not the one which implied the social utility of religion but the one which spoke of the Church as standing for the best in human life. Over 40 per cent of Protestants who attended church irregularly preferred this description.[11] The committee which made a confidential report on the condition of New South Wales Congregationalism in 1944 reported that there were 'not a few' associated with the Congregational churches who participated in various church activities and supported them financially but were seldom if ever seen at a Sunday service.[12] Though denominational newspapers and church records have little to say about such people they provided significant support for the churches. Probably the attitude of many Protestant men was reflected in this comment reported by the McIntyres. 'I don't go to church much, although I send along my contributions, you know. The wife and youngsters go, but it's the only day I've got free, and I must say I like to be out in the open air.'[13] Men like this one might easily become troubled if their wives did not go.

All this is suggestive of how deeply institutional Christianity has permeated and conditioned the values of Australians and New Zealanders. The churches were sufficiently strong to ensure that the standards of decency customary in the British Isles were transplanted and preserved for a century or more. But the Protestant churches have proved impotent by another, and more Christian, test: church leaders and churchgoers have not remoulded, on the whole have not even tried to remould, society in the image of the Kingdom of God.

An example of what I have in mind occurred in the early 1930s. As Australians faced the misery of the Great Depression Bishop Burgmann told his fellow Anglicans that the way they responded to the need of their neighbours would probably determine the Church of England's place in the nation for centuries to come. The temptation, thought Burgmann, would be to remain content with the institutional life of the church, ceremonies, doctrines, synods and the like. The truly Christian course was for the Church to go out to the nation and thereby know the cross and the resurrection of Jesus. The Church had to lose herself meeting the needs of 'that seventy five percent ... who are outside all Churches'.[14] Burgmann had the mind of Christ. But Anglican laymen and laywomen did not heed his appeal and they would not have done so even if more of their leaders had spoken as he had.

The Protestant churches were weathercocks of middle class opinion. When they adopted humanitarian causes it was because these had become or were becoming socially acceptable. An example from the 1880s and 1890s is concern about sweating and factory conditions. One or two ministers were ahead of general liberal opinion but the bulk of church leaders only came to condemn the exploitation of labour when there was no sacrifice associated with doing so. An example from today is concern in New Zealand with a bi-cultural or multi-cultural church. But how many were the Protestant church leaders who spoke loudly and pointedly during the late nineteenth century and early in this about the discrimination against coloured people in immigration policies? About the seizure of native lands? About commercial immorality? About gross inequalities in housing, in incomes, in education? Who urged love of enemies in time of war? True, if the leaders had spoken out on these issues probably few churchgoers would have been persuaded. But that in itself testifies to how little the Protestant churches have been able to make a creative, and above all, distinctively Christian impact upon their own people, much less society as a whole.

By and large the Catholic bishops were just as silent on these moral issues. The Catholic bishops had once, on the schools question, dared to lead their people against the mainstream of colonial opinion. But then the existence of the Catholic church itself seemed at stake. The bishops were not prepared for the institutional church to lose itself for the sake of the Kingdom of God any more than were the Protestant leaders. Nor perhaps were ordinary Catholic churchgoers any more ready to respond than their Protestant counterparts. It was as though the Catholic bishops had an unwritten agreement with their people: attend mass regularly, support your parish school, give to the church funds – and we will not make any untoward moral demands upon you. Protestant and Catholic leaders alike were in the habit of defining the Christian faith in narrowly individualistic and moral terms. It was easier for everyone that way.

REFERENCES

I. RELIGION AND THE IMMIGRANTS

1. John C. Caldwell and Lado T. Ruzicka, 'The Australian Fertility Transition: An Analysis', *Population and Development Review*, 4.1, 1976, p. 81; *N. Z. Census*, 1901, Ages of the people, table 12.

2. For the Australasian population in 1830: C. M. H. Clark, *Select Documents in Australian History 1788–1850*, Sydney: Angus and Robertson, 1950, pp. 405, 407, 409; Oliver, *The Oxford History of New Zealand*, p. 50.

3. Professor B. Bailyn, seminar, University of Auckland, 31 July 1984; cited with permission.

4. Thomas Walter Laqueur, *Religion and Respectability: Sunday Schools and Working Class Culture 1780–1850*, New Haven: Yale University Press, 1976, p. 191.

5. Ian Bradley, *The Call to Seriousness: The Evangelical Impact on the Victorians*, London: Cape, 1976, p. 37.

6. ibid., p. 15.

7. Alan D. Gilbert, *Religion and Society in Industrial England: Church, Chapel and Social Change, 1740–1914*, London: Longman, pp. 81–93.

8. ibid., pp. 31, 37.

9. W. S. F. Pickering, 'The 1851 Religious Census – A Useless Experiment?', pp. 393–94.

10. R. B. Walker, 'Religious Changes in Nineteenth Century Liverpool', *Journal of Ecclesiastical History*, 19.2, 1968, p. 203.

11. Obelkevich, *Religion and Rural Society*, p. 156.

12. Soloway, *Prelates and People*, pp. 50–52.

13. Obelkevich, *Religion and Rural Society*, pp. 139–40.

14. Keith Thomas, *Religion and the Decline of Magic*, London: Weidenfeld and Nicolson, 1971, p. 166.

15. Robert Currie, Alan Gilbert and Lee Horsley, *Churches and Churchgoers; Patterns of Church Growth in the British Isles since 1700*, Oxford: Clarendon Press, 1977, p. 141.

16. Obelkevich, *Religion and Rural Society*, ch. 6.

17. Inglis, *Churches and the Working Classes in Victorian England*, p. 3; Soloway, *Prelates and People*, pp. 445–46.

18. K. S. Inglis, 'Patterns of Religious Worship in 1851', *Journal of Ecclesiastical History*, 11.1, 1960, pp. 74–86.

19. McLeod, *Class and Religion in the Late Victorian City*, ch. 2.

20. Inglis, *Churches and the Working Classes in Victorian England*, p. 20.

21. Burleigh, *A Church History of Scotland*, pp. 311–13.

22. Hugh McLeod, *Religion and the People of Western Europe 1789–1970*: Oxford: Oxford University Press, 1981, p. 107.

23. Drummond and Bulloch, *The Scottish Church 1688–1843*, p. 158.

24. The Disruption and the build-up to it are covered in Burleigh, *A Church History of Scotland* and Drummond and Bulloch, *The Scottish Church 1688–1843*.

25. Andrew L. Drummond and James Bulloch, *The Church in Victorian Scotland 1843–1874*, Edinburgh: St Andrew Press, 1975, pp. 40, 321.

26. Boyd, *Scottish Church Attitudes to Sex, Marriage and the Family*, p. 18.

27. McLaren, *Religion and Social Class*; Boyd, *Scottish Church Attitudes to Sex, Marriage and the Family*.

28. Bowen, *The Protestant Crusade in Ireland, 1800–1870*.

29. John Bossy, *The English Catholic Community 1570–1850*, London: Dayton, Longman and Todd, 1975, pp. 303–13.

30. Connolly, *Priests and People in Pre-Famine Ireland*, pp. 100–08, 135–59.

31. ibid., p. 33.

32. ibid., pp. 36, 90.

33. Larkin, *The Making of the Roman*

Catholic Church in Ireland, deals
exhaustively with episcopal
differences over education.

34. Oliver MacDonagh, *Ireland*,
Englewood Cliffs, New Jersey:
Prentice Hall, 1968, p. 44.

35. Larkin, 'Economic Growth,
Capital Investment and the Roman
Catholic Church in Nineteenth-
Century Ireland', p. 877.

36. Connolly, *Priests and People in Pre-
Famine Ireland*, p. 23.

37. ibid., p. 33.

38. Larkin, 'The Devotional
Revolution in Ireland 1850–75'.
Larkin's concept of a devotional
revolution is contested by Keenan,
*The Catholic Church in Nineteenth-
Century Ireland*.

39. D. W. Miller, 'Irish Catholicism
and the Great Famine', *Journal of
Social History*, 9.1, 1975, pp.
83–88.

40. Keenan, *The Catholic Church in
Nineteenth-Century Ireland*, p. 99.

41. Larkin, 'The Devotional
Revolution in Ireland 1850–75',
p. 636.

42. Waldersee, *Catholic Society in New
South Wales 1788–1860*, p. 271;
L. L. Robson, *The Convict Settlers
of Australia*, Melbourne:
Melbourne University Press, 1965,
p. 4.

43. Oliver, *The Oxford History of New
Zealand*, p. 50.

44. Grocott, *Convicts, Clergymen and
Churches*, p. 28.

45. M. B. and C. B. Schedvin, 'The
Nomadic Tribes of Urban Britain:
A Prelude to Botany Bay', *HS*,
18.71, 1978, p. 254.

46. Grocott, *Convicts, Clergymen and
Churches*, pp. 49, 56.

47. ibid., pp. 55–57.

48. O'Farrell, *The Catholic Church and
Community in Australia*, pp. 42–43.

49. Pike, *Paradise of Dissent*, pp. 21–
22.

50. ibid., esp. p. 130; 'George Fife
Angas', in *ADB*, vol. 1; Clark,
A History of Australia, vol. 3, chs
3–4.

51. The population of Otago was less
than 4000 in 1856: Brooking, *And
Captain of Their Souls*, p. 117. For

a detailed account of the genesis of
the Otago settlement, McLintock,
The History of Otago.

52. James Hight and C. R. Straubel
(eds), *A History of Canterbury*, vol.
1, Christchurch: Christchurch
Centennial Association, p. 217–18.

53. Henry Brett and Henry Brook,
The Albertlanders, Auckland: Brett
Publishing Co., 1927, esp. pp. 16,
23.

54. Clark, *A History of Australia*, vol.
3, pp. 66–68; D. Van Abbe, 'A. L.
C. Kavel and G. D. Fritzsche', in
ADB, vol. 2.

55. G. H. Schofield (ed.), *A Dictionary
of New Zealand Biography*, vol. 2,
Wellington: Department of
Internal Affairs, 1940, pp. 38–39;
J. S. Gully, 'Norman McLeod',
in A. H. McLintock (ed.),
Encyclopaedia of New Zealand, vol.
2, Wellington: Government
Printer, 1966, pp. 372–74; Eric
Richards, 'Varieties of Scottish
Emigration in the Nineteenth
Century', *HS*, 21.85, 1985,
pp. 485–86.

56. McLay, *James Quinn*, pp. 48–49;
H. J. Gibney, 'James Quinn', in
ADB, vol. 5.

57. For the denominations of the
European-born of the Australian
population in 1911, *Australia
Census*, 1911, vol. 1, p. 152.
Moran, *History of the Catholic
Church in Australasia*, p. 364 gives
figures on the national extraction
of Catholics in the diocese of
Goulburn, apparently for around
1880.

58. McConville, 'Emigrant Irish and
Suburban Catholics', thesis, p. 42.

59. Larkin, 'The Devotional
Revolution in Ireland 1850–75',
pp. 651–52; the percentage was
calculated from the figures given in
McConville, 'Emigrant Irish and
Suburban Catholics', thesis, p. 42.

60. Russel Ward, *The Australian
Legend*, Melbourne: Oxford
University Press, 1958, p. 44.

61. Blainey, *The Rush That Never
Ended*, chs 10–11.

62. *Christian Advocate and Wesleyan
Record*, 10 Oct. 1861, p. 70.

63. John Metcalfe, 'Alexander Harris', in *ADB*, vol. 1.

64. James Bertram (ed.), *New Zealand Letters of Thomas Arnold the Younger*, London: Oxford University Press, 1966, pp. 207–19.

65. Chadwick, *The Victorian Church*, Part I, p. 487; Peter Lineham, 'Freethinkers in Nineteenth-Century New Zealand', *NZJH*, 19.1, 1985, pp. 63–64.

66. R. B. Madgwick, *Immigration into Eastern Australia, 1788–1851*, Sydney: Sydney University Press, 1937, p. 243.

67. Pike, *Paradise of Dissent*, pp. 181, 312, 517.

68. Serle, *The Golden Age*, p. 386.

69. ibid., pp. 386–87.

70. *South Australia Censuses*, 1846, 1855; Pike, *Paradise of Dissent*, p. 517.

71. *Statistics of New Zealand*, 1858, table 5.

72. David Fitzpatrick, 'Irish Emigration in the Later Nineteenth Century', *Irish Historical Studies*, 22.86, 1980, p. 132, n.13.

73. Coughlan, 'The Coming of the Irish to Victoria', p. 84.

74. Patrick O'Farrell, 'Writing the General History of Australian Religion', *JRH*, 9.1, 1976, p. 70.

II. IN A NEW WORLD

1. *Gleaner*, 19 Feb. 1848, p. 43.

2. *Proceedings of the Synod of the Presbyterian Church of Otago and Southland*, 1890, p. 35.

3. E.g. Gregory, *Church and State*, pp. 90–91; Kent, *Christian Life in Australia*, pp. 7–8; *Australian Christian World*, 30 July 1886, p. 281.

4. Hurley, 'Some Reasons why Catholics Lose Their Faith in New Zealand'; Phelan, 'The Irish Abroad: The Church in Australia'.

5. *Freeman's Journal*, 12 Jan. 1861, p.[2].

6. O'Farrell, *Letters from Irish Australia*, ch. 3; Brooking, *And Captain of Their Souls*, p. 66; Australasian Wesleyan Methodist Church, *Minutes of Annual Conference*, 1862, p. 34; *N. Z. Presbyterian*, 1 Feb. 1884, p. 153.

7. Kent, *Christian Life in Australia*, pp. 7–8.

8. McLintock, *The History of Otago*, p. 228.

9. Brooking, *And Captain of Their Souls*, p. 152.

10. *Christian Advocate and Southern Observer*, Nov. 1859, p. 67.

11. Kiddle, *Men of Yesterday*, p. 103.

12. Inglis, *The Australian Colonists*, p. 77.

13. *Gleaner*, 4 March 1848, p. 69.

14. Kiddle, *Men of Yesterday*, pp. 112–13; *Standard*, March 1860, p. 34; for Sunday as a 'handy day' John Collie, *The Story of the Otago Free Church Settlement*, Dunedin: Presbyterian Book Room, [1948], p. 59.

15. Grocott, *Convicts, Clergymen and Churches*, pp. 159, 164, 196.

16. *Report of the First New Zealand Church Congress Christchurch, May, 1923*, Christchurch: T. E. Fraser, 1929, p. 153.

17. *Reports of the Church Society for the Diocese of Sydney*, 1859, pp. 36–38.

18. Bruce A. W. Beckett, *A History of the Parish of Banks Peninsula, 1859–1959*, Auckland: Church Army Press, 1960, pp. 3–4. I owe this reference to Rev. W. Limbrick.

19. Matthews, *A Parson in the Australian Bush*, pp. 16–17, 121–22.

20. Wyatt, *A History of the Diocese of Goulburn*, pp. 219–20.

21. F. B. Boyce, *Fourscore Years and Seven: The Memoirs of Archdeacon Boyce . . .*, Sydney: Angus and Robertson, 1934, pp. 36–39.

22. H. T. Purchas, *A History of the English Church in New Zealand*, Christchurch: Simpson and Williams, 1914, pp. 220–21.

23. Percival, 'Methodism: Past and Present', p. 68.

24. *Month*, March 1920, p. 13.

25. Alison Alexander, 'Henry Hopkins and George Clarke: Two Tasmanian Non-

conformists', *Tasmanian Historical Research Association Papers and Proceedings*, 28.34, 1982, p. 118.

26. Watsford, *Glorious Gospel Triumphs*, p. 135.
27. Wyatt, *A History of the Diocese of Goulburn*, p. 160.
28. Buller, *Forty Years in New Zealand*, pp. 443–44.
29. Matthews, *A Parson in the Australian Bush*, p. 7.
30. V. A. Edgeloe, 'Sir James Fergusson', in *ADB*, vol. 4; Walter Phillips, 'Francis William Cox' in *ADB*, vol. 3.
31. *Australasian Baptist Magazine*, March 1859, pp. 172–76.
32. *Christian Advocate and Southern Observer*, 1 Dec. 1858, p. 50.
33. Cambridge, *Thirty Years in Australia*, pp. 43–44.
34. *The Thames Journals of Vicesimus Lush, 1868–1882*, (ed.) Alison Drummond, Christchurch: Pegasus, 1975, p. 108. The hireling comment is from *Church Gazette*, April 1873, p. 54. For other evidence of clerical resentment, *Church of England Messenger*, 11 Sept. 1888, pp. 11–12; Ruth Teale, 'By Hook and By Crook. The Anglican Diocese of Bathurst 1870–1911', MA thesis, University of Sydney, 1967, p. 271 and Appendix A.
35. Rollo Arnold, 'The Patterns of Denominationalism in Later Victorian New Zealand' in Christopher Nichol and James Veitch (eds), *Religion in New Zealand*, 2nd edn, Wellington: Christopher Nichol, 1983, p. 101.
36. Morley, *The History of Methodism in New Zealand*, pp. 413–14.
37. Bollen, *Australian Baptists*, pp. 18–19.
38. *Jubilee of Congregationalism in South Australia. Report of Intercolonial Conference Held in Adelaide, September, 1887*, Adelaide, 1887, p. 36; *Victorian Independent*, July 1897, p. 159.
39. Connolly, *Priests and People in Pre-Famine Ireland*, p. 25.
40. Bowen, *The Protestant Crusade in Ireland*, ch. 4; Connolly, *Priests and People in Pre-Famine Ireland*, pp. 86–87.
41. Coughlan, 'The Coming of the Irish to Victoria', pp. 78–83; Anon., *Waifs and Strays of Sea Life and Adventure Picked up between Liverpool and Melbourne*, Melbourne: Michael T. Gasson, 1857, p. 21; O'Farrell, *Letters from Irish Australia*, pp. 27, 28–29.
42. O'Farrell, *The Catholic Church and Community in Australia*, p. 82.
43. Mazzaroli, 'The Irish in New South Wales', thesis, ch. 1. On Victoria generally, Oliver MacDonagh, 'The Irish in Victoria, 1851–91: A Demographic Essay', *Australian National University Historical Journal*, nos 10 and 11, 1973–74, pp. 26–39.
44. Helen Wilson, *My First Eighty Years*, 3rd edn, Hamilton: Paul's Book Arcade, 1955, ch. 5; Helen Wilson, *Moonshine*, 2nd edn, Hamilton: Paul's Book Arcade, 1956, p. 29.
45. Chris McConville, 'The Victorian Irish: Emigrants and Families, 1851–91', in Grimshaw *et al.*, *Families in Colonial Australia*, pp. 2–4.
46. ibid., pp. 3–4. Mazzaroli, 'The Irish in New South Wales', thesis, p. 24.
47. Erik Olssen and Andrée Lévesque, 'Towards a History of the European Family in New Zealand', in Peggy G. Koopman-Boyden (ed.), *Families in New Zealand Society*, Wellington: Methuen, 1978, p. 5.
48. Hogan, *The Irish in Australia*, p. 165.
49. Chris McConville, 'The Victorian Irish', in *Australia 1888*, Bulletin no. 10, Sept. 1982, p. 71.
50. K. A. Pickens, 'Marriage Patterns in a Nineteenth Century British Colonial Population', *Journal of Family History*, 5.2, 1980, p. 189.
51. M. A. G. Ó Tuathaigh, 'The Irish in Nineteenth Century Britain: Problems of Integration', *Transactions Royal Historical Society*, 5th series, 31, 1981, p. 167.

52. Moran, *History of the Catholic Church in Australasia*, pp. 693, 773; *Austral Light*, 1900, pp. 137–41; *Month*, Jan. 1924, p. 9; Bourke, 'Catholic Fertility in Australia and New Zealand', thesis, pp. 181–82.
53. E.g. *Australia Census*, 1911, vol. 3, part 10, table 2.
54. O'Farrell and O'Farrell, *Documents in Australian Catholic History*, vol. 1, pp. 407–13.
55. Hogan, *The Irish in Australia*, p. 26.
56. *Chaplet and Southern Cross*, 27 May 1871, pp. 220–21. Bishop Geoghegan was also worried: Waldersee, *A Grain of Mustard Seed*, p. 109.
57. Moran, *History of the Catholic Church in Australasia*, p. 619.
58. Wilson, *The Church in New Zealand*, vol. 1, pp. 254–55; O'Sullivan, *An Apostle in Aotearoa*, p. 39; Byrne, *History of the Catholic Church in South Australia*, p. 101; G. H. Jose, *The Church of England in South Australia 1836–1856*, Adelaide: Church Office, 1937, pp. 56–57; *Advocate*, 8 Sept. 1888, p. 16; O'Kane, *A Path is Set*, pp. 4–5.
59. *Victorian*, 14 Nov. 1863, p. 460.
60. *N. Z. Tablet*, 25 Jan. 1884, p. 17.
61. O'Kane, *A Path is Set*, pp. 4–5.
62. O'Sullivan, *An Apostle in Aotearoa*, p. 56.
63. Byrne, *History of the Catholic Church in South Australia*, pp. 30–31.
64. E.g. O'Farrell, *Letters from Irish Australia*, pp. 57–58.
65. George Nadel, *Australia's Colonial Culture*, Melbourne: F. W. Cheshire, 1957, pp. 252–55; Lyons, 'Aspects of Sectarianism in N.S.W.', thesis, pp. 13–18.
66. Buller, *Forty Years in New Zealand*, p. 446.
67. Polding, *The Eye of Faith*, pp. 394–407.
68. *Catholic Times*, 14 Feb. 1890, p. 11.
69. *Chaplet and Southern Cross*, 24 June 1871, p. 236.
70. Archives Catholic Diocese of Auckland, LUC 24–1, Pastoral 12 Oct. 1885, p. 3. See also *Australasian Independent*, 15 May 1902, p. 11; Ruth Schumann, 'The Practice of Catholic Piety in Colonial South Australia', *Flinders Journal of History and Politics*, 9, 1983, p. 10.
71. For a detailed description of how mixed marriages had deleterious consequences according to the bishops, Moran, *History of the Catholic Church in Australasia*, pp. 692–95.
72. *Advocate*, 28 Sept. 1872, p. 16.
73. Grocott, *Convicts, Clergymen and Churches*, p. 193.
74. Moran, *History of the Catholic Church in Australasia*, pp. 139–40.
75. Hurley, 'Some Reasons why Catholics Lose Their Faith in New Zealand'.
76. Waldersee, *Catholic Society in New South Wales 1788–1860*, p. 213. See also e.g. Matthew Quinn to James Murray, 8 Jan. 1867, Irish College Rome Correspondence; Mazzaroli, 'The Irish in New South Wales', pp. 282–95.
77. For an Irish complaint about the French, Simmons, *In Cruce Salus*, p. 112.
78. *Chaplet and Southern Cross*, 29 June 1872, pp. 424–26.
79. O'Farrell, *The Catholic Church and Community in Australia*, pp. 122–23, 133.
80. Margaret M. Pawsey, *The Demon of Discord. Tensions in the Catholic Church in Victoria 1853–1864*, Carlton Vic.: Melbourne University Press, 1982.
81. Simmons, *In Cruce Salus*, pp. 83, 90.
82. James Hennesey, *American Catholics. A History of the Roman Catholic Community in the United States*, Oxford: Oxford University Press, 1981, pp. 75–77, 93–100.
83. Connolly, *Priests and People in Pre-Famine Ireland*, p. 57.
84. Liam Kennedy, 'Profane Images in Irish Popular Consciousness', *Oral History*, 7.2, 1979, pp. 42–47.

85. Connolly, *Priests and People in Pre-Famine Ireland*, p. 56.
86. Connell, *Irish Peasant Society*, p. 145.
87. Livingston, *The Emergence of an Australian Catholic Priesthood*, p. 64.
88. Hurley, 'Some Reasons why Catholics Lose Their Faith in New Zealand', p. 209; see also Long, 'A Word from Australia', p. 656.
89. Fr P. Gleeson, interview, 1983 speaking of a priest friend's experience.
90. *Proceedings of the First Australasian Catholic Congress*, pp. 340–41.
91. E.g. Fr P. Moore to Fr Fortune, 6 Oct. 1875, All Hallows College Correspondence.
92. *Australian Messenger of the Sacred Heart*, April 1891, p. 180.
93. Kent, *Christian Life in Australia*, p. 8.
94. Miles Fairburn, 'Local Community or Atomized Society: The Social Structure of Nineteenth Century New Zealand', *NZJH*, 16.2, 1982, p. 160.
95. *Australasian Independent*, 15 June 1896, p. 115.
96. Hugh Jackson, 'Moving House and Changing Churches: The Case of the Melbourne Congregationalists', *HS*, 19.74, 1980, pp. 74–85.
97. *N.S.W. Independent*, 15 April 1879, p. 58; Congregational Union and Home Mission of South Australia, *Annual Meetings . . .*, 1895, p. 63; Congregational Church, Brighton, Melbourne, *Church News*, May 1896, p. 2; *Victorian Independent*, June 1892, p. 136.
98. E.g. South Australian Wesleyan Methodist Church, *Minutes of Annual Conference*, 1879, p. 34; *New Zealand Presbyterian Church News*, Feb. 1874, p. 170; *Tribune*, 20 Jan. 1900, p. 4.
99. Inglis, *The Australian Colonists*, p. 19.
100. Kiddle, *Men of Yesterday*, pp. 26–27.
101. Mackray, *Revivals of Religion*, pp. 31–32.
102. J. Chandler, *Forty Years in the Wilderness: A Narrative of the Experiences of the Lord's Doings with an Early Colonist . . .*, Hartwell, 1893, p. 140.
103. South Australian Wesleyan Methodist Church, *Minutes of Annual Conference*, 1888, pp. 67–68.
104. O'Farrell and O'Farrell, *Documents in Australian Catholic History*, vol. 1, p. 410.
105. Polding, *The Eye of Faith*, pp. 116–23.
106. ibid., p. 392.
107. Oliver MacDonagh, 'The Irish in Australia: A General View', public lecture, Australian National University, 28 Aug. 1985.
108. *Australia Census*, 1933, *Statistician's Report*, p. 155.
109. Grocott, *Convicts, Clergymen and Churches*, pp. 219–20; Kenneth J. Cable, 'Australia and the Anglican Parson', in St Barnabas's Theological College, Belair, S.A., *Record of the Centenary Celebrations 11th and 12th June 1980 . . .*, n.p., n.d., p. 19; Prentis, 'The Presbyterian Ministry in Australia, 1822–1900, Recruitment and Composition', pp. 58–60.
110. A Layman, *Some Thoughts on the Duties of Christian Colonists in a New Country*, Nelson, 1868, p. 14; Prentis, 'The Presbyterian Ministry in Australia, 1822–1900: Recruitment and Composition', p. 54.
111. Alexis de Tocqueville, *Democracy in America*, London: Oxford University Press, 1946, ch. 27.
112. *N. Z. Presbyterian*, 1 July 1879, pp. 10–12.
113. Lawlor, *The Demanding God*, pp. 52–53.
114. Patrick O'Farrell, 'In Search of the Hidden Ireland', *JRH*, 12.3, 1983, pp. 322–30 places more emphasis than I on the survival of folk practices in Australia. See also Mazzaroli, 'The Irish in New

South Wales', thesis, pp. 278–81.

115. Pryor, *Australia's Little Cornwall*, pp. 165, 108; Blainey, *The Rush That Never Ended*, p. 127.

116. *Proceedings of the Synod of the Diocese of Auckland*, 1863, p. 7.

117. Grocott, *Convicts, Clergymen and Churches*, pp. 218–19.

118. Badger, *The Reverend Charles Strong and the Australian Church*.

119. H. J. Gibney, 'John Alexander Dowie', in *ADB*, vol. 4.

120. *Church Gazette*, Aug. 1875, p. 95, quoting Laurence J. Kennaway, *Crusts, a Settler's Fare due South*, London, 1874.

III. REVIVALISM

1. Mackray, *Revivals of Religion*, p. 33.

2. J. Edwin Orr, *Evangelical Awakenings in the South Seas*, Minneapolis, Minnesota: Bethany Fellowship Inc., 1976, p. 50; *Revival Record*, 2 July 1860, p. 3; 30 July 1860, p. 1.

3. Kent, *Holding the Fort*, pp. 104–05.

4. *Wesleyan Chronicle*, 19 March 1861, p. 37.

5. Special prayers and services for revival continued during 1861 and 1862: *Tasmanian Messenger*, Aug. 1861, p. 62; Sept. 1861, p. 86; Aug. 1862, pp. 375–76.

6. This judgement is based primarily upon a perusal of the files of *Primitive Methodist Miscellany* and *N. Z. Primitive Methodist*. For Primitive camp meetings in S.A., Hunt, *This Side of Heaven*, pp. 161–62.

7. The annual growth rates of the Wesleyans between 1850 and 1890 in S.A. and Victoria are not disgraced when placed alongside the annual growth rates of British and American Methodists 1790–1865. The latter are conveniently set out in Carwardine, *Transatlantic Revivalism*, pp. 46–47.

8. Lineham, *There We Found Brethren*, ch. 4.

9. *South Australian Wesleyan Magazine*, July 1865, pp. 131–33.

10. Watsford, *Glorious Gospel Triumphs*, pp. 119–20.

11. ibid., p. 123.

12. The following account of Taylor is based primarily on Taylor, *Story of My Life*, and newspaper and denominational periodical accounts.

13. Australasian Wesleyan Methodist Church, *Minutes of Annual Conference*, 1864, p. 43.

14. Taylor, *Story of My Life*, pp. 277–78, 320.

15. For a contrary view on Taylor's success, see the article on him, *ADB*, vol. 6.

16. John C. Symons, *Life of the Reverend Daniel James Draper*, London: Hodder and Stoughton, 1870, p. 267.

17. Smith and Blamires, *The Early Story of the Wesleyan Methodist Church in Victoria*, ch. 8, esp. p. 104. James Bickford was also enthusiastic, *An Autobiography of Christian Labour in the West Indies, Demerara, Victoria, New South Wales and South Australia 1838–1888*, London: Charles H. Kelly, 1890, pp. 181–82, 192–93.

18. Lineham, *There We Found Brethren*, pp. 59–62; Gordon Forlong, *The Life of Gordon Forlong*, n.p.: Printed by G.P.H. Society, 1975.

19. Lineham, *There We Found Brethren*, pp. 63–70.

20. Smith and Blamires, *The Early Story of the Wesleyan Methodist Church in Victoria*, p. 99.

21. Taylor, *Story of My Life*, p. 515.

22. Paul F. Bourke, 'Some Recent Essays in Australian Intellectual History', *HS*, 13.49, 1967, p. 101.

23. Pike, *Paradise of Dissent*, chs 11, 15, esp. p. 383; G. A. Wood, 'Church and State in New Zealand in the 1850s', *JRH*, 8.3, 1975, pp. 258–59. The New Zealand government did make land grants.

24. The following account is based on: *Yorke's Peninsula Advertiser*; Hunt, 'The Moonta Revival of 1875'; Hunt, *This Side of Heaven*,

pp. 124–26; Pryor, *Australia's Little Cornwall*; Jim Faull, *Cornish Heritage: A Miner's Story*, published by author, 6 Boundy Rd., Highbury, S.A., 1980; *Primitive Methodist Record*.

25. *Yorke's Peninsula Advertiser*, 27 April 1875.

26. Hunt, *This Side of Heaven*, pp. 124–25.

27. *Yorke's Peninsula Advertiser*, 22 June 1875.

28. Hunt, 'The Moonta Revival of 1875', p. 5.

29. T. A. Coghlan, *Labour and Industry in Australia. From the First Settlement in 1788 to the Establishment of the Commonwealth in 1901*, vol. 2, London: Oxford University Press, 1918, pp. 1034–35, 1040–41.

30. R. B. Walker, 'The Growth and Typology of the Wesleyan Methodist Church in New South Wales, 1812–1901', *JRH*, 6.4, 1971, pp. 337–38.

31. For a model, Paul E. Johnson, *A Shopkeeper's Millennium; Society and Revivals in Rochester, New York, 1815–1837*, New York: Hill and Wang, 1978.

32. E.g.: ibid.; Cross, *The Burned-Over District*; Carwardine, *Transatlantic Revivalism*, esp. pp. 54–56; J. M. Bumsted, 'Religion, Finance and Democracy: The Town of Norton as a Case Study', *Journal of American History*, 47, 1971, pp. 817–31; James Walsh, 'The Great Awakening in the First Congregational Church of Woodbury, Connecticut', *William and Mary Quarterly*, 3rd series, 28, 1971, pp. 543–62.

33. Ward, *Religion and Society in England 1790–1850*, p. 83; Harold Begbie, *Life of William Booth*, vol. 1, London: Macmillan, 1920, pp. 319–22; Shaw, *A History of Cornish Methodism*, p. 120.

34. Smith and Blamires, *The Early Story of the Wesleyan Methodist Church in Victoria*, pp. 209–14. D. A. Cowell provides information on the religious influence of the Cornish in his 'Methodism in New Zealand in the Late Nineteenth Century: Some Interactions of Religion and Society', MA thesis, University of Auckland, 1983.

35. Ward, *Religion and Society in England 1790–1850*, pp. 287–88.

36. Kent, *Holding the Fort*, ch. 3.

37. Cross, *The Burned-Over District*, pp. 4–8, 11, 68.

38. H. R. Taylor, *The Story of a Century: A Record of the Churches of Christ Religious Movement in South Australia, 1846–1946*, Melbourne: Australian Printing and Publishing Co., n.d., pp. 36–37.

39. Phillips, *Defending 'A Christian Country'*, ch. 3.

40. ibid., p. 67.

41. On occasion Taylor did draw crowds of over a thousand: Hunt, *This Side of Heaven*, pp. 92, 118.

42. McLoughlin, *Modern Revivalism*, pp. 159–60.

43. Phillips, *Defending 'A Christian Country'*, pp. 59–62.

44. *Otago Christian Record*, June–Aug. 1874.

45. Lemon, *The Young Man from Home*, p. 151.

46. McLoughlin, *Modern Revivalism*, pp. 272–73.

47. ibid., p. 377.

48. Phillips, *Defending 'A Christian Country'*, pp. 61, 64–65; Hilliard, *Popular Revivalism in South Australia*, pp. 15–16; Broome, *Treasure in Earthen Vessels*, p. 67.

49. See within, Graph 2, p. 116.

50. Hilliard, *Popular Revivalism in South Australia*, p. 30.

51. The text of the pastoral letter is given among other places in *Church of England Messenger*, 10 April 1924, pp. 170–71. Archbishop Lees was conscious of critics within the camp over Hickson: ibid., 12 April 1923, pp. 169–70, 23 Oct. 1924, p. 502. On the Hickson missions generally: Hansen, 'The Churches and Society in New South Wales: 1919–1939', thesis, pp. 176–82; Elkin, *The Diocese of Newcastle*, p.

704; Stewart Mews, 'The Revival of Spiritual Healing in the Church of England 1920–26', in W. J. Sheils (ed.), *The Church and Healing*, Oxford: Basil Blackwell, 1982, pp. 299–331.

52. Inglis, *Churches and the Working Classes in Victorian England*, p. 197.

53. Bolton, *Booth's Drum*, pp. 19–20.

54. Serle, *The Rush to Be Rich*, pp. 147–48.

55. Cambridge, *Thirty Years in Australia*, pp. 287–93.

56. Percival Dale, *Salvation Chariot: A Review of the First Seventy-One Years of the Salvation Army in Australia, 1880–1951*, Melbourne: Salvation Army Press, 1952, chs 2, 6, 7; Bolton, *Booth's Drum*, pp. 75–76; Serle, *The Rush to Be Rich*, p. 148.

57. Robert Sandall, *The History of the Salvation Army*, vol. 3, London: Thomas Nelson, 1955, ch. 1.

58. Bolton, *Booth's Drum*, pp. 63–66.

59. Inglis, *Churches and the Working Classes in Victorian England*, p. 197.

60. Powell, 'The Church in Auckland Society, 1880–1886', thesis, p. 77.

61. Paul Hasluck, *Mucking About: An Autobiography*, Melbourne: Melbourne University Press, 1977, ch. 3.

62. J. C. Pollock, *The Keswick Story: The Authorized History of the Keswick Convention*, London: Hodder and Stoughton, 1964; on holiness revivalism in general as well as Keswick in particular, Kent, *Holding the Fort*, ch. 8.

63. Ernest R. Sandeen, *The Roots of Fundamentalism: British and American Fundamentalism 1800–1930*, Chicago: University of Chicago Press, 1970, pp. 178–79.

64. *Truth and Progress*, 1868–71; Aug. 1874, pp. 90–91; *Spectator*, 16 Oct. 1875, p. 280.

65. *Southern Cross*, 30 Jan. 1875, p. 1.

66. *Missionary at Home and Abroad*, Sept. 1878, pp. 134–35.

67. Phillips, *Defending 'A Christian Country'*, pp. 80–81.

68. Bolton, *Booth's Drum*, p. 61; Phillips, *Defending 'A Christian Country'*, p. 81.

69. For accounts of Grubb's work in Australasia in 1890 and 1891–92: Edward C. Millard, *What God Hath Wrought: An Account of the Mission Tour of the Rev. G. C. Grubb, M. A. (1889–90) ...*, London: E. Marlborough, n.d.; Millard, *The Same Lord*.

70. Watsford, *Glorious Gospel Triumphs*, p. 272; South Australian Wesleyan Methodist Church, *Minutes of Annual Conference*, 1890, p. 82; Hannah MacNeil, *John MacNeil Late Evangelist ... A Memoir by His Wife*, London: Marshall Brothers, 1897, pp. 195–96.

71. *Reports of Addresses at the Christian Convention Geelong, September 15th, 16th, 17th, 1891*, Ballarat, n.d., pp. 83–84.

72. *Proceedings of the Christian Convention for the Deepening of the Spiritual Life, Held in the Centenary Hall, Sydney, January 5th ... 8th, 1892*, Sydney, 1892; *Reports of Addresses at the Christian Convention, Launceston, January 26th ... 29th, 1892*, Ballarat, 1892.

73. Millard, *The Same Lord*, pp. 62, 77, 122, 304.

74. Watsford, *Glorious Gospel Triumphs*, p. 293.

75. Chant, *Heart of Fire*, pp. 25–28.

76. Chant, *Heart of Fire*.

77. For a good study of revivalism in the USA, Dolan, *Catholic Revivalism*.

78. Keenan, *The Catholic Church in Nineteenth-Century Ireland*, pp. 156–58.

79. ibid., p. 158.

80. Press, *Julian Tenison Woods*, pp. 128–69 *passim*.

81. *N. Z. Tablet*, 19 Oct. 1877, p. 7. For his departure, ibid., 23 May 1879, p. 3. I am grateful to Father R. Gaertner C.PP.S., St Charles Seminary, Carthagena, Ohio, for information about Hennebery and also a photo of him. McLay, *James Quinn*, pp. 213–14 deals

with Hennebery in Queensland.

82. *N. Z. Herald*, 2 Dec. 1878, p. [3].
83. ibid., 26 Nov. 1878, p. [2].
84. ibid., 25 Nov. 1878, p. [2].
85. Wilson, *The Church in New Zealand*, vol. 1, p. 169.
86. *N. Z. Tablet*, 7 Dec. 1877, p. 9.
87. ibid., 10 Jan. 1879, p. 7.
88. ibid., 23 May 1879, p. 3.
89. *N. Z. Herald*, 25 Nov. p. [3], 26 Nov. p. [2], 5 Dec. p. [2], 10 Dec. p. [3], 1878.
90. *N. Z. Tablet*, 14 Nov. 1879, pp. 5–9.
91. Golden, *Some Old Waikato Days*, pp. 36–37; Wilson, *The Church in New Zealand*, vol. 1, p. 169.
92. Simmons, *In Cruce Salus*, p. 134.
93. Golden, *Some Old Waikato Days*, pp. 36–37.
94. O'Farrell, *The Catholic Church and Community in Australia*, p. 245.
95. E.g., Fr Benedict Tickell held missions in the Auckland diocese in 1901–05: Archives Catholic Diocese of Auckland LEN 43–1.
96. Moran, *History of the Catholic Church in Australasia*, p. 685.
97. Boland, *Faith of Our Fathers*, p. 66.
98. 'C.SS.R.', 'On Missions'.
99. Cardinal Moran was a critic: S. J. Boland, 'Very Reverend Father Edmund Vaughan C.SS.R. and the Foundation of the Redemptorists in Australia (1882–94)', Doctoral Dissertation, Pontifical Gregorian University, Rome, 1958, pp. 268–77.
100. The pastoral letter following the 1885 Plenary Council referred to 'a difficulty in confessing to the local pastors' which people experienced 'through one cause or another': Moran, *History of the Catholic Church in Australasia*, p. 685.
101. Thomas O'Farrell C.SS.R. to Fr McDonald, 7 Dec. 1882, copy in Catholic Historical Commission Archives, Melbourne, uncatalogued.
102. *Advocate*, 27 June 1885, p. 16.
103. Boland, *Faith of Our Fathers*, p. 56.
104. ibid., pp. 39–41.
105. *Advocate*, 4 July 1885, p. 15.
106. ibid., 23 Oct., pp. 15–16. The original notice is on display in the James Alipius Goold Museum, Fitzroy, Melbourne.
107. *Australian Messenger of the Sacred Heart*, Dec. 1922, p. 653; compare the careful teaching in Polding, *The Eye of Faith*, pp. 217, 358.
108. Fr Benedict Tickell O. P. to Bishop Lenihan, 30 May 1904: Auckland Catholic Diocesan Archives LEN 40–2.
109. Rowell, *Hell and the Victorians*; Kent, *Holding the Fort*, pp. 183–203.
110. Buckley, *Cutting Green Hay*, pp. 31–32.
111. Lawlor, *The Demanding God*, p. 21.
112. Fitzpatrick, *Solid Bluestone Foundations*, pp. 94–95.
113. Black notebook, unidentified on cover, of sermons and sermon sketches, uncatalogued, Redemptorist Archives, Pennant Hills, Sydney.
114. 'C.SS.R.', 'On Missions'.
115. Boland, *Faith of Our Fathers*, p. 58; *Advocate*, 27 Nov. 1886, p. 16.
116. Boland, *Faith of Our Fathers*, p. 64.
117. *N. Z. Tablet*, 25 Jan. 1884, pp. 17–18.
118. Boland, *Faith of Our Fathers*, p. 71.
119. *Advocate*, 23 Oct. 1886, pp. 15–16 reported that 6500 received Holy Communion in the cathedral; the number of confessions must have been far more since great numbers had made their confessions at the cathedral and taken Holy Communion in their own parish church.
120. ibid., 27 Nov. 1886, p. 16.
121. On the shift to maintenance in the USA, Dolan, *Catholic Revivalism*, pp. 54, 62, 182.
122. Boland, *Faith of Our Fathers*, p. 71.
123. Moran, *History of the Catholic Church in Australasia*, p. 524.
124. ibid., p. 535.

125. *N. Z. Tablet*, 21 Dec. 1877, p. 17.
126. ibid., 3 May 1973, pp. 48–49.
127. O'Farrell and O'Farrell, *Documents in Australian Catholic History*, vol. 2, pp. 396–97.

IV. SEPARATION AND IDENTITY

1. A non-sectarian ethos associated with the revivals of 1790–1840 was an important influence in undermining the old exclusiveness. On this non-sectarianism, both in England and the colonies, Jackson, 'Aspects of Congregationalism in South-Eastern Australia', thesis, pp. 28–36.
2. This makes the choice of title an unfortunate one in the case of a recent history of Congregationalism in New Zealand: J. B. Chambers, *A Peculiar People: Congregationalism in New Zealand 1840–1984 . . .*, Levin: Congregational Union of N.Z., 1984.
3. Jackson, 'Aspects of Congregationalism in South-Eastern Australia', thesis, p. 29; *These Hundred Years: A Short History of the Beresford Street Congregational Church, N.Z. 1852–1952*, Auckland, n.d., p. [17].
4. Jackson, 'Aspects of Congregationalism in South-Eastern Australia', thesis, pp. 37–38.
5. ibid., pp. 127–28.
6. Bollen, *Australian Baptists*, pp. 31, 33; Hilliard, 'The City of Churches: Some Aspects of Religion in Adelaide about 1900', p. 15.
7. Michael Petras, *Extension or Extinction: Baptist Growth in New South Wales 1900–1939*, Sydney: Baptist Historical Society of N.S.W., 1983, p. 82; Bollen, *Australian Baptists*.
8. In Melbourne the number of members per class leader increased as follows: 1862 13.4, 1865 14.3, 1870 17.1. The respective figures for Sydney were: 16.9, 16.9, 17.8.
9. *Wesleyan Chronicle*, 20 June 1865, p. 83.
10. Australasian Wesleyan Methodist Church, *Minutes of Annual Conference*, 1871, p. 64.
11. Obelkevich, *Religion and Rural Society*, p. 192; Robert Currie, *Methodism Divided*, London: Faber and Faber, 1968, p. 126; Frederick A. Norwood, *The Story of American Methodism. A History of the United Methodists and Their Relations*, Nashville: Abingdon Press, 1974, pp. 131–32, 235, 251, 257.
12. *N. Z. Wesleyan*, 1 Feb. 1873, p. 17.
13. *Spectator*, 29 May 1875, Supplement; ibid., p. 43.
14. R. B. Walker, 'Methodism in the "Paradise of Dissent", 1837–1900', *JRH*, 5.4, 1969, p. 338.
15. ibid., p. 337; Hunt, *This Side of Heaven*, p. 148.
16. Robert Potter, 'On the Relation of the State to the Ecclesiastical Bodies in Victoria', *Melbourne Review*, 1, 1876, pp. 12–14.
17. This was evident in many conference debates on the class meeting. See also H. T. Burgess, *The Class Meeting*, Adelaide: Wesleyan Book Depot, 1889; William G. Taylor, *Restore the Fellowship of the Church*, Sydney: Epworth, 1912.
18. Hunt, *This Side of Heaven*, p. 145.
19. Percival, 'Methodism: Past and Present', p. 70.
20. *Spectator*, 23 March 1888, pp. 141–42.
21. Erik Olssen, *A History of Otago*, Dunedin: John McIndoe, 1984, pp. 39–40.
22. *Proceedings of the Synod of the Presbyterian Church of Otago and Southland*, 1895, p. 42.
23. David Hilliard, 'The Transformation of South Australian Anglicanism, c. 1880–1930', *JRH*, 14.1, 1986; 'Omicron' estimated that not one in twenty of Church of England congregations were

communicants: *Church Chronicle*, 20 March 1865, p. 743.

24. Mol, *Religion in Australia*, p. 232.

25. The standardization procedure adopted was that recommended by Richard M. Bernard and John B. Sharpless, 'Analysing Structural Influence on Social History Data', *Historical Methods*, 11.3, 1978, pp. 113–21. Iteration was proceeded with until only marginal changes were occurring in the column and row totals.

26. This is obvious to anyone who has perused the denominational periodicals. It is also a necessary inference from the large number of all Protestant denominations who transferred their affiliation upon moving house or, to a lesser extent, upon marriage.

27. Hilliard, 'The City of Churches: Some Aspects of Religion in Adelaide about 1900', p. 8.

28. Porter, *Growing Together*.

29. *Advocate*, 30 Nov. 1918, p. 33, quoted Bourke, 'Catholic Fertility in Australia and New Zealand', thesis, p. 174.

30. The table compares 1891 with 1921 rather than 1933, for which figures are available, because the 1933 census data on religious affiliation are not strictly comparable with those of earlier censuses. At earlier censuses it was not made clear that the census question on religion was not compulsory. When the wording was changed in 1933 no reply was received from 12.8% of the Australian population, compared with a maximum of 0.9% in the period 1891–1921: Walter Phillips, 'Statistics on Religious Affiliation in Australia, 1891–1961', *Australian Historical Statistics*, Bulletin no. 4, 1981, pp. 5–15. It seems likely that among the non-repliers in 1933 out-marriers were much over-represented. This probably artificially pushed up the Catholic in-marriage level in 1933 relative to the earlier censuses. The format of the census question

adopted in 1933 was continued but no census information on mixed marriages is available between 1933 and 1961. For Australia as a whole the Catholic out-marriage level was slightly lower in 1961 than it was in 1933. This could mean that the earlier trend to increasing out-marriage among Catholics of Irish stock had been arrested. Another possible explanation of the change is the arrival of large numbers of European Catholic immigrants after 1947. Apparently, very largely these were Catholic in-marriers; see Mol, *Religion in Australia*, p. 235 and generally ch. 34, for useful information on out-marriage in the 1960s.

31. Colonial bishops who had been students at the Irish College included James and Matthew Quinn, James Murray, Patrick Francis Moran, Thomas Croke: Bowen, *Paul Cardinal Cullen and the Shaping of Modern Irish Catholicism*, pp. 28, 216.

32. John N. Molony, 'Paul Cullen', in *ADB*, vol. 3; McLay, *James Quinn*, p. 247 considers there is doubt in the case of James and Matthew Quinn.

33. Bowen, *Paul Cardinal Cullen and the Shaping of Modern Irish Catholicism*, p. 172.

34. Larkin, *The Making of the Roman Catholic Church in Ireland*; D. H. Akenson, *The Irish Education Experiment*, London: Routledge and Kegan Paul, 1970, pp. 202–14, 250–58, 294–303; E. R. Norman, *The Catholic Church and Ireland in the Age of Rebellion, 1859–1873*, Ithaca, New York: Cornell University Press, 1965, chs 1–2.

35. E. Jane Whately, *Life and Correspondence of Richard Whately, D.D.* (new edn in one volume), London: Longmans Green & Co., 1868, pp. 274, 275. For somewhat different interpretations, Lyons, 'Aspects of Sectarianism in N.S.W.', thesis, appendix VI and Phillips, *Defending 'A Christian*

Country', p. 231. It may be that Whately never in fact said what he was reported to have said. But it was not unnatural that Catholics should take as fact what Whately's daughter reported as being fact.

36. Moran, *History of the Catholic Church in Australasia*, p. 339.
37. ibid., pp. 467–74.
38. Press, *Julian Tenison Woods*, pp. 57, 69.
39. Fogarty, *Catholic Education in Australia 1806–1950*, vol. 1, p. 254.
40. W. G. McMinn, 'James Murray', in *ADB*, vol. 5.
41. O'Farrell, *The Catholic Church and Community in Australia*, p. 174.
42. Fogarty, *Catholic Education in Australia 1806–1950*, vol. 2, pp. 453–55. In 1950 there were 34 381 children in Catholic schools in N.Z., about 75% of the Catholic children of compulsory school age.
43. Moran, *History of the Catholic Church in Australasia*, pp. 871–74.
44. O'Farrell, *The Catholic Church and Community in Australia*, pp. 242–43; William A. Mullins, 'The Development of Catholic Education in New South Wales, Australia, 1900–1966. A Study of Catechetical Approaches . . .', PhD thesis, Catholic University of America, Washington, D.C., 1969.
45. Waldersee, *A Grain of Mustard Seed*, p. 108.
46. Phillips, *Defending 'A Christian Country'*, ch. 8; Simmons, 'Archbishop Francis Redwood: His Contribution to Catholicism in New Zealand', thesis, ch. 4; Ian Breward, *Godless Schools? A Study in Protestant Reactions to the Education Act of 1877*, Christchurch: Presbyterian Bookroom, 1967.
47. Bowen, *The Protestant Crusade in Ireland 1800–1870*, p. 269; Bowen, *Paul Cardinal Cullen and the Shaping of Modern Irish Catholicism*, p. 176; Keenan, *The Catholic Church in Nineteenth-Century Ireland*, p. 95.

48. Livingston, *The Emergence of an Australian Catholic Priesthood*, pp. 69–71.
49. This was suggested to me by Ms Fay Hercock.
50. On Moran, Hugh M. Laracy, 'The Life and Context of Bishop Patrick Moran', MA thesis, Victoria University of Wellington, 1964, pp. 98–103; on the Democratic party, O'Farrell, *The Catholic Church and Community in Australia*, pp. 346–47. See also Davis, *Irish Issues in New Zealand Politics*, ch. 8.
51. Mol, *Religion in Australia*, p. 246.
52. *Proceedings of the First Australasian Catholic Congress*, p. 145. For other defences of mixed marriages by priests: Fitzgerald, 'Is the Church Gaining Converts in Australasia?', pp. 461–62; *Austral Light*, 1907, p. 487.
53. O'Farrell, 'The Irish and Australian History', p. 19.
54. Serle, *The Rush to Be Rich*, p. 237.
55. Moran, *History of the Catholic Church in Australasia*, pp. 631–32.
56. O'Farrell and O'Farrell, *Documents in Australian Catholic History*, vol. 1, p. 340.
57. Campion, *Rockchoppers*, p. 47.
58. Colin McGeorge and Ivan Snook, *Church, State and New Zealand Education*, Wellington: Price Milburn, 1981, p. 13.
59. Campion, *Rockchoppers*, p. 48.
60. Lyons, 'Aspects of Sectarianism in New South Wales', thesis, p. 356.
61. Simmons, *In Cruce Salus*, pp. 106–07.
62. *N. Z. Tablet*, 25 Feb. 1898, p. 27. For similar comments Hurley, 'Some Reasons Why Catholics Lose Their Faith in New Zealand', p. 214; *Australian Messenger of the Sacred Heart*, May 1888, p. 158; Patrick O'Farrell, article on N.Z. Catholicism in the 1940s, *N.Z. Tablet*, 3 May 1973, p. 54; Buckley, *Cutting Green Hay*, pp. 10–15.
63. O'Farrell, 'The Irish and Australian History', p. 19; G. Haines, *Lay Catholics and the Education Question in the*

Nineteenth Century in New South Wales, Sydney: Catholic Theological Faculty, 1976, pp. 24–30; Davis, *Irish Issues in New Zealand Politics*, pp. 67–68, 104–05.

64. Mazzaroli, 'The Irish in New South Wales', thesis, ch. 7.

65. *N.Z. Tablet*, 25 Feb. 1898, p. 27.

66. Oliver MacDonagh, 'Irish Culture and Nationalism Translated: St Patrick's Day, 1888, in Australia' in Oliver MacDonagh, W. F. Mandle and Pauric Travers (eds), *Irish Culture and Nationalism*, New York: St Martin's Press, 1983, pp. 72, 80.

67. J. Whyte, 'Notes from My Uncle's Diary', *Australasian Catholic Record*, 14, 1908, pp. 416–17.

68. Up to 1930 there had been only four Australian-born bishops appointed to Australian dioceses: O'Farrell, *The Catholic Church and Community in Australia*, p. 366. For statistics on the training of priests, Livingston, *The Emergence of an Australian Catholic Priesthood*, pp. 55, 250. N.Z. lagged a little behind Australia as a whole in the proportion of the population who were native-born. It was between the censuses of 1901 and 1911 that the number of European adults born within N.Z. came to exceed the number born outside N.Z.

69. Connolly, *Priests and People in Pre-Famine Ireland*, p. 79.

70. The Fenian scare in N.Z. is handled in Davis, *Irish Issues in New Zealand Politics*, ch. 1. For N.S.W., see e.g., A. W. Martin, *Henry Parkes: A Biography*, Melbourne: Melbourne University Press, 1980, pp. 232–44, 246–50.

71. Murphy and Moynehan, *The National Eucharistic Congress Melbourne*.

72. For the idea of Catholic and Protestant teams, Michael Hogan, 'Whatever Happened to Australian Sectarianism', *JRH*, 13.1, 1984, pp. 83–91.

73. Long, 'A Word from Australia', pp. 654–55.

74. Anon., *The Good, the Unctious, or 'Jelly-fish' and the Bad Catholics . . .*, Sydney: E. J. Dwyer, n.d., pp. 7–8.

75. Rev. Thor Pedersen, personal communication.

76. Simmons, *In Cruce Salus*, pp. 225–27, 236. Bishop Liston, Cleary's coadjutor, was himself to receive many civic honours.

77. Herbert M. Moran, *Viewless Winds: Being the Recollections and Digressions of an Australian Surgeon*, London: Peter Davies, 1939, pp. 10, 22.

78. Moran, *History of the Catholic Church in Australasia*, pp. 686, 688, 691. The Young Men's Societies which Polding promoted in the late 1850s were designed to shield from anti-Catholic influences: O'Farrell, *The Catholic Church and Community in Australia*, p. 153.

79. *Proceedings of the Second Australasian Catholic Congress*, pp. 10–11.

80. For the estimated membership, ibid., p. 352. McConville, 'Emigrant Irish and Suburban Catholics', thesis, pp. 237–44 has a discussion of the Young Men's Societies movement.

81. Anon., 'Our Catholic Men – and Church Attendance', pp. 471–73.

82. *Australian Messenger of the Sacred Heart*, April 1920, p. 163.

83. J. T. McMahon, 'The Leakage Problem', *Australasian Catholic Record*, 2nd series, 14, 1937, p. 304.

84. *Australian Messenger of the Sacred Heart*, April 1921, p. 123.

85. The reports were published in issues of *Madonna*, 1920. The quotation is from May 1920, pp. 2–3.

86. Gregory Haines, 'Aspects of Australian Piety', *Australasian Catholic Record*, 2nd series, 55, 1978, p. 240.

87. *Advocate*, 18 Feb. 1899, pp. 8–9.

88. The quotation is from one of Cleary's Lenten Pastorals: *Month*, March 1920, pp. 7–9.

89. U. M. Bygott, *With Pen and Tongue: The Jesuits in Australia*

1865–1939, Carlton, Vic.: Melbourne University Press, 1980, pp. 215–17; James Griffin, 'William Philip Hackett' in *ADB*, vol. 9.

90. In 1888 Bishop Luck of Auckland noted 'the universal comment that Catholic journalists so frequently make in these colonies on the lack of support that is accorded to their efforts in the Catholic cause': Pastoral, 3 Feb. 1888, Archives Catholic Diocese of Auckland, LUC 24–1 (bound volume of Luck's published pastorals).

91. *Proceedings of the First Australasian Catholic Congress*, p. 255.

92. O'Farrell, *The Catholic Church and Community in Australia*, pp. 152–53.

93. E.g., *Advocate*, 2 March 1878, p. 13, 24 May 1879, p. 10, 17 Nov. 1883, p. 17; also Fitzpatrick, *Solid Bluestone Foundations*, pp. 70–71, for a breach of the rule of abstinence averted.

94. Fr Kevin Hannan, personal communication.

95. *Australian Messenger of the Sacred Heart*, Nov. 1920, p. 410.

96. ibid., Sept. 1926, p. 472.

97. Rumble, *Radio Replies in Defence of Religion*, pp. 289–92.

98. O'Farrell, *The Catholic Church and Community in Australia*, p. 211.

99. Buckley, *Cutting Green Hay*, p. 233.

100. The numbers of Roman Catholics in-married for every one out-married were as follows for N.S.W.: 1891 4.3, 1901 3.6, 1911 3.0, 1921 2.7. The level of in-marriage for Australia as a whole was lower in 1921 than in 1911. In a sample of Wellington wives studied in a 1967 survey, in the marriages celebrated between 1927 and 1952 which had at least one Roman Catholic partner 45% were Protestant-Catholic marriages: Miriam Gilson Vosburgh, *The New Zealand Family and Social Change: A Trend Analysis*, Wellington: Department of Sociology and Social Work, Victoria University of Wellington, 1978, p. 108.

101. Buckley, *Cutting Green Hay*, p. 233. See also Rumble, *Radio Replies in Defence of Religion*, pp. 289–90.

V. SUNDAY

1. Barrett, *That Better Country*.

2. I estimate that in 1850 26 per cent of the colonists of Australasia (W.A. excluded) were provided with seats and that 21 per cent were usual attenders. The reliability and completeness of at least some of the statistics are suspect. The sources for my calculations were as follows: N.S.W.: Barrett, *That Better Country*, p. 74, and Phillips, 'Religious Profession and Practice in N.S.W., 1850–1901', p. 385; Victoria: Barrett, *That Better Country*, pp. 76, 186; Tasmania (1849): ibid., pp. 76–77, 186; S.A. (1851): Pike, *Paradise of Dissent*, p. 387; N.Z.: Blue Books, 1852, New Munster and New Ulster, National Archives, Wellington, NM 11/4 and G 8/6, 31–75.

3. Serle, *The Golden Age*, p. 343; Phillips, 'Religious Profession and Practice in N.S.W., 1850–1901', p. 390.

4. Walter Phillips, 'Statistics on Churchgoing and Sunday School Attendance in Victoria 1851–1901', *Australian Historical Statistics*, Bulletin no. 5, May 1982, p. 36.

5. ibid., p. 36; Pike, *Paradise of Dissent*, p. 387; *Christian Weekly and Methodist Journal*, 24 Aug. 1888, for a census of attendance at evening services in Adelaide.

6. Total attendances (morning and evening) at places of worship of each religious group in each municipality were summed and expressed as a percentage of estimated adherents. The number of adherents in each municipality in 1887 was estimated by taking the total population of each municipality in 1887 and assuming

that the population was distributed across the denominations in the same way as at the 1891 census. Port Melbourne was included with the northern municipalities because of its working class character. Camberwell, Caulfield, Malvern and Coburg, all listed in the *Daily Telegraph* census, were excluded because their populations were too small in 1887; they were still classed as shires then. Essendon was grouped with Flemington and Kensington. Clifton Hill was taken as being within the municipality of Collingwood following the *Melbourne Directory*, 1888. In addition to Table 5 see Graeme Davison, *The Rise and Fall of Marvellous Melbourne*, Carlton, Vic.: Melbourne University Press, 1978, p. 208, table 19.

7. Phillips, *Defending 'A Christian Country'*, pp. 91, 92, 95; Eric W. Hames, *Out of the Common Way: The European Church in the Colonial Era, 1840–1913*, Auckland: Wesley Historical Society of N.Z., 1972, p. 116.

8. For a study of four Wesleyan congregations in Victoria, Renate Howe, 'Social Composition of the Wesleyan Church in Victoria during the Nineteenth Century', *JRH*, 4.3, 1967, pp. 206–17.

9. Phillips, 'Religious Profession and Practice in N.S.W. 1850–1901', p. 390; Serle, *The Rush to Be Rich*, p. 151.

10. Pickering, 'The 1851 Religious Census – A Useless Experiment?', pp. 393–94, for an estimate that 47 per cent of the population of England ten years and over attended public worship on the Sunday of the 1851 religious census. For church attendance in England later in the century, Hugh McLeod, 'Class, Community and Region: The Religious Geography of Nineteenth-Century England', in M. Hill (ed.), *A Sociological Yearbook of Religion in Britain*, 6, London: S.C.M. Press, 1973, pp. 29–72.

11. Jackson, 'Churchgoing in Nineteenth-Century New Zealand', pp. 56–58.

12. Exodus, 20:9–14.

13. Lemon, *The Young Man from Home*, p. 45.

14. John Christian Symons, *The Christian Sabbath; How It Should Be Spent . . .*, Melbourne: J. A. Smith, [1860], pp. 11–12.

15. Perry, *Parents and Children*, pp. 9–10.

16. Pike, *Paradise of Dissent*, p. 515.

17. *Presbyterian Magazine*, 1864, p. 313.

18. Cairns, *Family Religion*, p. 32.

19. E.g., Broome, *Treasure in Earthen Vessels*, p. 132; Lawrence Harold Barber, 'The Social Crusader: James Gibb at the Australasian Pastoral Frontier, 1882–1935', PhD thesis, Massey University, 1975, p. 181.

20. Robert Sutherland, *The History of the Presbyterian Church of Victoria from the Foundation of the Colony to the Abolition of State Aid in 1875*, London: Nisbet, 1877, pp. 353–59; the quotation is on p. 356.

21. *Proceedings of the Synod of the Presbyterian Church of Otago and Southland*, 1873, pp. 24–25.

22. James Augustus Hessey, *Sunday, Its Origin, History and Present Obligation . . .*, London, 1860.

23. Peter MacPherson, 'Presbyterianism in Victoria, A Collection of Newspaper Cuttings, MSS., etc. 1841–1883', 34 vols., La Trobe Library, Melbourne, *passim*.

24. Boyd, *Scottish Church Attitudes to Sex, Marriage and the Family*, p. 321, n. 150.

25. MacPherson, 'Presbyterianism in Victoria' (n. 23 above), 1866, p. 108, cutting, *Age*, 13 March 1866; 1866, pp. 547–48, cutting, *Argus*, 20 Nov. 1866.

26. E.g., during the controversy over the opening of the Athenaeum in Dunedin in early 1874 it was reprinted at least twice: *Otago Christian Record*, 7 March 1874, pp. 9–10; *The Religious Non-observance of the Sabbath. A Sermon by the Rev. F. W. Robertson . . .*, Dunedin, 1874.

27. *Proceedings of the General Assembly of the Presbyterian Church of Victoria*, 1871, p. 78; the circular, which is undated, is fixed between the *Argus* cuttings of 3 and 4 Oct. 1871 in MacPherson, 'Presbyterianism in Victoria' (n. 23 above); for the deputation, ibid., cutting, *Argus*, 31 Oct. 1871.

28. R. Douglas Brackenbridge, 'The "Sabbath War" of 1865–66: The Shaking of the Foundations', *Scottish Church Historical Society*, 17.1, 1969, p. 23.

29. Geoffrey Best, *Mid-Victorian Britain 1851–1875*, London: Weidenfeld and Nicolson, 1971, p. 262; Chadwick, *The Victorian Church*, Part I, pp. 455–68.

30. McLaren, *Religion and Social Class*, p. 42.

31. John Wigley, *The Rise and Fall of the Victorian Sunday*, Manchester: Manchester University Press, 1980, pp. 124, 131.

32. MacPherson, 'Presbyterianism in Victoria' (n. 23 above), 1874, pp. 357–62.

33. *Otago Daily Times*, 31 Jan., pp. 2–3; ibid., 12 Feb., pp. 2–3; 23 Feb. 1874, p. 2.

34. David Kennedy, *Kennedy's Colonial Travels . . .*, Edinburgh: Edinburgh Publishing Co., [1876], p. 164.

35. The openings included that of the Public Library and Museum in Adelaide in 1879. Developments in N.S.W. are covered in Phillips, *Defending 'A Christian Country'*, pp. 171–93.

36. Powell, 'The Church in Auckland Society', thesis, p. 123.

37. On Victoria, F. B. Smith, 'The Sunday Observance Controversy in Melbourne, 1874–1910', BA hons thesis, University of Melbourne, 1956; Serle, *The Rush to Be Rich*, pp. 156–60; Keith Dunstan, *Wowsers*, Melbourne: Cassell Australia, 1968, pp. 15–33.

38. G. A. Wilkes, *A Dictionary of Australian Colloquialisms*, Sydney: Sydney University Press, 1978, p. 365.

39. *Melbourne Punch*, 12 July 1860.

40. A writer for the *Argus*, 21 May 1861, referred to the Sabbath as 'an institution productive to the weaker classes of incalculable benefit', cutting, MacPherson, 'Presbyterianism in Victoria' (n. 23 above), 1861, pp. 140–41.

41. *Melbourne Review*, July 1883, pp. 308, 319.

42. For an almost lyrical exposition of this theme, Cairns, *Family Religion*, pp. 19–20.

43. H. R. Niebuhr, *Christ and Culture*, New York: Harper and Row, 1975, chs 5–6.

44. Lewis, *Sunday at Kooyong Road*, pp. 41–42.

45. Rhys Isaac, *The Transformation of Virginia 1740–1790*, Chapel Hill: University of North Carolina Press, 1982, pp. 168–70, provides a different interpretation of Sabbatarianism in another society.

46. Badger, *The Reverend Charles Strong and the Australian Church*, p. 56.

47. Porter, *Growing Together*, pp. 140, 145.

48. *Proceedings of the Synod of the Presbyterian Church of Otago and Southland*, 1882, Appendix, p. 7.

49. Margaret Olive Indian, 'Leisure in City and Suburb: Melbourne 1880–1900', PhD thesis, Australian National University, 1980, pp. 93–95, 268; Margaret Mutch, 'Aspects of the Social and Economic History of Auckland, 1890–1896', MA thesis, University of Auckland, 1968, pp. 375–78.

50. K. S. Inglis, 'The Colonial Religion', *Quadrant*, Dec. 1977, pp. 68–69.

51. *Australian Christian World*, 31 Jan. 1896, p. 1.

52. Presbyterian Church of N.S.W., *Minutes of Proceedings of the General Assembly*, 1895, p. 78.

53. *Australian Christian World*, 30 Sept. 1904, p. 4.

54. Church of England in New Zealand, *Proceedings of the Diocesan Synod of the Diocese of Wellington*, 1912, p. 62.

55. Hansen, 'The Churches and

Society in New South Wales: 1919–1939', thesis, pp. 222–24.

56. *Churchman*, 1 Jan. 1897, p. 94.

57. H. C. D. Somerset, *Littledene: Patterns of Change*, Wellington: New Zealand Council for Educational Research, 1974, pp. 35–36.

58. For a more detailed review of these censuses, see my articles 'Churchgoing in Nineteenth-Century New Zealand', pp. 43–49, and 'The Late Victorian Decline in Churchgoing: Some New Zealand Evidence', *Archives de Sciences Sociales des Religions*, 56.1, 1983, pp. 97–106. In the latter article, p. 100, I criticized Professor Hans Mol for calculating variations in the level of churchgoing using usual attenders as a proportion of total population, rather than usual attenders as a proportion of the population fifteen years and over. I am less sure on this point than I was. Broome, *Treasure in Earthen Vessels*, pp. x, 163, concludes that churchgoing in N.S.W. in the decade or so before 1914 did not decline but was merely 'stagnant'. See also R. L. Broome, 'Protestantism and New South Wales Society 1900–1914', PhD thesis, University of Sydney, 1974, pp. 565–71. The N.Z. statistics appear to be more reliable. They are also more consistent with the testimony of many at the time who believed that they were living through a decline in churchgoing. See also Michael E. Papesch, 'Church Attendance in New Zealand 1919–1939', BA hons research exercise, Massey University, 1983.

59. Methodist Church of N.Z., *Minutes of Annual Conference*, 1931, p. 54; *Proceedings of the Synod of the Presbyterian Church of Otago and Southland*, 1900, p. 48; *Congregational Union of N.Z. Yearbook*, 1895, pp. 26–27.

60. Elkin, *The Diocese of Newcastle*, p. 703; *Proceedings of the Synod of the Presbyterian Church of*

Otago and Southland, 1890, pp. 36–37.

61. *N.Z. Methodist Times*, 15 Jan. 1927, p. 8 (item from S.A.).

62. *Auckland Evening Star*, 24 April 1882.

63. Hilliard, 'The City of Churches: Some Aspects of Religion in Adelaide about 1900', p. 24.

64. Geoffrey Blainey, *A History of Camberwell*, Melbourne: The Jacaranda Press, 1964, p. 73.

65. *Mothers in Australia*, Sept. 1921, pp. 10–11.

66. Lewis, *Sunday at Kooyong Road*.

67. E.g., *Presbyterian Messenger*, 13 Feb. 1920, p. 103; Broome, *Treasure in Earthen Vessels*, pp. 131–32.

68. Lawlor, *The Demanding God*, p. 54.

69. Simmons, *In Cruce Salus*, p. 242.

70. Phillips, *Defending 'A Christian Country'*, p. 178.

71. *Australian Messenger of the Sacred Heart*, Sept. 1923, p. 570.

72. Calculated from the statistics in McConville, 'Irish Emigrants and Suburban Catholics', thesis, pp. 42–43.

73. Bishop Goold to Rev. Dr Geoghegan, 28 Dec. 1858, Catholic Diocese of Adelaide Archives, Episcopal and General Church Letters, copy of original.

74. Larkin, 'Economic Growth, Capital Investment and the Roman Catholic Church in Nineteenth-Century Ireland', p. 865, n. 32.

75. Patrick F. Murray, 'Calendar of the Overseas Missionary Correspondence . . .', Introduction, p. xiii, All Hallows College Correspondence.

76. Larkin, 'The Devotional Revolution in Ireland 1850–1875', pp. 626–27, 644, 651.

77. Larkin, 'Economic Growth, Capital Investment and the Roman Catholic Church in Nineteenth-Century Ireland', p. 865, n. 32.

78. The ratio for Victoria in 1880 is from Phillips, *Defending 'A Christian Country'*, p. 56. The ratios for the colonies in 1870 and again in 1930 have been calculated

from *The Irish Australian Almanac Directory*, 1871 and the *Australasian Catholic Directory*, 1931. Religious as well as secular priests are included. All figures are approximate.

79. Jules Lemire, 'The History of the Catholic Church in Australia', p. 47 of the unpublished translation by S. J. Boland C.SS.R., Redemptorist Archives, Pennant Hills, Sydney.

80. *Australian Messenger of the Sacred Heart*, Feb. 1922, p. 34; Fr Kevin Hannan, personal communication.

81. *Australian Messenger of the Sacred Heart*, Dec. 1922, p. 663; *Madonna*, March 1929, p. 76; Lawlor, *The Demanding God*, p. 15.

82. *Tribune*, 10 March 1900, p. 7; *Month*, 15 Nov. 1923, p. 23.

83. *Australian Messenger of the Sacred Heart*, Dec. 1923, p. 762.

84. Pastoral of 3 Feb. 1888, Archives Catholic Diocese of Auckland, LUC 24–1 (bound volume of Luck's printed pastorals).

85. *Month*, 15 Nov. 1923, p. 23.

86. O'Farrell and O'Farrell, *Documents in Australian Catholic History*, vol. 2, p. 467.

87. Simmons, *In Cruce Salus*, p. 211; Patrick O'Farrell, 'Piety and Prayer as Historical Problems', *Australasian Catholic Record*, new series, 55, 1978, p. 228; McConville, 'Emigrant Irish and Suburban Catholics', thesis, pp. 223–25.

88. *Auckland Evening Star*, 24 April 1882.

89. Moran, *History of the Catholic Church in Australasia*, p. 691.

90. Anon, 'Our Catholic Men – and Church Attendance'.

91. Hans Mol, *The Faith of Australians*, Sydney: George Allen & Unwin, 1985, pp. 108–21. Research so far has not conclusively demonstrated that where the home background is one of nominal Catholicism attendance at a parish school produces a significantly higher level of religious practice than where the home background is also one of nominal Catholicism

and there is no attendance at a Catholic school.

VI. DOCTRINE

1. *Presbyterian Messenger*, 20 Feb. 1920, p. 125.

2. Kenneth T. Henderson, *Khaki and Cassock*, Melbourne: Melville and Mullen, 1919, pp. 125, 127.

3. *Observer* (Adelaide), 26 March 1904, p. 43, H. T. H. Wightwick.

4. Alan Dougan, *A Backward Glance at the Angus Affair*, Sydney: Wentworth Books, 1971; Alan Dougan, 'Samuel Angus', in *ADB*, vol. 7.

5. Michael Roe, *Quest for Authority in Eastern Australia 1835–1851*, Melbourne: Melbourne University Press, 1965, pp. 149, 178. Roe's view, p. 130, is that the trend towards 'undisciplined individual judgement' amongst Protestants reached its peak in the mid-nineteenth century. This surely is an exaggeration.

6. George Higinbotham, *Science and Religion or the Relations of Modern Science with the Christian Churches. A Lecture*, Melbourne, 1883, p. 15.

7. Jackson, 'Aspects of Congregationalism in South-Eastern Australia', thesis, pp. 81–82; Mol, *Religion in Australia*, p. 168.

8. Jackson, 'Aspects of Congregationalism in South-Eastern Australia', thesis, esp. pp. 53–58.

9. John Legge, *Memorials of John Legge, MA*, London: James Clarke, 1880, pp. 261–63.

10. G. G. Howden and T. J. Pepper, '*Our Need of Ministers*' and '*The Unemployed Power in our Churches*' . . ., Sydney, [1872], p. 9.

11. *Victorian Independent*, Sept. 1874, pp. 688–89.

12. John Legge, *Attitude of Modern Science to the Theology of the Bible* . . ., Melbourne, 1874; John Legge, *Curious Results of Applying Sceptical Criticism to Itself as Seen in 'Supernatural Religion'* . . ., Melbourne: George Robertson, 1875; (W. R. Cassels), *Supernatural*

Religion. *An Inquiry into the Reality of Divine Revelation*, 2nd edn, Melbourne: George Robertson, 1875.

13. *Victorian Independent*, April–July 1873.

14. *N.S.W. Independent*, 15 Nov. 1876, pp. 178–81.

15. Gregory, *Church and State*, pp. 104–15; A. G. Austin, *Australian Education 1788–1900: Church, State and Public Education in Colonial Australia*, Melbourne: Isaac Pitman and Sons, 1961, pp. 181–84; Clark, *A History of Australia*, vol. 4, p. 294, on Andrew Garran in Sydney.

16. *Victorian Congregational Year Book*, 1867, p. 41.

17. 'Sir Richard Davies Hanson', in *ADB*, vol. 4; Richard Davies Hanson, 'Science and Theology' in his *Four Papers Read before the Adelaide Philosophical Society*, Adelaide, 1864 (the quote is at p. 71); *The Jesus of History*, London, 1869; *The Apostle Paul and the Preaching of Christianity in the Primitive Church*, London, 1875.

18. Walter Phillips, 'Thomas Roseby', in *ADB*, vol. 6.

19. Phillips, *Defending 'A Christian Country'*, p. 119.

20. *Jubilee Volume of Victorian Congregationalism 1888 . . .*, Melbourne, n.d., pp. 180–81.

21. For England during the nineteenth century, Rowell, *Hell and the Victorians*. For the effect upon children, Serle, *The Rush to Be Rich*, p. 129; Phillips, *Defending 'A Christian Country'*, pp. 113–14. If I remember correctly it was Professor John Kent who set me thinking about the disingenuousness of the ministers; I do not have the reference.

22. *Australian Independent*, 15 Oct. 1889, p. 194.

23. James Hill, *The Attitude of the Church to Modern Life and Thought . . .*, Sydney, 1886.

24. *Australasian Independent*, 15 Aug. 1893, pp. 143–44.

25. ibid., 15 June 1893, p. 106.

26. Anon., *'Robert Elsmere'. A Reply to the Rev. George Clarke's Lecture*, Hobart, 1889.

27. La Trobe Library MSS, 9239, 24, Congregational Ministers Association minutes, 1890–94, 5 Sept. 1892.

28. *S.A. Congregationalist*, Aug. 1907, p. 7.

29. *Victorian Independent*, July 1910, p. 127.

30. Jackson, 'Aspects of Congregationalism in South-Eastern Australia', thesis, pp. 184–85.

31. *Observer* (Adelaide), 30 March 1907, p. 44.

32. *Advertiser* (Adelaide), 15 Oct. 1909, p. 8; E. S. Kiek, *An Apostle in Australia*, London: Independent Press, 1927, pp. 183–87.

33. Mitchell Library MSS, 3145, 1, 'Notes on Visitation of the Churches of Australia by Rev. J. D. Jones . . .', p. 31, in packet labelled 'Documents relating to the Visit of Dr J. D. Jones etc. 1914'.

34. *Stow Church Magazine*, Dec. 1909, p. 11.

35. *Australasian Independent*, June 1896, p. 109.

36. ibid., 16 Sept. 1895, p. 148.

37. La Trobe Library MSS, 9239, 24, Congregational Ministers Association minutes 1901–07, 3 March 1902; J. Barton.

38. Congregational Union of South Australia, *Annual Meetings Reports of Proceedings, Reports of Organisations*, Adelaide, 1898, p. 15.

39. *Victorian Independent*, Nov. 1904, pp. 209–14.

40. *South Australian Congregational Year Book*, 1912, pp. 14–31; 1913, pp. 25–34; A. D. Sykes, *The Function of the Ministry*, Adelaide, 1905. The first quotation is from *The Function of the Ministry*, p. 6; the second is from *South Australian Congregational Year Book*, 1913, p. 26.

41. *Watchman*, Dec. 1896; *Daily Telegraph*, 26 Oct. 1896, p. 5, 27 Oct. 1896, p. 6.

42. *Outlook*, 16 April 1904, p. 28.

43. *Victorian Independent*, April 1902,

pp. 71–72; *Australasian Independent,* April 1902, p. 4.

44. M. L. Johnson, W. Mathison, and W. Cunliffe Jones, *'The Deity of Christ', Papers Read before the Congregational Union of New South Wales October 1913,* Sydney, 1913.

45. Congregational Union of Australia and New Zealand, *Volumes of Proceedings,* 1913, p. 53, L. D. Bevan; ibid., 1907, p. 26, A. Gosman; *Australian Christian World,* 9 April 1909, p. 1, J. Bongers.

46. *Congregationalist,* Nov. 1925, p. 10, H. Steele Craik.

47. *Church Notes,* Dec. 1926.

48. *Congregationalist,* 10 March 1928, p. 4.

49. ibid., 10 June 1929, p. 4.

50. *South Australian Congregational Year Book,* 1928–29, p. 9.

51. E. S. Kiek, *The Modern Religious Situation,* Edinburgh: Clark, 1926, ch. 7, esp. pp. 149, 154.

52. *Congregationalist,* 10 Jan. 1931, p. 2.

53. Karl Barth, *The Word of God and the Word of Man,* trans. by D. Horton, London: Hodder and Stoughton, n.d., was the first to be translated. It was reviewed in Oct. 1929: R. Birch Hoyle, *The Teaching of Karl Barth,* London: S.C.M. Press, 1930, p. 7.

54. *Austral Light,* 1904, pp. 597–608, 669–83.

55. Rumble, *Radio Replies in Defence of Religion,* pp. 245–53. 'E. M. O'B' [Eris O'Brien] in 1920 made a spirited defence of the doctrine of eternal punishment in hell and referred in passing to a 'material fire': *Austral Light,* 1920, pp. 17–21.

56. O'Farrell, *The Catholic Church and Community in Australia,* pp. 294–95; Simmons, 'Archbishop Francis Redwood: His Contribution to Catholicism in New Zealand', thesis, pp. 44–45.

57. Thomas Hayden, 'The Johannine Question', *Australasian Catholic Record,* 11, 1905, pp. 367–77; Thomas Hayden, 'Modernism as Condemned by the Church',

Proceedings of the Third Australasian Catholic Congress, pp. 84–88; Livingston, *The Emergence of an Australian Catholic Priesthood,* pp. 239–40; Kevin Livingston, 'In Those Days: Secular Priests and Earlier Catholic Periodicals', *Australasian Catholic Record,* new series, 50, 1973, pp. 283–90.

58. Walter Phillips, 'The Defence of Christian Belief in Australia 1875–1914: The Responses to Evolution and Higher Criticism', *JRH,* 9.4, 1977, p. 411.

59. *Catholic Press,* 25 July 1929, p. 22. Sheehy's lecture was one in a series of six reported in the *Catholic Press.*

60. *Catholic Magazine,* Jan. 1890, p. 39.

61. Fr Patrick Gleeson, interview, 1983.

62. *Australian Messenger of the Sacred Heart,* Sept. 1928, p. 514. See also, ibid., July 1922, p. 347.

63. Rumble, *Radio Replies in Defence of Religion,* p. 257.

64. Mol, *Religion in Australia,* p. 42.

65. *Proceedings of the Third Australasian Catholic Congress,* pp. 112–19.

66. Hurley, 'Some Reasons why Catholics Lose Their Faith in New Zealand', pp. 205–14; Phelan, 'The Irish Abroad: The Church in Australia', esp. p. 674.

67. Axel Clark, *Christopher Brennan: A Critical Biography,* Melbourne: Melbourne University Press, 1980, pp. 33–34; Christopher Brennan, 'Curriculum Vitae', Brennan Papers, Mitchell Library, p. 39.

68. Anon., 'Our Catholic Men – and Church Attendance', p. 470.

VII. THE FAMILY

1. At the censuses of 1871 42.1 per cent of the Australian population and 39.6 per cent of the N.Z. population were aged under 15.

2. Margaret Grellier, 'The Family: Some Aspects of its Demography and Ideology in Mid-Nineteenth Century Western Australia', in C. T. Stannage (ed.), *A New History of Western Australia,* Nedlands, W.A.: University of Western Australia Press, 1981, pp. 489–90. The figures include still births.

3. Patricia Grimshaw and Charles Fahey, 'Family and Community in Nineteenth-Century Castlemaine', in Grimshaw *et al.*, *Families in Colonial Australia*, pp. 96–97.

4. F. K. Crowley (ed.), *A New History of Australia*, Melbourne: William Heinemann, 1974, p. 183.

5. Peter McDonald and Patricia Quiggin, 'Life Course Transitions in Victoria in the 1880s', in Grimshaw *et al*, *Families in Colonial Australia*, p. 76.

6. John T. Noonan, Jr, *Contraception: A History of Its Treatment by Catholic Theologians and Canonists*, Cambridge, Mass.: Harvard University Press, 1965, esp. pp. 353, 409, and 490 for the Protestant position.

7. Bourke, 'Catholic Fertility in Australia and New Zealand 1880–1939', thesis, pp. 22–23; Judith Allen, 'Octavius Beale Reconsidered: Infanticide, Baby-Farming and Abortion in New South Wales, 1880–1939' in *What Rough Beast?: The State and the Social Order in Australian History*, Sydney: Allen and Unwin, 1982, pp. 111–29, esp. p. 119.

8. Hicks, *This Sin and Scandal*, gives an account of the Commission.

9. *Royal Commission on the Decline of the Birth Rate*, vol. 2, Q. 5990.

10. ibid., Qs. 6072–178.

11. Inglis, 'Religious Behaviour', pp. 459–60; Hicks, *This Sin and Scandal*, pp. 66–72.

12. *Royal Commission on the Decline of the Birth Rate*, vol. 2, Q. 5964.

13. ibid., Qs. 6168–78.

14. ibid., Qs. 6029–71, esp. 6040, 6070.

15. Fitzgerald, 'Is the Church Gaining Converts?', p. 452.

16. O'Farrell, *The Catholic Church and Community in Australia*, p. 376. Nash's paper was not published in the report of the Congress.

17. Neville Hicks, 'Theories of Differential Fertility and the Australian Experience, 1891–1911', *HS*, 16.65, 1975, table iv, p. 581.

18. Day, 'Family Size and Fertility', p. 157.

19. Bourke, 'Catholic Fertility in Australia and New Zealand 1880–1939', thesis.

20. Lincoln H. Day, *Analysing Population Trends: Differential Fertility in a Pluralist Society*, London and Canberra: Croom Helm, 1983, table 3.6, pp. 72–75.

21. Day, 'Family Size and Fertility', p. 159.

22. *Royal Commission on the Decline of the Birth Rate*, vol. 1, Appendix, p. 75; Evidence of Statisticians, p. 15, para. 532. See also Coghlan, *The Decline of the Birth Rate of New South Wales*, p. 41.

23. The average issue of all Irish-born wives was 5.06. *Australia Census*, 1911, vol. 1, pp. 281, 283. At the N.S.W. Census of 1901 there were 42 697 Roman Catholic wives and 16 143 Irish-born wives. Coghlan prepared an index based on the 1901 census, according to which if the average birth rate of a certain number of mothers of childbearing age of all denominations was set at 100 then the birthrate of Roman Catholic wives was 113 and for women born in Ireland 135: *Decline of the Birth Rate of New South Wales*, p. 42.

24. Ansley J. Coale, 'Factors Associated with the Development of Low Fertility: An Historic Summary', in *World Population Conference, 1965*, vol. 2, New York: United Nations, 1967, p. 209.

25. *Censuses of Population of Ireland 1946 and 1951 General Report*, Dublin: Government Stationery Office, 1958, p. 219.

26. ibid., p. 212; Day, 'Family Size and Fertility', p. 157.

27. Mol, *Religion in Australia*, p. 251.

28. Inglis, 'Religious Behaviour', p. 461.

29. ibid., pp. 461–62.

30. Boyd, *Scottish Church Attitudes to Sex, Marriage and the Family*, ch. 5, demonstrates the considerable interest in family religion in Scotland in the 1850s and 1860s.

31. Cairns, *Family Religion*; the quotation is at p. 4.

32. I owe the reference to Canterbury Anglicans to Professor W. H. Oliver. On the Henty family, Kiddle, *Men of Yesterday*, pp. 92–93. I owe confirmation of Jane and Stephen Henty's Anglicanism to Rev. Dr A. de Q. Robin.

33. *Church Chronicle*, March 1865, p. 743.

34. *Melbourne Church News*, May 1866, p. 40; 16 May 1866, p. 56. See also ibid., 18 June 1866, p. 88.

35. Cairns, *Family Religion*, pp. 3, 33–39.

36. *South Australian Wesleyan Magazine*, Oct. 1869, p. 74.

37. *Southern Spectator*, Oct. 1858, pp. 89–90. See also ibid., Nov. 1858, p. 124.

38. *Victorian Independent*, Nov. 1873, p. 520 (punctuation corrected).

39. In the home of James Balfour, Victorian merchant and politician, this was so: Andrew Harper, *The Honourable James Balfour, M.L.C.: A Memoir*, Melbourne: Critchley Parker, 1918, p. 268.

40. 'Recollections of William Smaill', p. 9, quoted R. R. McLean, 'Class, Family and Church: A Case Study of Interpretation, Otago 1848–1852', BA hons thesis, University of Otago, 1980, pp. 110–11.

41. Frank Fowler, *Southern Lights and Shadows*, first published London, 1859, Sydney: Sydney University Press, 1975, pp. 79–80.

42. New South Wales Wesleyan Methodist Church, *Minutes of Annual Conference*, 1877, pp. 50–51.

43. South Australian Wesleyan Methodist Church, *Minutes of Annual Conference*, 1878, p. 41.

44. *N.Z. Presbyterian*, 1 Dec. 1882, p. 108.

45. *Proceedings of the Synod of the Presbyterian Church of Otago and Southland*, 1896, pp. 55–60.

46. ibid., 1900, p. 47.

47. [J.L.] Rentoul and Hume Robertson, *The Church at Home: Prayers for Australian Family Worship*, London: Hodder and Stoughton, 1907; *Prayers for the Home Circle. With a Selection of Bible Readings*, Dunedin, [1917].

48. *Church of England Messenger*, 16 Oct. 1888, pp. 10–11.

49. H. L. Jackson, *Parents and Children*, Sydney, 1888.

50. From mid-1929 for more than two years the magazine ran a series to teach mothers how to teach their children religion.

51. *Mothers in Australasia*, Dec. 1926, p. 3.

52. Polding, *The Eye of Faith*, pp. 123–36.

53. Moran, *History of the Catholic Church in Australasia*, pp. 689–90.

54. *Madonna*, Feb. 1898, p. 35; Simmons, *In Cruce Salus*, p. 167.

55. *Australian Messenger of the Sacred Heart*, March 1928, pp. 177–79.

56. ibid., Feb. 1921, pp. 54–58.

57. ibid., July 1923, p. 445.

58. All the above instances of Sacred Heart piety are taken from ibid., Jan. 1921, pp. 24–25.

59. *Proceedings of the Third Australasian Catholic Congress*, p. 118.

60. John O'Brien, *Around the Boree Log: A Selection ...*, illustrated by Patrick Carroll with biographical details by Father F. A. Mecham, London: Angus and Robertson, 1978; G. P. Walsh, 'Patrick Joseph Hartigan', in *ADB*, vol. 9.

61. *Tribune*, 27 Feb. 1904, p. 6.

62. Dan Davin, *No Remittance*, London: Michael Joseph, 1959, pp. 143–44.

63. *Presbyterian Magazine*, Nov. 1865, pp. 348–49.

64. Perry, *Parents and Children*, pp. 5–7.

65. *Testimony*, July 1866, p. 110.

66. *Wesleyan Chronicle*, 14 Sept. 1861, p. 124.

67. *Christian Outlook*, 21 March 1896, p. 92.

68. Perry, *Parents and Children*, pp. 5–6.

69. *Christian Outlook*, 21 March 1896, p. 92.

70. *Christian Advocate*, Sept. 1859, p. 35.

71. McLachlan, 'Larrikinism: An Interpretation', thesis, p. 10.

72. R. E. N. Twopeny, *Town Life in Australia*, first published London, 1883, Penguin, 1973, p. 101.
73. Quoted McLachlan, 'Larrikinism', thesis, p. 78. The quote does not appear in the *Bulletin*, 10 Jan. 1885, p. 13, the reference McLachlan gives.
74. Perry, *Parents and Children*, pp. 3–4.
75. Polding, *The Eye of Faith*, p. 127.
76. *Tribune*, 7 March 1903, p. 3.
77. *Catholic Press*, 21 July 1927, p. 18.
78. Jessie Ackermann, *Australia from a Woman's Point of View*, first published London, 1913, Cassell Australia, 1981, p. 71.
79. Morven S. Brown, 'Changing Functions of the Australian Family', in Elkin, *Marriage and the Family in Australia*, pp. 82–114.
80. R. D. Arnold, 'The Country Child in Later Victorian New Zealand', *Comment*, April 1982, p. 23.
81. Raewyn Dalziel, 'The Colonial Helpmeet. Woman's Role and the Vote in Nineteenth-Century New Zealand', NZJH, 11.2, 1977, pp. 112–23.
82. Strong, *Present-Day Responsibilities*, pp. 4–5, 8.
83. A. P. Elkin, 'The Family – A Challenge', in *Marriage and the Family in Australia*, p. 206.
84. Charles Strong is to a degree an exception. See his *Religion and the Home: An Address to Parents and Young People . . . 5th November 1905*, [Melbourne], n.d.; also his *Present-Day Responsibilities*.
85. E.g. *Proceedings of the Synod of the Presbyterian Church of Otago and Southland*, 1882, Appendix 6; 1891, p. 69; 1900, p. 49. See also *Proceedings of the General Assembly of the Presbyterian Church of N.Z.*, 1908, p. 61, for a report on a statistical inquiry.
86. *Proceedings of the Synod of the Presbyterian Church of Otago and Southland*, 1890, p. 37.
87. *Christian Outlook*, 22 Aug. 1896, p. 357.
88. *Proceedings of the Synod of the Presbyterian Church of Otago and Southland*, 1899, p. 44.
89. Strong, *Present-Day Responsibilities*, p. 12. For a later comment that parents were unwilling to interfere with their children's religious freedom, F. C. Spurr, *Australian Family Life*, Sydney: Watchman Newspaper Ltd., 1910, p. 11.
90. *Outlook*, 11 Jan. 1926, p. 26.
91. *Catholic Church Record* (Gosford), Oct. 1922, p. 5. This remark occurred in the first of a series of articles on the Catholic home in 1922–23. Cusack also ran the series in the *St Kevin's Church Record* in 1929–30 and at least one other parish paper that he edited during his career.
92. Mol, *Religion in Australia*, p. 172.

CONCLUSION

1. William H. McNeill, *The Shape of European History*, New York: Oxford University Press, 1974, p. 24.
2. Geoffrey Blainey, *The Tyranny of Distance*, Melbourne: Sun Books, 1966, ch. 8.
3. For the dating of Pusey's letter, Henry Parry Liddon, *Life of Edward Bouverie Pusey*, vol. 4, London: Longmans and Green, 1897, p. 40.
4. Alan D. Gilbert, *The Making of Post-Christian Britain: A History of the Secularization of a Modern Society*, London and New York: Longman, 1980.
5. I am in agreement here with McLeod, *Class and Religion in the Late Victorian City*, pp. 284–85.
6. Connell, *Irish Peasant Society*, p. 131.
7. *St Kevin's Church Record*, Dec. 1932, p. 6.
8. *N.Z. Methodist Times*, 15 Jan. 1927, p. 8 (item from S.A.).
9. McIntyre, *Country Towns in Victoria*, p. 178.
10. Kenneth C. Dempsey, 'Minister-Lay Relationships in a Methodist Country Community', *St. Mark's Review*, no. 65, Aug. 1971, p. 16.
11. Mol, *Religion in Australia*, pp. 23, 322.

12. Congregational Union of New South Wales, *Report and Recommendations of Forward Movement Commission*, n.p., 1944, pp. 17–18.

13. McIntyre, *Country Towns in Victoria*, pp. 176–78.

14. E. H. Burgmann, *The Opportunity of the Church of England*, Morpeth: St John's College Press, n.d., p. 8.

BIBLIOGRAPHY

Two lists of sources are given below. The first is of books, theses and articles cited more than once in the text. The second is of religious periodicals (mainly weeklies and monthlies) cited at least once in the references. Full references to manuscript and archival material are given in the references.

I drew material for this book from the archives of the Catholic archdioceses of Sydney, Melbourne and Adelaide and the diocese of Auckland and the Redemptorist archives, Pennant Hills, Sydney. I also used microfilms of All Hallows College, Dublin, correspondence and that of the Irish College, Rome. Work on Protestant denominational archives was restricted to Congregational church and union records in the Mitchell Library, the La Trobe Library and the State Library of South Australia.

In trying to explore the vast amount of material in the religious press, I tried to cover the 1860s, around 1890 and the 1920s as well as I could. In following up particular themes I wandered hither and thither.

ABBREVIATIONS
ADB   Australian Dictionary of Biography
HS   Historical Studies
JRH   Journal of Religious History
NZJH   New Zealand Journal of History

1. BOOKS, ARTICLES AND THESES

Anon., 'Our Catholic Men – and Church Attendance', *Australasian Catholic Record*, 13, 1907, pp. 466–75.

Badger, C. R., *The Reverend Charles Strong and the Australian Church*, Melbourne: Abacada Press, 1971.

Barrett, John, *That Better Country: The Religious Aspect of Life in Eastern Australia 1833–1850*, Carlton, Vic.: Melbourne University Press, 1966.

Blainey, Geoffrey, *The Rush That Never Ended: A History of Australian Mining*, 3rd edn, Carlton, Vic.: Melbourne University Press, 1978.

Boland, S. J., *Faith of Our Fathers*, Armadale, Vic.: published for the Redemptorist Fathers, produced by H. H. Stephenson, 1982.

Bollen, J. D., *Australian Baptists: A Religious Minority*, London: Baptist Historical Society, 1975.

Bolton, Barbara, *Booth's Drum. The Salvation Army in Australia 1880–1980*, Sydney: Hodder and Stoughton, 1980.

Bourke, Joanna, 'Catholic Fertility in Australia and New Zealand 1880–1939', MA thesis, University of Auckland, 1985.

Bowen, Desmond, *Paul Cardinal Cullen and the Shaping of Modern Irish Catholicism*, Dublin: Gill and Macmillan, 1983.

The Protestant Crusade in Ireland, 1800–1870: A Study of Protestant Catholic Relations between the Act of Union and Disestablishment, Dublin: Gill and Macmillan, 1978.

Boyd, Kenneth M., *Scottish Church Attitudes to Sex, Marriage and the Family*, Edinburgh: John Donald, 1980.

Brooking, Tom, *And Captain of Their Souls: An Interpretive Essay on the Life and Times of Captain William Cargill*, Dunedin: Heritage Books, 1984.

Broome, Richard, *Treasure in Earthen Vessels: Protestant Christianity in New South Wales Society 1900–1914*, St Lucia, Queensland: University of Queensland Press, 1980.

Buckley, Vincent, *Cutting Green Hay: Friendships, Movements and Cultural Conflicts in Australia's Great Decades*, Ringwood, Vic.: Penguin Books, 1983.

Buller, James, *Forty Years in New Zealand . . .*, London: Hodder and Stoughton, 1878.

Burleigh, J. H. S., *A Church History of Scotland*, London: Oxford University Press, 1960.

Byrne, F., *History of the Catholic Church*

in *South Australia*, Adelaide: E. W. Cole, 1896.

Cairns, Adam, *Family Religion*, Melbourne, n.d.

Cambridge, Ada, *Thirty Years in Australia*, London: Methuen, 1903.

Campion, Edmund, *Rockchoppers: Growing up Catholic in Australia*, Ringwood, Vic.: Penguin Books, 1982.

Carwardine, Richard, *Transatlantic Revivalism: Popular Evangelicalism in Britain and America 1790–1865*, London: Greenwood Press, 1978.

Chadwick, Owen, *The Victorian Church*, Part I, 3rd edn, London: Adam and Charles Black, 1971, Part II, 2nd edn, 1972.

Chant, Barry, *Heart of Fire: The Story of Australian Pentecostalism*, Fullarton, S.A.: Luke Publications, 1973.

Clark, C. M. H., *A History of Australia*, vols. 3 and 4, Carlton, Vic.: Melbourne University Press, 1973, 1978.

Coghlan, T. A., *The Decline of the Birth Rate of New South Wales and Other Phenomena of Child-Birth*, Sydney: N.S.W. Government Printer, 1903.

Connell, K. H., *Irish Peasant Society*, Oxford: Clarendon Press, 1968.

Connolly, S. J., *Priests and People in Pre-Famine Ireland 1780–1845*, Dublin: Gill and Macmillan, 1982.

Coughlan, N., 'The Coming of the Irish to Victoria', *HS*, 12.45, 1965, pp. 68–86.

'C.SS.R.', 'On Missions', *Australasian Catholic Record*, 1, 1895, pp. 321–36.

Cross, Whitney R., *The Burned-Over District: The Social and Intellectual History of Enthusiastic Religion in Western New York, 1800–1850*, New York: Harper and Row, Harper Torchbook edn, 1965.

Davis, Richard P., *Irish Issues in New Zealand Politics*, Dunedin: University of Otago Press, 1974.

Day, Lincoln H., 'Family Size and Fertility' in A. F. Davies and S. Encel, *Australian Society: A Sociological Introduction*, Melbourne: Cheshire, 1965, pp. 156–67.

Dolan, Jay P., *Catholic Revivalism*, Notre Dame: University of Notre Dame, 1978.

Drummond, Andrew L., and Bulloch, James, *The Scottish Church 1688–1843: The Age of the Moderates*, Edinburgh: St Andrew Press, 1973.

Elkin, A. P. (ed.), *The Diocese of Newcastle: A History of the Diocese of Newcastle, New South Wales, Australia*, Sydney: Australasian Medical Publishing Co., 1955.

Marriage and the Family in Australia, Sydney: Angus and Robertson, 1957.

Fitzgerald, T. A., 'Is the Church Gaining Converts in Australasia?', *Australasian Catholic Record*, 7, 1901, pp. 451–63.

Fitzpatrick, Kathleen, *Solid Bluestone Foundations and Other Memories of a Melbourne Girlhood 1908–1928*, South Melbourne: Macmillan, 1983.

Fogarty, Ronald, *Catholic Education in Australia 1806–1950*, 2 vols. Carlton, Vic.: Melbourne University Press, 1959.

Golden, John, *Some Old Waikato Days*, Dunedin: N.Z. Tablet Printing Co., 1922.

Gregory, J. S., *Church and State; Changing Government Policies towards Religion in Australia*, North Melbourne, Vic.: Cassell, 1973.

Grimshaw, Patricia, McConville, Chris and McEwen, Ellen (eds), *Families in Colonial Australia*, Sydney: George Allen and Unwin, 1985.

Grocott, Allan, M., *Convicts, Clergymen and Churches: Attitudes of Convicts and Ex-Convicts towards the Churches and the Clergy in New South Wales from 1788 to 1851*, Sydney: Sydney University Press, 1980.

Hansen, Donald Edgar, 'The Churches and Society in New South Wales: 1919–1939. A Study of Church Activities, Socio-Religious Issues, Community-Church and Inter-Church Relations', PhD thesis, Macquarie University, 1978.

Hicks, Neville, *'This Sin and Scandal': Australia's Population Debate 1891–*

1911, Canberra: Australian National University Press, 1978.

Hilliard, David, *Popular Revivalism in South Australia from the 1870s to the 1920s*, Adelaide: Uniting Church Historical Society, 1982.

'The City of Churches: Some Aspects of Religion in Adelaide about 1900', *Journal of the Historical Society of South Australia*, no. 8, 1980, pp. 3–30.

Hogan, James Francis, *The Irish in Australia*, Melbourne: George Robertson, 1888.

Hunt, Arnold D., *This Side of Heaven: A History of Methodism in South Australia*, Adelaide: Lutheran Publishing House, 1985.

'The Moonta Revival of 1875', *The Uniting Church in South Australia Historical Society Newsletter*, no. 7, 1980.

Hurley, P. E., 'Some Reasons why Catholics Lose Their Faith in New Zealand', *Irish Ecclesiastical Record*, 3rd series, 8, 1887, pp. 205–14.

Inglis, K. S., *The Australian Colonists: An Exploration of Social History 1788–1870*, Carlton, Vic.: Melbourne University Press, 1974.

Churches and the Working Classes in Victorian England, London: Routledge and Kegan Paul, 1963.

'Religious Behaviour' in A. F. Davies and S. Encel (eds), *Australian Society: A Sociological Introduction*, 2nd edn, Melbourne: Cheshire, 1970, pp. 437–75.

Jackson, H. R., 'Aspects of Congregationalism in South-Eastern Australia circa 1880 to 1930', PhD thesis, Australian National University, 1978.

'Churchgoing in Nineteenth-Century New Zealand', *NZJH*, 17.1, 1983, pp. 43–59.

Keenan, Desmond J., *The Catholic Church in Nineteenth-Century Ireland: A Sociological Study*, Dublin: Gill and Macmillan, 1983.

Kent, C. S., *Christian Life in Australia: Its Dangers, Difficulties and Duties*, Sydney: 1869.

Kent, John, *Holding the Fort: Studies in Victorian Revivalism*, London: Epworth Press, 1978.

Kiddle, Margaret, *Men of Yesterday: A Social History of the Western District of Victoria 1834–1890*, Carlton, Vic.: Melbourne University Press, 1961.

Larkin, Emmet, 'Economic Growth, Capital Investment and the Roman Catholic Church in Nineteenth-Century Ireland', *American Historical Review*, 72.3, 1967, pp. 852–84.

'The Devotional Revolution in Ireland 1850–75', *American Historical Review*, 77.3, 1972, pp. 625–52.

The Making of the Roman Catholic Church in Ireland 1850–1860, Chapel Hill: University of North Carolina, 1980.

Lawlor, Pat, *The Demanding God: Some Boyhood Reflections*, Dunedin: N.Z. Tablet Co., 1972.

Lemon, Andrew, *The Young Man from Home: James Balfour 1830–1913*, Carlton, Vic.: Melbourne University Press, 1982.

Lewis, Brian, *Sunday at Kooyong Road*, Richmond, Vic.: Hutchinson Group, 1976.

Lineham, Peter, *There We Found Brethren: A History of the Assemblies of the Brethren in New Zealand*, Palmerston North: Gospel Publishing House Society, 1977.

Livingston, K. T., *The Emergence of an Australian Catholic Priesthood 1835–1915*, Sydney: Catholic Theological Faculty, 1977.

Long, M., 'A Word from Australia', *Irish Ecclesiastical Record*, 3rd series, 4, 1883, pp. 653–61.

Lyons, Mark, 'Aspects of Sectarianism in New South Wales circa 1865 to 1880', PhD thesis, Australian National University, 1972.

McConville, Chris, 'Emigrant Irish and Suburban Catholics: Faith and Nation in Melbourne and Sydney, 1851–1933', PhD thesis, University of Melbourne, 1981.

McIntyre A. J. and J. J., *Country Towns in Victoria: A Social Survey*, Carlton, Vic.: Melbourne University Press, 1944.

McLachlan, N. D., 'Larrikinism: An Interpretation', MA thesis, University of Melbourne, 1950.

McLaren, A. Allan, *Religion and Social Class: The Disruption Years in Aberdeen*, London: Routledge and Kegan Paul, 1974.

McLay, Yvonne Margaret, *James Quinn First Catholic Bishop of Brisbane*, Armidale, Vic.: Graphic Books, 1979.

McLeod, Hugh, *Class and Religion in the Late Victorian City*, London: Croom Helm, 1974.

McLintock, A. H., *The History of Otago*, Dunedin: Otago Centennial Historical Publications, 1949.

McLoughlin, William G., *Modern Revivalism: Charles Grandison Finney to Billy Graham*, New York: The Ronald Press, 1959.

Mackray, Archibald N., *Revivals of Religion: Their Place and Power in the Christian Church*, Sydney: John L. Sheriff, 1870.

Matthews, C. H. S., *A Parson in the Australian Bush*, Adelaide: Rigby, 1973.

Mazzaroli, Louise Ann, 'The Irish in New South Wales, 1884 to 1914; Some Aspects of the Irish Sub-Culture', PhD thesis, University of New South Wales, 1979.

Millard, Edward C., *The Same Lord: An Account of the Mission Tour of the Rev. George Grubb, MA in Australia, Tasmania and New Zealand, from April 3rd, 1891, to July 7th, 1892*, London: E. Marlborough, 1893.

Mol, Hans, *Religion in Australia: A Sociological Investigation*, Melbourne: Nelson, 1971.

Moran, P. F., *History of the Catholic Church in Australasia*, Sydney: The Oceania Publishing Co., n.d.

Morley, William, *The History of Methodism in New Zealand*, Wellington: McKee, 1900.

Murphy J. M. and Moynehan, F., *The National Eucharistic Congress Melbourne, Australia 2–9 December 1934*, Melbourne: Advocate Press, 1936.

Obelkevich, James, *Religion and Rural Society: South Lindsey 1825–1875*, Oxford: Clarendon Press, 1976.

O'Farrell, Patrick, *The Catholic Church and Community in Australia: A History*, West Melbourne: Nelson, 1977.

Letters from Irish Australia 1825–1929, Sydney: New South Wales University Press, 1984.

'The Irish and Australian History', *Quadrant*, 22.12, 1978, pp. 17–21.

O'Farrell, Patrick and Deidre (eds), *Documents in Australian Catholic History 1788–1968*, 2 vols, London: Geoffrey Chapman, 1969.

O'Kane, F., *A Path is Set: The Catholic Church in the Port Phillip District and Victoria 1839–1862*, Carlton, Vic.: Melbourne University Press, 1976.

Oliver, W. H. with Williams, B. R. (eds), *The Oxford History of New Zealand*, Wellington: Oxford University Press, 1981.

O'Sullivan, Owen, *An Apostle in Aotearoa. A Biography of Jeremiah Joseph Purcell O'Reily O.F.M. Cap. Wellington's First Catholic Pastor*, Auckland: The Word Publishers, 1977.

Percival, G. C., 'Methodism: Past and Present', *Journal and Proceedings of the Australasian Methodist Historical Society*, 2.2, Oct. 1933, pp. 64–73.

Perry, Charles, *Parents and Children: A Paper Read before the Congress [of the Society for the Promotion of Morality] Held in the Assembly Hall, Melbourne, on 29th October, 1870*, Melbourne, 1870.

Phelan, Michael, 'The Irish Abroad: The Church in Australia', *Irish Ecclesiastical Record*, 3rd series, 14, 1893, pp. 33–45, 498–511, 673–89.

Phillips, Walter, *Defending 'A Christian Country': Churchmen and Society in New South Wales in the 1880s and after*, St Lucia, Queensland: University of Queensland Press, 1981.

'Religious Profession and Practice in New South Wales, 1850–1901: The Statistical Evidence', *HS*, 15.59, 1972, pp. 378–400.

Pickering, W. S. F., 'The 1851 Religious Census – A Useless Experiment?', *British Journal of Sociology*, 18.4, 1967, pp. 382–407.

Pike, Douglas, *Paradise of Dissent*, 2nd edn, Carlton, Vic.: Melbourne University Press, 1967.

Polding, John Bede, *The Eye of Faith: The Pastoral Letters of John Bede Polding*, Gregory Haines *et al.* (eds), Kilmore, Vic.: Lowden Publishing Co., n.d.

Porter, Una B. (ed.), *Growing Together. Letters between Frederick John Cato and Frances Bethune 1881 to 1884*, Carlton, Vic.: Queensberry Hill Press, 1981.

Powell, Michael J., 'The Church in Auckland Society, 1880–1886', MA thesis, University of Auckland, 1970.

Prentis, Malcolm D., 'The Presbyterian Ministry in Australia, 1822–1900: Recruitment and Composition', *JRH*, 13.1, 1984, pp. 46–65.

Press, Margaret, M., *Julian Tenison Woods*, Sydney: Catholic Theological Faculty, 1979.

Proceedings of the First Australasian Catholic Congress Held at St Mary's Cathedral, Sydney, 10 September 1900, Sydney: published at St Mary's Cathedral, 1900.

Proceedings of the Second Australasian Catholic Congress Held in the Cathedral Hall, Melbourne, October 24th to 31st, 1904, Melbourne: published at St Patrick's Cathedral, 1905.

Proceedings of the Third Australasian Catholic Congress Held at St Mary's Cathedral, Sydney, 26th September–3rd October 1909, Sydney: published at St Mary's Cathedral Book Depot, n.d.

Pryor, Oswald, *Australia's Little Cornwall*, Adelaide: Rigby, 1962.

Rowell, Geoffrey, *Hell and the Victorians*, Oxford: Oxford University Press, 1974.

Royal Commission on the Decline of the Birth Rate and on the Mortality of Infants in New South Wales, vol. 1, Report and Statistics, Sydney: N.S.W. Government Printer, 1904.

   vol. 2, Other evidence, exhibits, etc.

Rumble, L., *Radio Replies in Defence of Religion*, Sydney: Missionaries of the Sacred Heart, Kensington, 1934.

Serle, Geoffrey, *The Golden Age: A History of the Colony of Victoria, 1851–1861*, Carlton, Vic.: Melbourne University Press, 1963.

   The Rush to Be Rich: A History of the Colony of Victoria, 1883–1889, Carlton, Vic.: Melbourne University Press, 1971.

Shaw, Thomas, *A History of Cornish Methodism*, Truro: D. Bradford Barton, 1967.

Simmons, E. R., *In Cruce Salus. A History of the Diocese of Auckland 1848–1980*, Auckland: Catholic Publications Centre, 1982.

Simmons, Nicholas Anthony, 'Archbishop Francis Redwood: His Contribution to Catholicism in New Zealand', MA thesis, Massey University, 1981.

Smith, J. B. and Blamires, W. L., *The Early Story of the Wesleyan Methodist Church in Victoria*, Melbourne: Wesleyan Book Depot, 1886.

Soloway, R. A., *Prelates and People: Ecclesiastical Social Thought in England 1783–1852*, London: Routledge and Kegan Paul, 1969.

Strong, Charles, *Present-Day Responsibilities. A Sermon*, Melbourne: Samuel Mullen, 1877.

Taylor, William, *Story of My Life*, New York: Eton and Mains, 1895.

Waldersee, James, *A Grain of Mustard Seed: The Society for the Propagation of the Faith and Australia, 1837–1977*, Kensington, N.S.W.: Chevalier Press, 1983.

   Catholic Society in New South Wales 1788–1860, Sydney: Sydney University Press, 1974.

Ward, W. R., *Religion and Society in England 1790–1850*, London: B. T. Batsford, 1972.

Watsford, John, *Glorious Gospel Triumphs as Seen in My Life and Work*, London: Charles H. Kelly, 1900.

Wilson, J. J., *The Church in New Zealand*, vol. 1, Dunedin: Tablet Printing and Publishing Co., 1910.

Wyatt, R. T., *A History of the Diocese of Goulburn*, Sydney: Edgar Bragg & Sons, 1937.

2. RELIGIOUS PERIODICALS
In some cases publication ceased before 1930, not always at a certain date. Some of the periodicals underwent name changes which can make them difficult to track down. Some of the items cited under 'Protestant, Interdenominational' were weighted towards one denomination in their content.

(i) Baptist
Australasian Baptist Magazine. Melbourne, 1858–
Truth and Progress. Adelaide, 1868–

(ii) Church of England
Churchman. Sydney, 1894–
Church Chronicle for the Diocese of Adelaide. Adelaide, 1859–
Church Gazette. Auckland, 1872–
Church of England Messenger. Melbourne, 1869–
Melbourne Church News. Melbourne, 1866–70
Mothers in Australia (later *Mothers in Australasia*). Sydney, 1917–

(iii) Congregational
Australasian Independent (see *Australian Independent*).
Australian Independent. Sydney, 1888–1907
Church News. Brighton, Melbourne (local church) 1893– (held by Baillieu Library, University of Melbourne)
Church Notes. Melbourne (Independent Church, Collins Street) 1911–
Congregationalist. Sydney, 1908– (also *New South Wales Congregationalist*)
New South Wales Independent. Sydney, 1875–87
South Australian Congregationalist. Adelaide, 1905–
Stow Church Magazine. Adelaide, 1909–
Victorian Independent. Melbourne, 1870–
Watchman. Sydney (Pitt Street Church), 1895– (held by Mitchell Library)

(iv) Methodist
Christian Advocate and Wesleyan Record. Sydney, 1858–
Christian Weekly and Methodist Journal. Adelaide, 1881–
New Zealand Methodist Times. Auckland, Christchurch, 1910–
New Zealand Primitive Methodist. Wellington, Dunedin, 1878–
New Zealand Wesleyan. Christchurch, 1871–
Primitive Methodist Miscellany. Melbourne, 1863–
Primitive Methodist Record. Adelaide, 1866–
South Australian Wesleyan Magazine. Adelaide, 1864–
Spectator and Methodist Chronicle. Melbourne, 1875–
Wesleyan Chronicle. Melbourne, 1857–

(v) Presbyterian
Christian Outlook. (see *Outlook*).
New Zealand Presbyterian. Dunedin, 1879–93
New Zealand Presbyterian Church News. Auckland, 1873–
Outlook. Dunedin, 1894– (1901–10 issued jointly by Presbyterian, Methodist and Congregational churches of New Zealand)
Presbyterian Magazine. Sydney, 1863–
Presbyterian Messenger. Melbourne, 1865–
Standard: Free Presbyterian Magazine. Melbourne, 1859–

(vi) Protestant, Interdenominational
Australian Christian World. Sydney, 1885–
Christian Advocate and Southern Observer. Adelaide, 1858–
Gleaner. Sydney, 1847–48
Missionary at Home and Abroad. Melbourne, 1873–
Otago Christian Record. Dunedin, 1873–
Revival Record. Melbourne, 1860–63
Southern Cross. Melbourne, 1874–
Southern Spectator. Melbourne, 1857–
Tasmanian Messenger. Hobart, 1859–
Testimony. Sydney, 1865–

(vii) Roman Catholic
Advocate. Melbourne, 1868–
Austral Light. Melbourne, 1892–
Australasian Catholic Record. Sydney, 1895–

Australian Messenger of the Sacred Heart.
Melbourne, 1887–
Catholic Church Record. Gosford,
N.S.W., 1922– (held Sydney
Archdiocesan Archives)
Catholic Magazine. Melbourne, 1888–91
Catholic Press. Sydney, 1895–
Catholic Times. Wellington, 1888–
Chaplet and Southern Cross. Adelaide,
1870–

Freeman's Journal. Sydney, 1850–
Madonna. Melbourne, 1897–
Month. Auckland, 1918–
New Zealand Tablet. Dunedin, 1873–
St Kevin's Church Record. Eastwood,
N.S.W., 1929– (held Sydney
Archdiocesan Archives)
Tribune. Melbourne, 1900–
Victorian. Melbourne, 1862–

INDEX

Ackermann, Jessie   161
Act of Union with Ireland   13, 86
Advocate   84, 101
Albertland   17–18
Alexander, Charles   58
Alfred, Prince (Duke of
  Edinburgh)   30, 94
All Hallows College   120
Anderson, Francis   141
Angas, George Fife   16–17, 18
Angus, Samuel   126
Annual Register   6
Arnold, Matthew   20
Arnold, Thomas (the Younger)   20
Ashford, W. J.   137
Austral Light   98, 101
Australasian Catholic Record   70, 138,
  141, 144
Australian Catholic Hymnal   72
Australian Christian World   114
Australian Independent   131, 134
*Australian Messenger of the Sacred
  Heart*   101, 120, 155, 157

Backhouse, James   24, 25
Balfour, James   109
Ballance, John   41
Baptists   78, 83, 84, 85
Barnabo, Cardinal Alessandro   35, 85
Barth, Karl   137
Bethune, Frances   84
Bevan, Llewelyn David   33, 133, 135
Bible Christians   54, 55
Bible classes   3, 163
Bicheno, J. E.   40
Binney, Thomas   128
Blamires, W. L.   53
Board of National Education
  (Ireland)   87
Booth, Herbert   61
Booth, R. T.   57
Booth, General William   60, 61, 62, 63
Bossy, John   12
Bourke, Paul F.   54
Boyce, Francis Bertie   26
Boylan, Eustace   98, 100, 102, 120,
  139
Brennan, Christopher John   140–1
Brethren   49–50, 53, 55, 75
Buckley, Vincent   73, 103

Buller, James   36
Bulletin   112, 118, 160
Bulloch, W.   25
Burgmann, Bishop Ernest Henry   172
Burke, Robert O'Hara   42
Burned-Over District (New York)
  56–7
Burnett, Matthew   57
Burns, Thomas   17
Byrne, F.   36

Cairns, Adam   108, 112, 148, 150
Cambridge, Ada *see* Cross, Ada
Camden College   137
Campbell, R. J.   133
Cargill, William   17
Carlow College   120, 121
Carr, Archbishop Thomas Joseph   98,
  101, 138
Casely, Rev.   55
Catholic Association   13
Catholic devotional associations   69,
  75, 98–100
Catholic devotions   15, 155–7
Catholic Evidence Guild   139, 161
Catholic Guild (Sydney)   87
Catholic Magazine   98
Catholic religious orders   3–4, 65, 66,
  69, 86 *see also* Redemptorists
Catholic Young Men's Societies   98
Cato, Frederick John   84
Chalmers, Thomas   10
Chandler, John   42
Chapman, J. Wilbur   58, 60
children and young people   50, 51,
  52–3, 73–4, 90, 91, 98–100,
  Chapter 7
Children of Mary   98–100
Christian Advocate   160
Christian Conventions   64–5
Christian Outlook   159
Christian Review and Messenger   148
Church Acts   54
church attendance   7, 8, 11, 13, 15, 58,
  Chapter 5
Church Chronicle   150, 169
Church of England brotherhoods   25
Churchman   114
Clarke, George (Congregational
  minister)   132–3

Clarke, George (evangelist) 57
Cleary, Bishop Henry William 92, 97, 101
clergy, lay attitudes to 30–2, 39–41, 143, 144; supply of 12, 15, 25, 38, 120–1
Clough, Arthur Hugh 20
Cockburn, Lord Henry 10
Coghlan, Sir Timothy Augustine 145
Colonization Commission (South Australia) 16
contraception 142–7, 165, 167–8, 169
convicts 15–16, 22
Conwell, Bishop Henry 39
Corbett, Bishop 100, 101
Cornish 20, 45, 54–7
Coughlan, Neil 21–2
Croke, Bishop Thomas William 86, 92
Cross, Ada 61
Cullen, J. F. 129
Cullen, Cardinal Paul 33, 85–91, 102, 139
Cunningham, Peter Miller 16
Cusack, J. M. 122, 124, 165, 170

Daily News 8
Daily Telegraph 105
Davin, Dan 158
Delany, Bishop Patrick 91
Democratic Party 91
Dempsey, Kenneth 171
denominational affiliations 2, 19–20, 21
Disruption (of Church of Scotland) 11
Dowie, John Alexander 46
Dowling, Patrick 140, 157
Dowty, Henry 80
Draper, Daniel James 53
Dublin Evening Mail 86
Dunedin Athenaeum 110
Dunne, Patrick 19, 33

education (Catholic) 13, 69, 87–94, 124, 154, 173
d'Eichthal, Gustave 10
Elkin, Adophus Peter 162
Evangelicals (Church of England) 6
Evangelicals (Church of Scotland) 10

family 113, Chapter 7, 167–8
family limitation *see* contraception

family worship 11, 142, 147–58, 165, 167–8
fasting 121–2
Finney, Charles Grandison 51-2
First Church of Otago, Dunedin 46
Fisher, Sir James Hurtle 17
Fitzgerald, T. A. 101, 144
Fitzpatrick, Kathleen Elizabeth Pitt *see* Pitt, Kathleen
Fletcher, William Roby 128, 131
folk religion 8, 11, 12, 44–5, 93
Fordyce, John 131
Forlong, Gordon 53
Forrest, M. D. 102
Fowler, Francis Edmund Town 151
Freeman's Journal 23

Gallagher, Bishop John 40
Geoghegan, Bishop Patrick Bonaventure 36, 88, 89
Gilroy, Cardinal Norman Thomas 92
Godley, John Robert 17
Goold, Archbishop James Alipius 39, 72, 120
Gosman, Alexander 134
Graham, William Franklin (Billy) 60
Great Famine 13–5
Grey, Sir George 18
Grubb, George Carleton 64–5
Guinness, Harry Grattan 57
Guthrie, Thomas 11

Hamilton, William 25
Hampson, Margaret 57, 58
Hanson, Richard Davies 128–30, 138
Harpur, Charles 126, 137
Harris, Alexander 20, 24, 38
Hayden, Thomas 138
hell 66, 73–4, 129–31, 138, 140, 141, 168, 169
Helping Hand Mission Hall 59
Henderson, A. M. 128
Henderson, Kenneth T. 125, 126
Hennebery, Patrick 66–9, 76
Hennessy, N. M. 143
Henty, Jane 150
Hessey, James Augustus 108–9
Hickson, James Moore 60
Higinbotham, George 126
Hill, James 131
Hindmarsh, John 17
Hinterocker, Rev. 76
Hird, David 135
Hogan, James Francis 35

Hopkins, Henry 30
Hurley, P. E. 38, 40, 140

ideas (religious) 5, 20, 36–7, Chapter 6, 167–8
Independent (Congregational) church, Collins St, Melbourne 78
Inglis, Kenneth Stanley 114

Jackson, D.G.M. 76
Jackson, Henry Latimer 153
James, J. E. 136
Johnson, Eli 57

Kench, W. T. 136
Keswick convention movement 62–5
Kiek, Edward Sidney 117, 136–7, 170
Kirby, Joseph Coles 134
Kirk, W. 79

Landers, Michael 68
Lanigan, Bishop William 88
Lawlor, Patrick Anthony 44, 74
Legge, John 127
Leigh, Richard 26
Lewis, Brian Bannatyne 113, 119
Lindsay, Sir Lionel Arthur 118
Linus, Rev. 161
Long, M. 97
Loyalist League (Victoria) 96
Luck, Bishop John Edmund 37, 122
Lush, Vicesimus 30, 32
Lutherans 18, 145

Macartney, Hussey Burgh 63, 109
Macartney, Hussey Burgh (the Younger) 63–4
MacDonagh, Oliver 43
McEncroe, John 38
McGlashan, John 24
McIntyre, A. J. and J. J. 171–2
McKenzie, Thomas 36
McKillop, Mary Helen 35, 43, 88
Macky, Dill 144
McLaren, A. Allan 11
McLeod, Donald 18
MacLeod, Norman (Scottish divine) 109
McLeod, Norman (Waipu leader) 18
McNeill, William H. 168
Madonna 101
Manly *see* St Patrick's College, Manly
Mannix, Archbishop Daniel 94, 96
marriage patterns 82–5, 97 *see also* mixed marriages

Marsden, Bishop Samuel Edward 32
Mateer and Parker 57
Mathew, Theobald 68
Matthews, C.H.S. 25
Mayhew, Henry 9, 16
Mead, Silas 63
Melbourne art gallery *see* Public Library and National Gallery (Melbourne)
Melbourne Central Catholic Library 101
Melbourne Church News 150
Melbourne Eucharistic Congress 94–5
Melbourne Punch 112
Melbourne Review 112
membership (Protestant understanding of) 77–82, 85, 167–8
Merritt, H. T. 152
Methodist class meeting 52, 78–80
Methodist Holiness Association 64
Missionary at Home and Abroad 64
mixed marriages 34–5, 37, 38, 82, 83, 90–1, 94, 102–3, 146–7, 169
Moderates (Church of Scotland) 10
Moody, Dwight Lyman 55, 57–8, 73
Moody Bible Institute (Chicago Bible Institute) 58
Moonta revival 54–7
Moore, Bishop James 75, 161
Moran, Dr Herbert Michael 97
Moran, Bishop Patrick 86, 91
Moran, Cardinal Patrick Francis 75, 86, 120, 139, 144
Mothers' Union 153
Mothers in Australasia 153
Mountain, J. and Mrs 57
Murray, Bishop James 70, 71, 86, 87–8, 102
Murray, Archbishop Daniel 87
Murray, John 111

Nash, John B. 145
Ne Temere 90, 94, 102
New South Wales Independent 129
New South Wales Royal Commission on the decline of the birth rate 143–5
New Zealand Constitution Act 39
New Zealand Herald 66
New Zealand Presbyterian 44
Newman, John Henry 126
Noble, William 57
Norton, John 112

Norton, Bishop John   123

Obelkevich, James   8
'O'Brien, John' (Patrick Joseph Hartigan)   157
O'Connell, Daniel   13, 91
O'Farrell, Rev.   71, 72
O'Farrell, Patrick   22
O'Reily, Jeremiah Joseph Purcell   36
O'Shanassy, John   33
Otago Lay Association   17
Oxford Movement   6, 17

Palmer, J. H.   134
Parkin College   136
Pentecostalism   65
Pepper, T. J.   128
Perry, Bishop Charles   158, 159, 160
Perry, Joseph   61
Phelan, Michael   140
Pirie Street Methodist church, Adelaide   118
Pitt, Kathleen   74
Pius IX   85, 87
Pius X   138
Plunkett, Sir Horace   169
Polding, Archbishop John Bede   16, 39, 43, 65, 88, 89, 90, 154, 160
Pompallier, Bishop Jean Baptiste Francois   39
Potter, Robert   80
Presbyterian Magazine   158
Price, C.S.Y.   150
Price, J. Howell   143, 144
Primitive Methodists   8, 49, 54, 55
Protestant-Catholic relations   35-8, 88, 97, *see also* sectarianism
Protestant converts to Rome   75-6
Public Library and National Gallery (Melbourne)   110, 113
Pusey, Edward Bouverie   168

Quinn, Bishop James   19, 35, 91
Quinn, Bishop Matthew   87-8

Redemptorists   36, 65, 69-75
Redwood, Archbishop Francis   37, 69, 86
religious equality   16-17, 28, 30, 32-3
Rentoul, J. L.   112
Revival   49
Revival Record   49
revivals and revivalism   5-8, 10-11, 14-15, 18, 77, Chapter 3, 167-8

Reynolds, Bishop Christopher Augustine   76
Robertson, Frederick William   109
Robertson, Joseph   134
Roe, Michael   126
Romaine, William   6
Roseby, Thomas   129
Rumble, Leslie   102, 138, 139
rural-urban differences   58, 114-15, 116, 126, 169
Ryan, Philip   40

St Canute's Catholic church, Streaky Bay   123
St Francis's Catholic church, Thames   68
St James's Church of England, Sydney   153
St John's Presbyterian church, Wellington   36
St Mary's Cathedral, Sydney   88
St Mary's Catholic church, St Kilda   71-2
St Patrick's Cathedral, Melbourne, 72, 75
St Patrick's College, Manly   138
St Patrick's Day   92-3
Salvation Army   56, 60-2, 63, 64, 75
Sankey, Ira D.   55, 57-8
Scammett, F. G.   134
sectarianism   2, 36, 93-7
Selwyn, Bishop George Augustus   45
Sheehy, P. J.   139
Slattery, Rev. Dr   139
Smaill, William   150-1
Smith, J. B.   53
Smith, Robert Pearsall   63
Smith, Sydney   15
Somerset, H.C.D.   114
Sommerville, Alexander N.   57-8, 60
South Australian Company   17
South Australian Congregationalist   133
South Australian Wesleyan Magazine   150
Southern Spectator   150
Southwell, Charles   20
Sprott, Bishop T. H.   114
Steel, Robert   108, 158
Stephens, Mr   55
Strong, Charles   46, 113, 162, 164
Sunday Liberation Society   113
Sunday observance   11, 24, Chapter 5, 148, 167-8
Supernatural Religion   127

Sutherland, Robert   108
Sykes, Alfred Depledge   133, 135
Syllabus of Errors   87
Symons, John C.   109
Synge, E.   25

Taylor, Peter   110
Taylor, William 'California'   51–4,
   57, 60, 66
temperance   27, 68, 69
Test and Corporation Acts   16
Testimony   158
Thomas, Dr   63
Thomson, Mrs   164
Thurles (synod of, 1850)   13, 15
Tocqueville, Alexis de   39, 44
Torrey, Reuben A.   58
Tribune   101
Trimmer, Sarah   6
Truth   112
Twopeny, Richard Ernest Nowell
   160

Vardon, Joseph   134
Varley, Henry   57
Vaughan, Edmund   72

Vaughan, Archbishop Roger William
   Bede   86, 88, 92
Verdon, Bishop Michael   86
Victorian Congregational College   134
Victorian Independent   127, 128, 135

Wakefield, Edward Jerningham   161
Walsh, Frank   109
War Cry   62
Ward, Mrs Humphry   132
Watsford, John   50–1, 64
Watt, Michael   23, 163
Webster, Geoffrey   76
Wesley, John   10, 63, 80
Wesleyan Chronicle   49, 79
Whately, Archbishop Richard   87
Williams, George   57
Williams, Jane   42
Wilson, Helen   34
women   25, 66, 73, 78, 117–9, 124,
   131, 141, Chapter 7, 172
Woods, Julian Edward Tenison   35,
   37, 38, 66, 88
Wooler, Patience   62
wowser   111, 112